David Andersen

Martin Luther
The Problem of Faith and Reason

Christliche Philosophie heute
Christian Philosophy Today
Quomodo Philosophia Christianorum
Hodie Estimatur
Band 10

Band 1
John Warwick Montgomery
Tractatus Logico-Theologicus

Band 2
John W. Montgomery
Hat die Weltgeschichte einen Sinn?
Geschichtsphilosophien auf dem Prüfstand

Band 3
John W. Montgomery
Jésus: La raison rejoint l'histoire

Band 4
Horst Waldemar Beck
Marken dieses Äons:
Wissenschaftskritische und theologische Diagnosen

Band 5
Ross Clifford
John Warwick Montgomery´s Legal Apologetic:
An Apologetic for All Seasons

Band 6
Thomas K. Johnson
Natural Law Ethics: An Evangelical Proposal

Band 7
Lydia Jaeger
Wissenschaft ohne Gott? Zum Verhältnis zwischen
christlichem Glauben und Wissenschaft

Band 8
Thomas K. Johnson und Ron Kubsch
Herman Bavinck. Christliche Weltanschauung

Band 9
John Warwick Montgomery
La Mort De Dieu

David Andersen

Martin Luther
The Problem of Faith and Reason

A Reexamination in Light of the
Epistemological and Christological Issues

Preface by John Warwick Montgomery
Foreword by Paul Helm

Christliche Philosophie heute

Christian Philosophy Today

Quomodo Philosophia
Christianorum Hodie Estimatur

Band 10

WIPF & STOCK · Eugene, Oregon

MARTIN LUTHER
The Problem of Faith and Reason

This edition published by Wipf and Stock Publishers by arrangement with Verlag für Kultur und Wissenschaft.

Wipf & Stock
An imprint of Wipf and Stock Publishers
199 W. 8th Avenue, Suite 3
Eugene OR, 97401
www.wipfandstock.com

ISBN:978-1-62032-600-8

Manufactured in the U.S.A.

For my amazing wife, Jeana, and wonderful children,
Alexandra, Christian, Katherine, and Elizabeth

Acknowledgements

It is a great pleasure for me to acknowledge several people who have helped me in preparing the present work. I want to thank first of all my Ph.D. supervisor, Professor Alister E. McGrath, for his guidance of this project during my studies at Wycliffe Hall, Oxford. Without his support and encouragement, this work would never have come to fruition. In addition, I would like to thank Professor John Warwick Montgomery for his role as my secondary supervisor and his insightful guidance as I was researching and writing this work. Professor Paul Helm has been invaluably helpful in reading earlier drafts of this work and offering important points that needed clarification. Professor Erik Ankerberg deserves special mention for reading the final draft and helping me prepare its completed form, as well as for his support and friendship. Professor Rod Rosenbladt stands behind this work as an inspirational friend and mentor who was instrumental in awakening in me an interest in Luther studies during my undergraduate work. Of the various libraries which were used during the course of this work, I wish to acknowledge the assistance of the staff of the Bodleian Library, Oxford, as well as the Taylor Institution Library, Oxford. I also owe Professor Thomas Schirrmacher and Ron Kubsch thanks for their encouragement and support during the closing stages of this work.

Finally, I would like to thank my wonderful wife, Jeana, for her love, friendship, and support – as well as my children Alexandra, Christian, Katherine, and Elizabeth. Their love is truly a gift from God.

Table of Contents

PART THREE
Faith and Reason

PART FOUR
Secondary Literature: Another Look

Preface by John Warwick Montgomery

Luther has long been regarded, both by secular philosophers and by misguided believers, as an irrationalist. To take only a few examples: Luther's insistence on the real presence of Christ's body in the Sacrament has been seen as a physical impossibility (in spite of the Einsteinian revolution in physics!). His confidence in the literal facticity of Scripture has been viewed as hopelessly naïve (even though the same view was clearly maintained by Jesus himself!). And Yale historian Jaroslav Pelikan – who, at the end of his career, moved from Lutheranism to mystical Eastern Orthodoxy – titled one of his early works *From Luther to Kierkegaard*, thereby transmuting Luther into a kind of pre-modern existentialist.

Thus the great importance of the present work. David Andersen rightly shows that Luther "places himself well within an empiricist tradition," that for Luther "a love for our own presuppositions is often the greatest hindrance to reaching reasonable conclusions," and that "Luther is utterly convinced that it [the Christian religion] has the empirical support of eyewitnesses concerning the very Word of life" – Christ's resurrection constituting "the foremost proof of his claim to deity and thereby the ground for all Christian discourse."

A careful reading of Dr Andersen's book will surely give the lie to all existentialisings of the Reformer. It will also demonstrate that Luther cannot be classified as one who would today replace insistence on clear thinking with post-modern refusals to allow, even in principle, the establishing of objective truth.

Not without reason did Luther's followers – one thinks of Tycho Brahe and Johannes Kepler, to name only two – give us the scientific perspective which has so profoundly influenced the development of the western Christian world.

Following Luther's insights, as accurately portrayed by Dr Andersen, the reader can identify such endemic contemporary fallacies as that "all religions are saying the same thing" and that "all spiritual roads lead up the mountain to the same religious summit." Dr Andersen shows Luther's continuing ability to point lost worlds – ours as well as that of the 16th century – to the unique and demonstrable claim of Jesus Christ to be the sole path to religious Truth and Life.

John Warwick Montgomery

Ph.D. (Chicago), D.Théol. (Strasbourg, France), LL.D. (Cardiff, Wales); Barrister-at-Law, England and Wales; Avocat à la Cour, Paris; Professor Emeritus of Law and Humanities, University of Bedfordshire (U.K.); Distinguished Research Professor of Philosophy and Christian Thought, Patrick Henry College, Virginia (U.S.A.)

Foreword by Paul Helm

It's a great pleasure to be asked to welcome and commend David Andersen's book on Luther's view of faith and reason. In my estimate it marks a most welcome departure from traditional studies of this topic. He approaches faith and reason not, in the first instance, through a soteriological lense, Luther's theology of the Cross, or the Law-gospel dialectic, say, or justification by faith alone, but in terms of his basic understanding of epistemology. He places Luther's understanding of faith's relation to reason in the epistemological and logical tradition starting in Ancient Greece, and developed and modified in patristic and medieval theology. For all his uniqueness, Luther was a child of the great logical and epistemological traditions arising from classical culture. The author explores, initially in a fairly abstract, analytic mode, what according to Luther, human reason is, what we may know as a result of the exercises of our reason, and how we may know it. This involves Andersen in an innovative work, reconstructing Luther's general epistemology from stray remarks and underlying assumptions.

He notes Luther's confidence in our capacities to gain historical knowledge as well as the knowledge of nature, stressing its a posteriori character. For Luther, the knowledge of God is likewise a posteriori. Using many examples, Andersen notes the Reformer's positive estimate of logic, and of the mind's power to draw valid inferences provided that reason is properly subordinated to grammar and to reality. This is all in pursuit of knowledge acquired a posteriori, by means, though not the sole means, of reason. But reason is fallen. The properly subordinate role of both reason in its epistemological sense and in the sense of logic is overturned when the mind inquisitively speculates about God. Fallen reason overextends itself, and itches to know what cannot be known. Yet to gain the knowledge of God reason itself must not be abandoned; it must be made subordinate to the Word of God and especially to the Incarnate Word, who, Andersen claims, especially through his Resurrection, both ensures and mediates the knowledge of God. Only with difficulty, and by the grace of God, can the true role of reason in matters of faith be realised.

The result of this many-sided approach to the Reformer is a refreshingly positive re-evaluation of Luther's estimate of reason and of the often-reproduced portrait of Luther as fideistic and pessimistic. This new orientation also succeeds in revealing the complexity of Luther's thought, its nuances as well as its tensions, and the fact that he thinks of reason and faith on various levels. Reason is majestic, but it is to be subordinate to the will of God. It is majestic, but it is also fragmented and distorted by the Fall.

In pursuing the theme of the positive elements in Luther's epistemology, Andersen offers a subtle account of Luther's motifs of the revealed and hidden God which, as they develop, are not intended to promote scepticism about God, but instead to make Christology the sole source of such knowledge. The knowledge of God is to be sought and found in the revealed God, not in what we may speculate about the hidden God nor by taking as theologically axiomatic what is not itself a revealed item. Luther's use of the *communicatio* is simply his way of emphasising that the Incarnate God is no other than God himself. The humanity is the valid expression of the divinity. This is true knowledge of God, and reason fulfils its true role when it functions subordinately in its articulation.

Andersen shows that the seeming incommensurability of Luther's various estimates of faith and reason can be reconciled if we patiently attend to the nature of faith and to Luther's explanation of the extravagances of reason. Reason in faith must remain within the limits of the Word. Faith restores reason's right function. The contrast is not between faith and reason but between faith and sight. So Luther's epistemology is not confined to 'things below' while 'things above' are left to be appropriated fideistically.

The book is noteworthy for its clarity and for the detailed attention that it pays both to primary and secondary sources. In stepping out into territory where theological commentators on Luther have habitually feared to tread, Andersen succeeds in offering a persuasive new reading of the Reformer, and in raising issues and offering insights that will, it is hoped, give rise to further constructive debate about Luther, faith and reason.

Paul Helm
Paul Helm is a Teaching Fellow at Regent College, Vancouver. From 1993–2000 he was Professor of the History and Philosophy of Religion at King's College, London.

Introduction

The subject of the present study, the relation between reason and faith in the later works of Martin Luther, is a problematic one that originates primarily from Luther's own hand. This is in other words not a problem superficially raised by Luther's critics, but one that finds its roots in the very expressions Luther employs to distinguish between faith and unaided natural reason. Regarding the issue of reason alone, for instance, we find many passages in which Luther embellishes it with unqualified praise, and yet others in which he uses terminology that many would level only against their worst enemy. One sufficient example of the former is found in *Die Disputation de homine* where Luther says that reason is truly divine, possessing a certain form of majesty. Perhaps more often though Luther's remarks tend to be negative, and one need only recall some of his more famous invectives against reason to the effect that it is, by its very nature, a "schedliche Hure;" or, even more shocking, that it is the "Teuffels Braut." Evaluating the precise relation between his various, often completely contradictory, comments on reason proves difficult enough, but it is complicated all the more with his consistent antithesis between faith and reason. How are we to understand his odd statements that faith literally conquers (or to make things worse, kills) reason? One is naturally left wondering what he could possibly mean by the terms "faith" and "reason." Given the fact that these terms are highly volatile, it will be our main purpose to define as accurately as possible what reason is and its scope of significance within Luther's later thought, and then examine its consequences for the faith/reason relation. However, it must be pointed out at the beginning that attention will not primarily be directed toward examining Luther's distinction between philosophy and theology, as other works have examined this topic with some detail (though of course some comments on this will be impossible to avoid). Rather, our focus will be directed toward examining the epistemological issues involved in Luther's notion of reason; an area that has been severely neglected in recent research with the result that Luther's position on reason is dealt with one-sidedly and thus improperly. As Marius correctly observed in his recent work, the question "How do we keep reason at bay and God with us?" runs through Luther's life's work like a flood, "and it may not be too much to say that his answers to it gave him his theology and his significance in history."[1] Given its importance, the epistemological question deserves not just passing mention but rather our full attention.

Although one might think that the faith/reason relation in the thought of the Reformer – and perhaps the most influential thinker of the Christian Church – has been thoroughly exploited, it has in fact surprisingly been widely neglected, aside from special mention in works such as Wilhelm Link's *Das Ringen Luthers um die Freiheit der Theologie von der Philosophie* (Berlin, 1954) and Bengt Hägglund's *Theologie und Philosophie bei Luther und in der occamistischen Tradition* (Lund, 1955). Of the more extensive works on our topic in the young Luther we should mention Bernhard Lohse's *Ratio und Fides. Eine Untersuchung über die ratio in der Theologie Luthers* (Göttingen, 1958), R. Kuhn's *Luthers Lehre von der ratio*. Diss (Erlangen, 1957), and W. Joest's *Ontologie der Person bei Luther* (Göttingen, 1967).[2] Given the fact however that I have restricted the present work to the mature Luther, only brief mention (if any) will be made of the above works.

Studies on the mature Luther are just as scarce as those on his younger years in this particular area.[3] Of the few that do examine the problem it must be said at the outset that they all, in one way or another, focus on Luther's soteriological orientation in order to explain his seeming distaste for natural reason. This is so whether the position is presented under the form of reason's inseparable connection with the law or the now very familiar two kingdom approach. Due to this orientation they all tend to downplay or minimize the epistemological issues.[4] They can be specified as follows: Robert Fischer's essay "A Reasonable Luther" in

---

[1] Richard Marius, *Martin Luther: The Christian Between God and Death* (Cambridge, Massachusetts, 1999) p. 104.

[2] For a brief overview of these works see Karl-Heinz zur Mühlen *Reformatorische Vernunftkritik und neuzeitliches Denken: Dargestellt am Werk M. Luthers und Fr. Gogartens* (Tübingen, 1980) pp. 70–75.

[3] This point however cannot be restricted solely to the issue of reason. As Siggins pointed out in 1974 modern Luther research has practically ignored the theology of the mature Luther. I think his claim is significant, as well as highly accurate, that we find the real genius of Luther as a theologian and stylist precisely in these later years. Furthermore, that the thought of the young Luther has become the norm by which the mature Luther is judged has also been pointed out by scholars such as Pelikan. Given this, we need to ask (as does Siggins), Did Luther achieve new insights as an elderly man? As I will argue, this question has to be answered in the affirmative. See Ian D. Kingston Siggins, *Luther* (New York, 1972) pp. 178, 188 and Jeroslav Pelikan's Introduction to *Luther's Works* (Saint Louis, 1958) Vol. 1, p. xii.

[4] In being critical of this it will not be my intention to commit the opposite error of minimizing the force of Luther's soteriology. Rather, it will be my intention to balance the scale, so to speak, and examine the force of both these issues in their proper places.

Reformation Studies: Essays in Honor of Roland H. Bainton ed. Franklin H. Littell (Richmond, Va., 1962) deals briefly with the faith/reason issue. Fischer claims that Luther's attacks on reason were shaped by his early theology of the cross and were directed at reason's efforts "to storm the citadel of God." Luther is thus seen to have criticized epistemology by means of his theology of the cross.[5] Another essay that seems far too brief is Hans-Walter Krumwiede's "Martin Luther: Die Kompetenz der Vernunft" in *Jahrbuch Der Gesellschaft für Niedersächsische Kirchengeschichte* (Blomberg, 1985) vol. 83, pp. 55–74. Like Fischer, Krumwiede does not restrict himself to the mature Luther and the few direct remarks he makes about reason are set within the context of the two kingdom theory and the spiritual lordship of Christ.[6] A much more extensive work that deals in greater detail with Luther and reason (though it must be said that this is not his primary focus) is Herbert Olsson's *Schopfung, Vernunft und Gesetz in Luthers Theologie* (Uppsala, 1971), in which the author provides a critical analysis of the views of Harnack and Holl in respect to their positions on Luther's understanding of the law e.g., they each see in the natural experience of the law a revelation of God's will. Olsson's analysis leads him to propose a soteriological approach to Luther's notion of natural reason (i.e., in roughly the same manner as the above examinations). Briefly, he claims that for Luther the Gospel is a crucial and necessary precondition for a genuine knowledge of the law as the Creator's will. One possesses a correct understanding from human reason only if he knows in what relation he stands to faith. In other words, one can grasp the meaning of the law and its works only in connection with an understanding of the Gospel. Thus the goodness of the Creator is concealed from natural reason and requires enlightenment through the Gospel. Furthermore, the natural light of reason is composed from the Law, and thereby knows nothing other than the Law. It is an inherent notion of reason therefore that it ought to do good and avoid evil, and that it should acquire justice through the works of the Law. In short, reason concludes that God is pleased with man through his works; man's knowledge of God is knowledge through the Law. Accordingly, Luther always puts reason and the Law together. Olsson's soteriological approach comes out clearly when he claims that reason is naturally composed of ignorance and hostility with respect to God because it is in a constant restless activity to please God through its works. The natural light of reason on this account stands

---

[5] For example, pp. 33–35. It is an interesting feature of Fischer's analysis that he uncritically moves from the young to the mature Luther (e.g., as early as 1513 to as late as 1539) with the naive assumption that Luther never changed or significantly developed his position on some the these matters. This is a mistake that, I will maintain, we cannot afford to make in regard to both the subjects of Luther's theology of the cross and most importantly his conception of epistemology.

[6] See pp. 59–64.

opposed to the Gospel, as from reason springs the wrong understanding that it ought to attain righteousness through works of the Law. Thus reason is the driving force of man's self-righteousness and is an enemy of God. The Gospel however announces that God gives mercy to all and in doing so provides judgment over man's self-righteousness. When man receives the Gospel in faith, he forsakes his own self-righteousness:

> D.h. das Evangelium zerschlägt gerade das, was charakteristisch für die natür- liche Vernunft ist. Deshalb muss die natürliche Vernunft auch das Evangelium hassen. Un je mehr der Mensch von seiner natürlichen Vernunft beherrscht ist, umso mehr hasst er das Evangelium. Darum muss der Mensch ein neues Licht (das Evangelium) erhalten, wenn er eine wahre Kenntnis von Gott und seinem Willen erhalten soll.[7]

Because Olsson views Luther's invectives against reason from a purely soterio- logical standpoint he fails, as the other works in this area, to tackle the episte- mological issues that are so important to a proper examination of reason. A more recent work that deals with our topic is Karl-Heinz zur Mühlen's *Reformatorische Vernunftkritik und neuzeitliches Denken: Dargestellt am Werk M. Luthers und Fr. Gogartens* (Tübingen, 1980). Mühlen however spends very little time on the mature Luther and follows prior works (e.g., Olsson and Gerrish) in identifying Luther's harsh attacks on reason with his soteriological orientation.[8] In fact, up to date, the only *major* study on reason in the mature Luther is Brian Gerrish's *Grace and Reason*[9] (Oxford, 1962). Gerrish's work is by far the most extensive study on this topic and is also the clearest statement of the soteriological approach. Moreover, because of its limited scope it appears to be regarded as more or less definitive on the subject and has therefore wielded considerable influence on sub- sequent treatments.[10] Due to its significance it is necessary to devote considerable time to Gerrish's thesis, and in fact we will deal mostly with his work. In doing so however I do not wish to suggest that another significant work, such as Ols- son's, suffers from exactly the same defects as Gerrish's. For example, one might

[7] See Olsson, pp. 506ff.

[8] See for example pp. 68–69, 73, 75, 93, 129–137.

[9] Gerrish also wrote the article "Martin Luther" in *The Encyclopedia of Philosophy* (New York, 1967) but this, for the most part, simply reflects his position in Grace and Reason.

[10] For example: Dennis Bielfeldt's recent unpublished Ph.D. dissertation *Luther, Logic, and Lan- guage: An Inquiry into the Semantics of Theological Language in the Writings of Martin Luther* (1987, University of Iowa); Ake Bergvall's recent article "Reason in Luther, Calvin, and Sidney" in *The Sixteenth Century Journal* XXIII/1 (1992); Ian D. Kingston Siggins, in his *Martin Luther's Doc- trine of Christ* (New Haven and London, 1970) also relies on Gerrish's study in his brief comments on the subject (strange bedfellows in my opinion); others will be cited later.

object that my criticisms of Gerrish's elevation of the two kingdoms are not an essential part of Olsson's thesis and should thus not be subsumed under Gerrish's approach. That Olsson does not deal at any great length with Luther's distinction between the two kingdoms is true. However, all the soteriological approaches mentioned above end up in the same strange predicament; namely, they discard almost completely the issue of epistemology in a subject that in itself is laden with epistemological questions. In addition, to one degree or another all the prior studies effectively suggest a more exclusive connection between reason and the law in the later Luther than I think justifiable.[11] Therefore, because Gerrish's study is by far the most extensive and the clearest presentation of the soteriological view, this study can be seen as interacting mainly with his work.

As I hope to show, there is reason to believe that Gerrish's evaluation – and in effect all previous evaluations – is flawed at several critical junctures, necessitating an overall reevaluation of the later works of the Reformer. In summary, Gerrish's work suffers from two main problems: (1) an improper elevation of the so-called two kingdom theory and the forgiveness of sins, and (2) the supposition that Luther subordinates the epistemological question "How do I know God?" to the soteriological question "How am I saved?"[12] Gerrish's thesis creates two distinct but intimately related problems. First, by taking as his framework the two kingdoms and the forgiveness of sins he is forced to the conclusion that Luther's various remarks are to be understood in light of a "fundamental dualism" between the Earthly and Heavenly Kingdoms.[13] Second, by proposing a subservient role to epistemology, Gerrish fails to give adequate attention to Luther's implicit epistemology. He therefore attempts to lay bare the *theological* presuppositions which lay behind Luther's notion of reason.[14] My response is fairly straightforward and can be summed up as follows: the problem of "reason" is, in and of itself, primarily a philosophical issue, not theological. That, of course, is not to deny that Luther often speaks of reason and its direct relation to God, but this fact does not somehow excuse us from detailing the philosophical issues pregnant within the very notion of reason. Gerrish's failure to develop in full the epistemological issues seems to me a crucial flaw in his thesis. This is to say, in short, that he collapses two distinct issues by neglecting to distinguish the fundamental question, "What is Luther's *implicit* epistemology?" (subordinate or not) from, "*Did*

---

[11] To establish this one need only show that his attacks on reason were very often directed against epistemological rationalism and not only against man's self-righteousness. We will see that Luther in fact spends a great deal of time undermining the presuppositions of rationalism.

[12] Gerrish, *Grace and Reason* p. 55.

[13] Gerrish, *Grace and Reason* pp. 8, 13.

[14] Gerrish, *Grace and Reason* p. 4 (emphasis mine).

Luther tend to subordinate the epistemological question to the soteriological?"
One simply cannot with any degree of accuracy avoid evaluating the philosophical presuppositions of reason and, at the same time, claim to have provided an
adequate definition. What results from Gerrish's method, in my estimation, is a
Luther that teeters on the brink of theological schizophrenia. That is, he has effectively manufactured an epistemological gulf in Luther's thought between two
kingdoms that contains no bridge from ordinary human experience to the truth
of God's revelation.[15]

Doubtless, the contributing factor to Gerrish's ambiguity on these issues is
his proposal that Luther's governing framework consists of the two-kingdoms
and the forgiveness of sins. Although in principle I can appreciate his assertion
that Luther's religious ideas "must be seen in relation to the basic structure of his
thought and to what he himself regarded as the centre of the Christian Faith,"
I must nevertheless take issue to what he actually regards as Luther's center of
faith. It will be one of the main components of this work to insist that the center
for all of Luther's theologizing – that which forms the foundation and justification
of his thought as a whole – is and can be nothing other than the historic person
of Christ. More recently, Ian Siggins has (rightfully) insisted on precisely this
reorientation:

> Hence our claim that the uniqueness, necessity, and all-sufficiency of Christ is
> "the focus and pivot of all his theology, to which even the doctrine of justifica-
> tion is ancillary." To call *sola fide* the material norm of his theology would be
> unequivocally correct, if only Luther's disciples (old and new) had remembered
> his injunction, "Christ and faith belong together." For Luther *sola fide* is simply
> another way of saying *a solo Christo*. Faith is an empty vessel and justifies
> because of Christ alone. Unfortunately, in the hands of others justification – the
> doctrine of justification – has been allowed to usurp the pivotal position which
> belongs to Christ alone in Luther's doctrine (as in Paul's). Justification is only
> one aspect – even if a most important aspect – of that clinging to Christ which
> is faith: for Christ is our righteousness. But to elevate the formal content of
> justification (imputation of righteousness) to the level of dominant importance
> as a normative principle is inevitably to distort Luther's passionate concern...
> Hence the peculiarly dogmatic form into which the doctrine of justification is
> cast for polemical purposes is an inadequate key to the richness of Luther's faith.
> Not justification, but Christ alone, is the material norm of his theology and the
> lifeblood of his faith.[16]

[15] On this important observation see John Warwick Montgomery, "Lutheranism and the Defense of
the Christian Faith," *Lutheran Synod Quarterly* vol. 11, no. 1, Special Issue (Fall, 1970) p. 29.
[16] Siggins, *Martin Luther's Doctrine of Christ* pp. 79, 104–105.

I quote Siggins at length here to highlight the fact that such ancillary concepts as the two-kingdoms and justification depend of necessity on the more central notion of Christ. Luther's understanding of Christ in other words must take not only doctrinal primacy but logical primacy as well, as there can be no concept of justification (and, to say the least, the two kingdoms) without a logically prior Christology. It may seem a trivial shift in emphasis on my part, but it is one that ultimately sets the findings of this study against Gerrish's; differences in fact of the most fundamental type. In light of this shift, my analysis should effectively eliminate Gerrish's apparent insurmountable epistemological gulf between the earthly and heavenly kingdoms, and alleviate the corresponding (also manufactured) burden concerning the precise nature of the faith/reason relation.

Method of Present Study

In order to elaborate on the method adopted in this work, two things need to be mentioned. First, as stated above our examination will be restricted to the mature Luther. Though placing a precise line of demarcation between Luther's mid and later thought can be somewhat arbitrary due to obvious overlap and continuity of concepts, it is nevertheless an unfortunate necessity in a limited project such as this. However, despite this obvious problem, I do think there is a good case to be made for taking as our point of departure the year 1527 with Luther's treatise *Das diese wort Christi (Das ist mein leib etce) noch fest stehen widder die Schwermgeister.* Briefly, my reasoning is as follows: Luther's 1544 *Kurzes Bekenntnis vom heiligen Sakrament,* written not long before his death and indisputably part of his mature works, begins with these sober remarks:

> Denn ich, als der ich nu auss der Gruben gehe, wil dis zeugnis und diesen rhum mit mir fur meins lieben Herrn und Heilands Jhesu Christi richtstuel bringen, das ich die Schwermer und Sacraments feinde, Carlstad, Zwingel, Ecolampad, Stenckefeld und yre Jünger zu Zürich und wo sie sind, mit ganzem ernst verdampt und gemidden habe, nach seinem befelh [Luther quotes Titus 3:10–11]... Sie sind offt gnug, auch ernstlich gnug, vermanet von mir und vielen andern, die Bücher sind am tage.[17]

---

[17] WA LIV 141.17–25.

In this brief confession Luther explicitly refers back several times to his two earlier works on the subject of the sacraments (with his complete stamp of approval)[18]
– i.e., *Das diese wort Christi (Das ist mein leib etce) noch fest stehen widder die
Schwermgeister* (1527) and *Vom abendmal Christi, Bekendnis* (1528) – and even
quite boldly declares (with reference to the latter) that his earlier treatise was a divine warning and admonition which regrettably had no effect on the fanatics' final
position.[19] (Luther also continuously refers, in his 1528 treatise, back to points he
had already sufficiently proven in his 1527 treatise.)[20] There are also external considerations leading to this starting date, namely, that from 1526 onwards Luther
was forced to deal, mostly due to his Protestant opponents, with the issues of the
sacraments and the hypostatic union. Some of his clearest statements on these
subjects originate from this time period and continue to be of major importance to
him right up to his death in 1546. That is, his clearest mature utterances on both
the hypostatic union in Christ and his bodily presence in the Eucharist – arguably
the two most significant topics of Luther's later career – have their roots in these
important earlier works. In short, then, 1527 appears to be a relatively secure place
to begin our task of ascertaining Luther's so-called mature view.

Second, due to the goal of the present work i.e., accurately defining Luther's
mature view, it has been necessary to reexamine completely the topic of reason
and the faith/reason relation. Therefore, in order that full weight is given to my
critique of previous approaches – e.g., Gerrish – I will for the most part suspend
judgment on those works until the final chapter (Part IV). My criticisms in other
words will follow of necessity from my own reexamination of Luther's thought
and can be properly understood only in light of those conclusions.

Very briefly, my conclusions can be summarized as follows: Luther's understanding of human reason is much more complicated than at first appears. As
our brief overview of the western tradition will highlight, the problem of reason
necessarily involves issues of epistemology and logic. We will maintain in these
important matters that Luther is squarely within an empiricist tradition concerning our knowledge of a factual nature and, as a result of that position, his view of
logic is heavily geared towards a critique of the *premises* in the deductive process,
a process that was so important to both his predecessors and contemporaries.
His understanding of epistemology and logic – illustrated from his philosophi-

---

[18] The fact that the mature Luther stamps his complete endorsement on these earlier works is seen in
several places e.g., WA LIV 144.30–145.6; 152.1–153.31.

[19] WA LIV 155.18–21 (regarding Luther's other references see n. 13). Although Luther states that this
treatise was published fifteen years earlier, Martin E. Lehmann points out that it was, to be more precise, published sixteen years earlier. See *Luther's Works* (Philadelphia, 1971) Vol. 38, p. 304 n. 35.

[20] e.g., WA XXVI 261.26–29; 262.8–12; 265.2–11; 279.22–24; 296.16–29.

cal and theological positions – reflect much less of a dependence on pure syllogistic reasoning than his forerunners and more of an emphasis on observation as means to reasonable argumentation. This in itself is a noticeable shift within medieval thought. A key element in Luther's thinking is that reason is a compulsive speculator in that it often pushes for conclusions that do not have any basis in fact. Left to its own devises reason creates thoughts which ultimately prey upon themselves (to use Knowles' expression) and is therefore in desperate need of objective information not only for scientific advance, but more importantly, for its knowledge of God. Luther would have wholeheartedly agreed with Chesterton when he remarked that detached intellectualism is all moonshine, because it is ultimately light without heat, reflected from a dead world. Accordingly, Luther's indisputable emphasis on the person and work of Christ surfaces to the foreground to answer man's need for both epistemological and soteriological clarification, as knowledge that has its origins in the brightness of the sun. This aspect of his thought can be illustrated both from his more theoretical model of the hypostatic union and his concrete emphasis on the historicity of Christ's resurrection. His corollary emphasis on the sacraments as the very connection between the risen Christ and his earthly church adds another important piece to the puzzle. Here at the elements Christians are to bring their reason captive to the external Word of Christ and train their thoughts and memory to reflect, not on its own self-created premises, but on Christ's victorious resurrection in the midst of doubt and despair. This involves an exhausting battle within every believer, and faith is simply that which believes God's Word pronounced in Word and Sacrament and appropriates the promise of forgiveness in the elements. In so doing, the Christian acknowledges God's righteousness and thereby his faithfulness in honoring his promise. The faith/reason problem on this account should be viewed not according to an epistemological rift between the two, but as the struggle for the believer to keep his own ideas in check in favor of God's secure promise, based ultimately on our knowledge of the resurrection (thus Marius' question, how do we keep reason at bay and God with us?).

Having made these preliminary remarks we can now fully detail our methodology. In order to reach our objective of reexamining Luther's understanding of reason and its consequent impact on the faith/reason problem, I will attempt to answer two basic questions that, for lack of better terms, I shall call the "core" and "internal" questions (the former will encompass Part I and the latter Parts II and III). By core I mean those basic epistemological questions that cannot be avoided when attempting to define reason without committing the fallacy of *petitio principii*. The internal is simply the question of how one's particular position on reason holds together i.e., that which is more or less peculiar to one's own position. Distinction between these two is meant to highlight the fact that, on the one hand, one cannot avoid those core epistemological issues without severely begging the more central questions while, on the other hand, different thinkers tend to bring the notion of reason into differing conceptual relations (what I mean by this will become clear below). To do justice to one's overall thought therefore *both* of these issues must be analyzed.

In order to satisfy these criteria I have separated the present work into four major parts. Part I deals with the presuppositions of reason, that is, with epistemology and logic. In chapter one we will briefly examine the problem of reason in its historical context, noting the significant contributions of Plato and Aristotle to the distinctly western notion of reason. Their influence on the medieval period will be highlighted and will thus provide the necessary background with which we can then evaluate Luther's particular view on the subject. The subsequent three chapters in Part I – in fact, the rest of the thesis – will examine Luther himself.

To answer the so-called core question as it relates to Luther's thought three topics will be examined. The first of these (chapter two) is probably the least obvious, yet relatively important for this study; namely, an assessment of Luther's notion of the Garden of Eden and the Fall. Though perhaps this discussion, strictly speaking, belongs in the internal evaluation there are two reasons it is included here: (1) Luther's discussions on these *Genesis* passages provide the historical basis i.e., the biblical data, for his epistemology and clearly reveal his notion of limits, a notion that plays an integral part in his epistemological focus. (In fact, it will quickly become evident that one of the primary characterizations of Luther's understanding of reason is the reality that it possesses certain definable limits which cannot be traversed this side of heaven. Examination of this element of his thought will accordingly take up both the first and last parts of our more restricted examination of reason i.e., Part I and II.) (2) Luther describes, with surprising detail, what reason was like before man's fall from Paradise. The benefit of this approach is that of being able to clarify what he sees as "right reason" from the very outset, which in turn should help clarify his consistent comparisons between man's pre and post-fallen state. Given these two factors it is advantageous to include the discussion in Part I as a backdrop for Luther's understanding of epistemology, in addition to the fact that it will serve to clarify the rest of the work.

The second topic (chapter three) will deal head-on with the question of Luther's epistemology. Previous approaches to Luther's thought have almost completely ignored the epistemological issues pregnant within the topic of reason and have, in my opinion, begged the more central questions. Important to this issue is the influence of William of Ockham on Luther's epistemological position. Much attention is therefore directed toward Ockham's epistemology and the related charge of scepticism. It will be observed here that it is now of general consensus that Ockham was not, as previously charged, a sceptic concerning knowledge in general.

This is a rather important point for the present study as previous approaches have suggested the opposite.[21] Assuming then that Luther was positively influenced by Ockham in the area of epistemology, as I believe he was, he is no longer open to the charge of scepticism latent in other studies.

Finally, the third topic (chapter four) will examine Luther's understanding of the nature and legitimacy of formal reasoning within his epistemological framework. I focus here on such questions as, What does Luther regard as a *reasonable* use of logical analysis? Of particular importance is the relation between deductive and inductive inference. This chapter also deals with the important connection Luther noted between our actual use of language and the way in which we draw logical inference. What I hope to provide in Part I is Luther's basic philosophical framework with which we can then examine his peculiar approach to the issue of human reason.

In Part II the so-called internal question will be evaluated by noting those peculiar elements connected to reason, and its associated limitations, within the general structure of Luther's thought. We will begin this portion of the work (chapter five) – having already established the fact that Luther believes logical analysis necessary to both philosophy *and* theology – by asking the obvious question: Exactly what does Luther have in mind when he calls reason the "devil's whore?" His often used synonyms for reason, speculation and imagination, are highly significant in this regard. He believes that reason is naturally prone to speculate about the nature of God's divine majesty apart from any objective source of information. Reason's natural impulse, in other words, is to "imagine" false premises from which it then draws invalid conclusions. Without an objective, external source of knowledge, man cannot reason his way to God. This aspect of Luther's thought will naturally bring us to the subject of the next chapter – the person and work of Christ.

It will be shown in chapter six that there is an internal link within Luther's thought between fallen reason and the person and work of Christ. The link begins in Eden, where reason is created to the sole end that it may instinctively know and love God. However, in his fall from Paradise man now faces the horrible reality that his reason becomes perverted and loses the function for which it was created. Man no longer understands God's character, that he is a God who wills to have mercy on those who call on him. As such fallen reason now has need of both soteriological and epistemological clarification, thereby requiring an external source of knowledge consonant with the limitations of human comprehension. In other words, man is in the most desperate of situations, one in which he cannot answer *either* the question of "How do I know God?" *or* that of "How am I saved?"

---

[21] See for instance Gerrish, *Grace and Reason* p. 55.

The one hinges upon the other. In the midst of this dilemma reason is restored, though only partially, through that historic event of the incarnation in which God graciously reveals his heart, finding its ultimate expression on the cross. Only here is reason's created function restored in which it obtains a true knowledge of God, or more centrally, knows God as Savior. Luther's later understanding of the *Deus absconditus* and the hypostatic union will be thoroughly examined in this chapter. In chapter seven we will briefly consider the logical centrality of Christ's resurrection for Christian theology as Luther understands it.

Chapter eight will conclude our overall discussion of reason by examining in detail Luther's notion of limits. Reason, according to Luther, was not satisfied to stay within the boundaries that God had originally imposed in Eden and consequently turned inward for further speculation. This speculative disease of the human mind is innate as a result of man's fall, which means that it is common to both the unbeliever and believer. As a result, Luther often warns Christians to keep their own ideas in check and to beware of overestimating the significance of their own thoughts and wisdom. For, as he relentlessly points out, to leave the manger of the God-man is nothing less than a separation from the one true God. But given the fact that Christians do not have a daily direct access to Christ himself, how does Luther suggest that we actually carry out his advice? In this regard he could hardly be clearer: As he consistently bids reason be taken captive to the person of Christ – revealed only in the eyewitness accounts of the Apostles – so he also urges that Christians bring their reason captive in the Holy Sacraments. Luther insists that God works solely through the oral Word and Sacraments, thereby highlighting his epistemological position that knowledge of God is not innate. In a life-long use of these visible means of grace Christians combat their single worst problem, a love for their own wisdom, on a practical and obtainable level. Thus, says Luther, God gathers us together and encloses us within the limits of the Word, both oral and visible, so that we are not tossed about by false doctrine or go astray in our own self-chosen works and speculations.

Part III will conclude our examination of Luther by reevaluating the peculiar features in his understanding of the faith/reason relation. In chapter nine we will see that he believes, on the one hand, that reason judges only on the basis of what it sees and hears and, on the other hand, that it also – because of its sinful nature – often forms bizarre ideas purely on the basis of its own inward speculation. Based on this, he characterizes the battle between faith and reason as the believer's fight to hold on to the kernel of faith he has in the midst of a world that seems to discredit the Gospel's claims. But the Gospel's claim is well substantiated, Luther proposes, by the historicity of Christ's resurrection. Therefore a large part of this struggle consists in concentrating on this fact – one which gives the *reason* for all of Christian doctrine – through Word and Sacrament. On this account, there are ample reasons to believe in Christ but reason continually draws man's thinking back to the hardships of the present. Thus to counter this innate weakness faith, through an exhausting battle, draws the believer back to the simple Word of God. The supposed antithesis is therefore not one characterized by an epistemological gulf between what can be known by reason and what can be known only through faith. Faith in this sense actually arrests man's unreasonableness by concentrating on that which is objective, rather than on the mind's self-created premises and illegitimate conclusions.

Chapter ten will deal solely with the subject of Luther's place in philosophical theology. Specifically, his relation to the fideist tradition is examined in detail. Generally speaking, I will contend that Luther, despite seeming affinities with a fideist tradition, is unequivocally outside this line of thinking insisting as he does on proof for one's theological position. To conclude Part III, chapter eleven will detail my own summary and conclusions. Finally, secondary literature will constitute the focus for all of Part IV (because, however, this has already been mentioned in some detail above I will not summarize my findings here).

To conclude, a word needs to be said about the primary sources utilized for this work. In order to minimize an artificial elevation of factors that may otherwise prove secondary in Luther's thinking, I have employed a broad base of his later works, including not only his major later commentaries but also some of his important later academic disputations and polemical treatises, in addition to some of his final sermons. One of those sources frequently cited is Luther's *Genesis* lectures. While I recognize that some particular aspects of these lectures have been called into doubt, I nevertheless maintain that for the most part the lecture series is substantially and unmistakably the voice of Luther (to use Pelikan's phrase). My opinion is based on the fact that the thought pattern displayed in the series meshes almost exactly with that expressed in other works of the same time period. Given that it can hardly be denied, in my opinion, that it is one of the richest sources we possess of Luther's later thought. At any rate, we cannot afford simply to ignore the vast amount of information it contains. However, it must also be emphasized that I have not cited anything from those lectures that cannot be found – at least to some extent – in other works of our proposed time period, and cannot therefore be found guilty of total dependence on that work.

PART ONE

Epistemology and Logic

CHAPTER
ONE

The Problem in
its Historical Context

It might be said that the Western philosophical tradition has to a large extent been a continuing conversation about the scope and legitimacy of human reason, necessarily entailing the broader issues involved in epistemology and logic. What "reason" actually is and to what extent its powers are valid has been hotly debated from at least as far back as the ancient Greeks and continues right up to the present, and doubtlessly will continue to be an issue of contention far into the future. Because the Greeks made such a strong impact and could be even said to have set the stage for every following generation concerning this great debate, it will be helpful to highlight very briefly their contributions. Without a doubt though, a more important reason for us to summarize their thought is because it was their contributions to western civilization that, to a large extent, fixed the pattern of Christian philosophy in the middle ages, and is therefore a firm component of Luther's heritage. With that said let us turn to the fathers of the debate, followed by a short evaluation of their influence in the Middle Ages.

Modern scholarship is in overall agreement concerning most of the issues lying at the heart of the Greek conception of reason, logic, and epistemology. These issues can be characterized roughly as follows: Generally speaking, it is acknowledged that behind the Greek concept of reason lay the conception of form. Form is identity of structure, a one in many, a pattern that maintains itself through diversity and change. This form, or order, is not seen or heard as sound and color are; that is, it is not sensed at all, but apprehended in a different way that is called intelligence. Reason, on this view, is that which sees the abstract in the concrete and the universal in the particular.[1] To Aristotle, for example, the notion of form as end is fundamental to his ethics. Man is a half-grown being trying to become what he is not yet, and if we are to define the essence of what he is we must project ourselves forward and catch the form, in the sense of goal or ideal, which he is attempting to realize. You can determine, in other words, what man is only through what he is striving to become. Aristotle would thus not endorse any cleft between naturalism and ethics, or between fact and value. "Nor was there any conflict for the Greek between the scientist or moralist on the one hand and the metaphysician on the other. How were you to determine what the world as a whole was like? Simply by carrying through to the end the process that revealed to you the nature of a bed or the nature of man. Having discovered the essential natures or purposes of these and other things, we must try to put these purposes together, to discover the joint design, the over-arching purpose, of the whole."[2]

Concerning the more specific area of science, Plato regarded geometry as the ideal of scientific knowledge, and he was so thoroughly a rationalist that he believed all scientific knowledge would in the end prove to be of this necessary type. It appears that he viewed things this way for the following reasons.[3] For one, knowledge of such a kind is certain. Plato assumes from the outset that knowledge is attainable and that it must be both infallible and of the *real* i.e., any state of mind that cannot vindicate its claim as such cannot be true knowledge. Plato accepts Protagoras's view that sense-perception is relative, that is, it is elusive and subject to the influence of temporary influences on part of both subject and object. Moreover, he accepts Heraclitus's view that the objects of sense-perception are always in a state of becoming and are unfit to be the objects of true knowledge. And in that the objects of sense-perception pass away and cannot be clearly defined, they cannot be the objects of scientific knowledge. It thus follows not only that sense-perception does not possess the marks of true knowledge and cannot therefore be equated with true knowledge, but also that true knowledge of sensible objects cannot even be obtained.[4] If it is understood what is being said in geometry, on the other hand, it quickly becomes evident that we are not, indeed cannot be, mistaken. In fact, in mathematics we see that a conclusion is true only when

[1] Brand Blanshard, *Reason and Analysis* (London, 1962) p. 55. Quoting Thomas Whittaker, Blanshard says that the widest sense of reason is "the relational element in intelligence, in distinction from the element of content, sensational or emotional." Whittaker also points out that both the Greek term *logos* and the Latin *ratio,* from which "reason" has largely drawn its meaning, were sometimes used to denote simply "relation" or "order" (p. 25).

[2] Blanshard, *Reason and Analysis* p. 59.

[3] Blanshard, *Reason and Analysis* pp. 60–62.

[4] Frederick Copleston, *A History of Philosophy* (London, 1976) Vol. 1, pp. 143–149.

we also see that is *must* be true. Second, such thinking gives new truth. Purely *a priori* reasoning, so thought Plato, provides us fresh knowledge about the world. Third, such knowledge is independent of sense. Although this does not mean that sensible things are of no aid, it does mean that the sensible figure – for example a triangle – is a mere approximation or vehicle of the *real;* in short, *the* triangle can never be caught or confined in any of its sensible disguises. And finally, such knowledge on Plato's account must be knowledge of the universal and abiding, as it is only this that fulfills the requirements for being an object of knowledge.[5] By this Plato means that there are no exceptions to it, and thus the same for all men. This fact follows from necessity e.g., if we see that the Pythagorean theorem about triangles must be true, then we need not worry about a triangle turning up in the future that proves anomalous. "Plato would have said, as Bosanquet did, that the solidarity of mankind lies in the intellectual life."[6]

The fact that reason gives the same answers everywhere, when clearly thought through, is thought by Plato to show that knowledge is objective. This means that when men lay hold of the same laws it is because they are out there to grasp; concepts or universals are found, not manufactured. One cannot change at will the laws discovered by reason because they belong to the very nature of things, or, to the "bony structure of the world."[7] Plato had hoped to reach in his ultimate idea of reason an understanding which grasped things as a complete and necessary system, where everything is made intelligible through the part it played in the whole. This kind of insight, the "nous", is beyond even the mathematical, and consists of ideas and their relations apprehended only by intelligence. "The framework of the world was not a dead system of logic or geometry. It was alive."[8]

Aristotle on the other hand held that there are different degrees of knowledge.[9] Knowledge, on his view, does in fact start from sense; that is, it starts from the particular and ascends to the general or universal.[10] This can be partially illustrated in the following manner. The man of "mere experience" may know that a

---

[5] Any time, according to Plato, that we attain stable and abiding knowledge we find that it concerns the universal. That is, definition concerns the universal; thus true knowledge is knowledge of the universal. See Copleston, *A History of Philosophy* Vol. 1, pp. 150–151.

[6] Blanshard, *Reason and Analysis* p. 62.

[7] Blanshard, *Reason and Analysis* pp. 62–63. For an excellent discussion concerning Plato's concept of the ascent of knowledge, see Copleston, *A History of Philosophy* Vol. 1, pp. 151–162.

[8] Blanshard, *Reason and Analysis* pp. 65–67.

[9] Copleston, *A History of Philosophy* Vol. 1, pp. 287–288.

[10] Copleston, *A History of Philosophy* Vol. 1, p. 281. "Thus it is clear that we must get to know the primary premises by induction; for the methods by which even sense-perception implants the universal is inductive." *Anal. Post.,* II 19, 100 b (as quoted by Copleston). This however must be understood

certain medicine had done good to X without knowing the reason for it. But the man of "art" knows the reason and as such he knows a universal i.e., he knows that the medicine will tend to cure all who suffer from that particular ailment. But this in itself is not Wisdom according to Aristotle, for the highest Wisdom is not utilitarian; rather, it is that which apprehends the first principles of Reality. On this account, Wisdom deals with the first principles and causes of things and is therefore universal knowledge in the highest degree. Yet this means also that it is the science which is furthest removed from the senses, or the most abstract, and is the most difficult of the sciences because it involves the greatest effort of thought. Nevertheless, it is the most exact of the sciences and is in itself the most knowable since it deals with the first principles of all things. These principles are in themselves more knowable than their applications (as they depend upon the first principles), though this does not mean that they are the most knowable *to us,* since we necessarily start with things of sense.[11] In actual discovery we usually have to reverse the process and argue from the "familiar to us," highly complex facts, to the "more knowable in its own nature," the simpler principles implied in the facts.[12] From sense-perception however it requires a considerable effort of rational abstraction to proceed from what is directly known to us – sense-objects – to their ultimate principles.

We have seen that when Plato referred to science he had in mind an ideal science, that is, mathematics. But what of the sciences that do not appear to possess such a governing necessity about them, say astronomy and physics? While Plato had little to say concerning the natural sciences, Aristotle did in fact formulate how these two disparate fields are related. By science Aristotle had in mind proved knowledge, that is, the knowledge of *conclusions* from premises. The "proof" is simply the pointing out of the connection between the truth we call the conclusion and others that we call the premises of our demonstration: "Science points out the *reason why* of things, and this is what is meant by the Aristotelian principle that to have science is to know things through their *causes* or *reasons why.*" In a properly ordered system of scientific truths we should begin with the simplest

in light of Taylor's remarks that "Aristotle insists that Induction does not yield scientific proof. 'He who makes an induction points out something, but does not demonstrate anything'." The reasons for this are discussed below. See A. E. Taylor, *Aristotle* (London and Edinburgh, 1919) p. 41.

[11] Copleston observes that Aristotle recognizes that there is a difference between logical priority or priority *in se* and epistemological priority *quoad nos:* "He expressly states that 'prior' and 'better known' are ambiguous terms, for there is a difference between what is prior and better known in the order of being and what is prior and better known to man. I mean that objects nearer to sense are prior and better known to man; objects without qualification prior and better known are those further from sense." See *A History of Philosophy* Vol. 1, p. 281–282.

[12] Taylor, *Aristotle* p. 40.

and most widely extended principles and reason down – through successive inferences – to the most complex propositions, "the reason why of which can only be
exhibited by a long chain of deductions."[13] For him, scientific knowledge means
deducing the particular from the general or the conditioned from its cause, in
order that we know both the cause on which the particular fact depends and the
necessary condition between the fact and its cause. This implies that we have scientific knowledge when we know the cause as the cause of that fact and no other,
and, that the fact could not be other than it is.[14] Genuine scientific knowledge
thus has the status of necessary truth,[15] as the first principles of any science must
be indemonstrable.[16] It follows from this that sense-perception of itself can never
give us scientific truth because it can only assure us that a fact is so. It cannot in
other words explain the fact by showing its connection with the rest of the system
of facts i.e., it does not give us the *reason* for the fact. Science in Aristotle's estimation is not just a catalog of things and events, but is the inquiry into the real
essences and characteristics of things and laws of connection between events.[17]
(Taylor in particular argues that, in this regard, Aristotle's theory of knowledge
only begins in naturalism but ultimately ends in Platonism.)

Let us take as a concrete example the familiar syllogism, "All men are mortal,
Socrates is a man, Therefore Socrates is mortal." The conclusion, Aristotle points
out, is linked to the premise by necessity. But, we may ask, is there really any
necessity in the major premise that all men are mortal? Aristotle thought in fact

---

[13] Taylor, *Aristotle* p. 40.

[14] Copleston, *A History of Philosophy* Vol. 1, pp. 281.

[15] John Losee, *A Historical Introduction to the Philosophy of Science* (Oxford, New York, 1993)
p.15. Losee goes on to say that "Aristotle bequeathed to his successors a faith that, because the first
principles of the sciences mirror relations in nature which could not be other than they are, these
principles are incapable of being false."

[16] Taylor, *Aristotle* p. 43.

[17] Taylor, *Aristotle* p. 41. Taylor goes on to say that all science is then the search for "middle terms" of
syllogisms by which to connect the truth which appears as a conclusion with the less complex truths
which appear as the premises from which it is drawn. And as the middle term must be taken univer-
sally, the search for middle terms may also be described as the search for universals; we may thus
speak of science as knowledge of the universal interconnections between facts and events (p. 42).

there was and held that there is such a thing as intuitive induction[18] by which one can see that such and such a character implies or necessitates another.[19] Blanshard comments on this in the following:

> The causal laws of science are commonly assumed to be mere fixed conjunctions in which we link A and B together for no better reason than that we have never found them apart. Regarding many of these laws, Aristotle would have conceded that we do not see their necessity; we have no idea, for example, why horned animals should all be ruminants. Regarding many others he would have insisted that we are not wholly in the dark about them; flesh and blood as put together in the human body form the sort of thing that would disintegrate. But he would have said that where we had a genuine law before us, we could always, if we looked sharply enough, see the bright thread of necessity running through the causal link. This conviction, like so much else in Aristotle, comes from Plato, of whom it may be said that 'wherever he finds law, and he finds it everywhere, he finds rationality and the Good'.[20]

Although there is an emphasis on inductive inference in Aristotle in the sense that syllogism through induction is clearer *to us,* his ideal is clearly that of deduction, of syllogistic demonstration. He did see that the premises in deduction themselves need proof, but if, he thought, every principle needs proof then we will be involved in a *processus in infinitum* and nothing will be proved. Accordingly, he held that there are particular principles that are known intuitively and immediately without demonstration, the highest of these being the principle of contradiction and one for which no proof can be given. The first principles of any science must be indemonstrable and must be known immediately. But how do we come to know them? Aristotle avoids possible internal inconsistency here by maintaining that the sole function of the induction is to fix our attention on a principle which it does not prove – ultimate principles neither permit nor require proof. When the induction has done its work in calling attention to the principle, you have to see for yourself that the principle is true. "You see that it is true by immediate inspection, just as in sense-perception you have to see that the color before your eyes is red or blue.

---

[18] An example of this is the case of a scientist who notices on several occasions that the bright side of the moon is turned toward the sun and who concludes that the moon shines by reflective sunlight. "The operation of intuitive induction is analogous to the operation of the 'vision' of the taxonomist. The taxonomist is a scientist who has learned to 'see' the generic attributes and differentiae of a specimen...This is an ability which is achieved, if at all, only after extensive experience." See Losee, *A Historical Introduction to the Philosophy of Science* p. 8. Losee cites the above example from the *Posterior Analytics* 89b10–20.

[19] Blanshard, *Reason and Analysis* p. 63.

[20] Blanshard, *Reason and Analysis* pp. 63–64.

This is why Aristotle holds that the knowledge of the principles of science is not itself science (demonstrated knowledge), but what he calls intelligence, and we may call intellectual intuition."[21] (Taylor points out here that Aristotle's theory of knowledge is therefore sharply distinguished not only from empiricism but also from theories of the Hegelian type.)

With this in mind then Aristotle's epistemological progression – as presented by Copleston – can be characterized as follows: (1) first principles; (2) what is derived necessarily from first principles; and (3) what is contingent and could be otherwise. But as we have already alluded to above Aristotle clearly saw that the major premise of a syllogism, for instance, "All men are mortal," cannot be derived immediately from the first principles; it depends also on induction. It is this important aspect of Aristotelian epistemology that involves a realist theory of universals, and Aristotle declares that induction exhibits the universal as implicit in the clearly known particular.[22] Thus although Aristotle passes adverse judgment on Plato's theory of Ideas, he is in full agreement with Plato that the universal is not merely a subjective concept or a mode of oral expression. What Aristotle intends by this is that, to the universal in the mind, there corresponds the specific essence in the object, though this essence does not exist in any state of separation outside of the mind.[23] It is separated in other words only in the mind and through the mind's activity. Therefore Aristotle, along with Plato, believed that the object of science is the universal. Copleston sums this up nicely: "Strictly speaking, therefore, there is no objective Universal for Aristotle, but there is an objective foundation in things for the subjective universal in the mind. The universal 'horse' is a subjective concept, but it has an objective foundation in the substantial forms that inform particular horses."[24]

Besides theoretical reason as briefly summarized above, both Plato and Aristotle recognized a practical reason whose influence is direct and permeating, and interestingly it appears in the list of virtues under the name of "wisdom." For Plato, it is the charioteer, keeping a firm and equal reign upon the black and white

[21] Taylor, *Aristotle* pp. 43–45.

[22] Copleston, *A History of Philosophy* Vol. 1, p. 283. Copleston also points out that Aristotle carried analysis of deductive processes to a high level and very completely, but the same cannot be said for induction. It is a fact however natural in a time where mathematics was so much more developed than the natural sciences.

[23] "While admitting the general Platonic position that the universal element, or essential form, is the object of science, of rational knowledge, he identified this universal element with the immanent essential form of the sensible object, which, together with its matter, constitutes the object and which is the intelligible principle in the object." Copleston, *A History of Philosophy* Vol. 1, p. 375. See also Taylor, *Aristotle* p. 39.

[24] Copleston, *A History of Philosophy* Vol. 1, pp. 301–302.

horse, the appetites and the passions. Both philosophers however agree as to the court of appeal: form as end is to prescribe form as law or rule. Man is a bundle of impulses which should be dealt with, according to wisdom, by developing in harmony in the interest of the man as a whole. There is an appropriate form of life for the individual human being, as its course will allow for differing emphases with differing talents. But how is this form discovered? Partly by studying one's powers experimentally, but it is wisdom which tells us what to do with it. How did it proceed according to Plato and Aristotle? Blanshard says that "just as a sculptor at work on a statue knows, though perhaps dimly, the ideal figure he wants to embody, and knows that in the light of it a larger nose or an extended arm would be unfitting, so men generally, who are the sculptors of their fate, know dimly the form of life that in the end will satisfy them..." Aristotle's ethics has been described as aestheticism since the beauty of a life was the test of its goodness, and Plato, somewhat more mystically, held that if we ever achieve the final truth about things we have to set them under the form of the good. Thus reason for Plato was far more than framing an argument; more precisely it was "that in us upon which we must call if we would form an adequate notion of the ends of our life, or plan that life completely."[25]

Blanshard observes that these Greek conceptions of reason have been dominant ideas throughout western culture, so much so that they contain all the major elements that later philosophers have found in reason. Western thought can be seen on this view as little more than a series of footnotes to Plato. "It is Greek rationalism again, this time in its Aristotelian form, that was taken over by Thomas Aquinas and used as the instrument for systematizing Christian belief. Aristotle's account of reasoning was almost as canonical as Scripture in the Middle Ages, and remained so till the sixteenth century."[26]

The Christian Era

The revival of dialectic in the eleventh century well illustrates the plausibility of Blandshard's remarks. It was then that, for the first time in the middle ages, some of the great problems of metaphysics and epistemology had to be faced, and the classical world of Plato and Aristotle proved so important to formulating sufficient answers that they were almost canonized as the ruling authority in such

[25] Blanshard, *Reason and Analysis* pp. 68–69.

[26] Blanshard, *Reason and Analysis* p. 69.

matters.[27] So much so that no medieval thinker started to build a system from the postulates of his own mental experience.[28] Aristotle's system in particular came to be regarded as a corpus of rational, natural truths, which are as ascertainable and valid in their degree as is the body of revelation. (Even as scholasticism declined with Ockham and his followers, the greatest reverence is still shown to Aristotle; this is shown in the attempts to represent their ideas as a more faithful interpretation of the "Philosopher.")[29]

Significantly, it is here with the mental awakening of the mid-eleventh century masters of logic that the age of scholasticism may be said to begin. Knowles argues that in using the term "scholastic" we should not have in mind content as opposed to the method of medieval philosophy, as it is better defined as a term of method. "If by a scholastic method we understand a method of discovering and illustrating philosophical truth by means of dialectic based on Aristotelian logic, then 'scholastic' is a useful and significant term." This medieval dialectic typically followed a basic pattern of question *(quaestio),* argument *(diputatio)* and conclusion *(sententia).*[30] It is the revival of this very dialectic, Knowles points out, that is perhaps the most remarkable element of this awakening. The growing self-confidence of the schools found expression in their assertions concerning the supremacy of reason. It seemed that there were no limits to the field which the human mind could master, with the result that all arguments that were not strictly logical and formal seemed worthless. "Rationalism in the modern sense made its appearance, with its accompaniments in individuals of scepticism and pessimism." Berengar of Tours, for instance, was prepared to state that reason, not authority, is mistress and judge. For him dialectic is the art of arts (a position

---

[27] Although it must be mentioned that a distinct move towards the supremacy of dialectic was made by John Scotus Erigena in the ninth century. Erigena saw dialectic as "the mother of the arts" and held that it is not a product of human invention but has been established in the very nature of things by God. Jaroslav Pelikan observes that in "the history of philosophy, 'Erigena was not so much the first medieval as the last ancient philosopher'; but he was nevertheless the theologian who decisively raised, for the first time in the Middle Ages, the theological question of the claims of reason in the formulation of Christian doctrine, especially in the interpretation of the relation of God and the world." See *The Growth of Medieval Theology (600–1300)* (Chicago and London, 1978) pp. 95–98.

[28] David Knowles, edited by D. E. Luscombe and C. N. L. Brooke (Second Edition), *The Evolution of Medieval Thought* (London and New York, 1988) pp. 82–83. Knowles goes on to say that "If that, in its totality, is learnt, accepted and practiced, a whole great system of thought becomes available. It is at once the strength and the weakness of Aristotelian thought, both in the Middle Ages and in more modern times, that a tightly bound network of syllogisms radiates from a single great axiom, and that within that network every part appears, logically speaking, to be the inevitable consequence of its neighbor."

[29] Knowles, *The Evolution of Medieval Thought* p. 81.

[30] Knowles, *The Evolution of Medieval Thought* p. 79.

that would soon become widely accepted), and it is the sign of an eminent mind that it turn all things to dialectics, including the mysteries of faith. The reason for this is that dialectic is the exercise of reason, and reason is incomparably superior to authority when it is a question of ascertaining the truth.[31]

While the masters of the eleventh century had inherited only the so-called "old" logic of Aristotle – mainly in translation and with the commentaries of Boethius – the middle decades of the twelfth century marked the arrival of the "new" logic, completing the Aristotelian corpus on the subject. These new sources[32] were mainly concerned with the modes of propositions, the syllogism in all its forms, the various methods of argument, and the detection of fallacies. Its subsequent impact is clearly seen in that dialectical logic was soon to become the be-all and end-all in liberal arts, and along with it the "question" and "disputation" as the basic form of all teaching and discovery was canonized for the whole of the middle ages and beyond. Great emphasis was put upon the manipulation of syllogisms, as well as demolishing false arguments and pressing valid conclusions. The syllogism therefore became the "steel framework" of argumentation to the extent that is was all pervasive not only as the foundation of all assertions and criticisms, but also to the amazing extent that is was capable of indefinite extension and inevitably supported the construction of cosmology and deep theological speculation.[33]

The importance of Aristotle's "dialectical" reasoning is further demonstrated in the medieval Aristotelianism of the schoolmen with whom it became a regular method. For them, the best point of departure was to begin their consideration of a doctrine by a preliminary rehearsal of all the arguments they could find or devise against the conclusion they meant to adopt. We see this, for instance, in the *Summa Theologiae* of St. Thomas, where the first division of any article is regularly constituted by arguments based on the premises of actual or possible antagonists, and is in that sense strictly dialectical. The reason for such an approach, as we have seen, is that no genuine simple principle according to Aristotle admits of demonstration. So all that can be done in answer to the man who denies the "self-evident truth" of an alleged "principle" is to examine the consequences of a denial of the axiom and show that they include some that are false. One indirectly establishes the truth of a given principle in other words by showing the

---

[31] Knowles, *The Evolution of Medieval Thought* pp. 85–87.

[32] Knowles lists them as the *Analytica priora,* the *Analytica posteriora,* the *Topica* and the *De elenchis sophisticis.*

[33] Knowles, *The Evolution of Medieval Thought* pp. 171–172. Logic was now a separate academic subject such that the student went to logic at the earliest possible convenience, as it easily lent itself not only to exercises in mental agility but also to deep speculation.

falsity of consequences that follow from its denial. This is dialectical reasoning in
Aristotle's sense of the word i.e., reasoning not from your own but from someone
else's premises.[34]

It has been suggested by Knowles that it was this very erection of logic and
dialectic as the sole training and method behind every intellectual discipline in the
twelfth and thirteenth centuries that proved to be the partial cause of the decline of
scholastic philosophy. Such an emphasis gradually brought about the divorce between life and thought, and the physical universe no longer continued to supply the
philosopher with impetus for thought. Scripture itself and the traditions of the past
had an even smaller place in the theologian's interests. "Thought divorced from
life must always wither, and the philosopher of the fourteenth century withdrew
more and more into his own world, in which definitions and conclusions were no
longer controlled by all other kinds of human experience. Ideas and principles
were strained to the limit, and ultimately thought preyed upon itself, and suffered
fragmentation."[35] Though this is certainly at least partially true, there was an important shift in thinking on these topics which occurred in the fourteenth century
e.g., Ockham, that forever changed the face of epistemology and logic and has
been appropriately characterized as follows:

> As physics became released from metaphysics, and as the laws of nature were
> explored through the study of this world, rational and scientific investigation
> and experimentation were able to develop – and God's freedom was revalued
> when the older framework of necessary laws of nature had been loosened by
> criticism. The struggles in the fourteenth century between the *via antiqua* of
> realism and the *via moderna* of nominalism, together with all their implications
> in logic, epistemology, metaphysics, ethics, theology and politics, have cast long
> shadows reaching down to the present – and disagreements can be expected to
> continue into the future.[36]

As Ockham is such a pivotal figure in this development we will reserve special
comment for a later chapter. For now it is enough to note the change that takes
place as a result of Ockham's work away from metaphysical notions of reason and
epistemology towards one that places a great deal of importance on observation.

---

[34] Taylor, *Aristotle* pp. 46–47.

[35] Knowles, *The Evolution of Medieval Thought* (London and New York, 1988) p. 309. His remarks
here are doubtless valuable, yet, as has been pointed out by Luscombe and Brooke, Knowles was
generally unsympathetic towards the nominalist criticisms of earlier metaphysics, "not least because
it removed the basis of a demonstrable theology." See their "Introduction to the Second Edition" of
the above work, p. xxv.

[36] D. E. Luscombe and C. N. L. Brooke (ed.), *The Evolution of Medieval Thought* (London and New
York, 1988) p. xxv.

And even though Ockham gives the Philosopher such high honor as he does, this is nevertheless the *beginnings* of a movement away from Aristotelian epistemology. This evolution marks an important change in reason's significance and the role it plays in ascertaining truth, and is therefore of decisive importance to our present topic, as it is within this milieu that Luther's understanding of epistemology and reason takes its shape. Luther was despondent over the fact that ideas and principles were indeed strained to the uttermost limit, and it became one of the hallmarks of his criticisms of reason, as conceived both by the scholastics and his rationalist Protestant opponents, that their own thoughts did in fact prey upon themselves ultimately to create an unrealistic view of human reason and logic. The peculiar features of Luther's notion cannot be fully appreciated if disconnected from this emergent western tradition. As I hope to show, the complexity of his thought at this point has been widely neglected and misunderstood both by his critics and his advocates. His understanding of these issues can and should be seen as both a continuation of Ockham's breakthrough in epistemology *and* a peculiar refinement of that epistemology; and an understanding, if I may be so bold, that is at points much clearer than Ockham's (particularly in the area of religious epistemology).

With Luther however we find an additional element that is not at first easy to explain, and thus complicates the task of identifying the key elements of his thinking. Specifically, the problem consists in his seemingly unqualified condemnations of reason as a "schedliche Hure" and "Teuffels Braut."[37] This is all the more perplexing when juxtaposed with other comments (e.g., *Die Disputation de homine*) regarding reason's divine derivation and its possession of a certain divine "majesty." One naturally asks how reason can be, at the same time, both divine and the devil's whore? Whatever answer is offered one thing remains clear: the tension between Luther's various remarks permeates his writings, and intensifies with his repeated assertion that faith ultimately conquers (or kills) reason. So our task appears to be doubly complicated.

[37] See WA LI 129.19–21; 126.29.

CHAPTER

TWO

Luther's Beginning: Eden and the Fall

As stated earlier, a major objective of this project will be to provide an adequate definition of reason according to Luther's later understanding. To do so, I have chosen to begin the evaluation, not by adducing Luther's various comments on reason's legitimacy, but rather by evaluating his stance on man's state in the Garden of Eden. This may seem a bit odd, but I think it will prove valuable because Luther goes into some detail about what reason's majestic qualities were, and why they were so important to Adam and Eve pre-fall. That is, it can be truly said that in the Garden reason functioned according to its created purpose. The strength of this method is that of being able to define what reason was before man's corruption, and in turn to clarify the comparisons Luther consistently makes between man's pre- and post-fallen state. In other words, it is hoped that this will provide a backdrop, so to speak, that we may then use to evaluate Luther's well-known condemnations of reason. We will therefore begin with a brief discussion of the Garden of Eden followed immediately with Luther's discussion of the fall.

The Garden

Luther's remarks on man's pre-fallen state manifests two striking features: (1) reason is viewed in direct relation to God[38] and, (2) there is an almost inseparable

---

[38] Bernard Lohse observes a "certain parallelism" between reason and conscience in this regard, "yet conscience is the larger concept," as he sees conscience in direct relation to God. Quoting Hirsch, Lohse says that conscience is the "bearer of man's relationship to God." See Lohse's "Conscience

relation between reason and will. First, what does Luther mean by the potentially ambiguous terms "reason" and "will" within his discussion of Paradise?

Fortunately, his definitions are fairly straight-forward: Briefly, reason or intellect[39] is primarily that part of Adam's make-up which enabled him to *know* God and his will, and the ability to "perceive" his works.[40] This does not, of course, imply that reason's ability to compute and calculate is somehow excluded from his definition.[41] What Luther seems to mean is that the former qualities constituted

---

and Authority in Luther" in *Luther and the Dawn of the Modern Era* (Leiden, 1974), ed. Heiko A. Oberman, pp. 161, n. 5, 163. Lohse cites additional references in his *Ratio und Fides* (Göttingen, 1958), p. 90, n. 6.

[39] Reason and intellect are often used synonymously as in the following: "quod omnis culpa sit tuae concupiscentiae, et tum voluntatis, tum rationis depravatae" WA XLII 510.21–22. In the next paragraph the same sequence is used except for the fact that *intellectus* is used instead of *rationis*: "convincunt nos de corruptione naturae nostrae, quod neque voluntas, nec intellectus rectus sit..." (510.26–28). This is cited to show that there is not always a discernible difference between the two words, and *intellectus* must also be examined as it relates to Luther's understanding of *ratio*. Also in the following reference the two have the same function in man: intellect no longer knows God and His will and no longer "perceives" His works, and further down Adam had a keen intellect and knew the origin of Eve: "Sed peccatum originale est vere totus lapsus naturae humanae, quod est intellectus obscuratus, ut non agnoscamus amplius Deum et voluntatem eius, ut non animadvertamus opera Dei." WA XLII 86.18–21. *Intellectu* no longer knows God, thus does not differ from the way Luther uses reason. The same function is said of *rationis* WA XLII 124.11–12: "Sicut enim natura oculi est videre, Ita natura rationis et voluntatis in Adamo fuit nosse Deum, fidere Deo, timere Deum." Lohse, quoting early Luther, also shows that Luther did not make many significant distinctions between man's various functions: "What, then, is our lantern which enlightens with this light of the Word? Without a doubt it is our heart, and it makes no difference whether you call it conscience or intellect" WA V 525.11–13. Steven Ozment observes the same of the young Luther concerning the separate terms *spiritus, mens, cor* and *conscientia;* these prove to be concepts correlative with *anima,* and not independent parts of the soul, which he uses to designate as comprehensively as possible the life and activity of the human being. *See Homo Spiritualis: A Comparative Study of the Anthropology of Johannes Tauler, Jean Gerson, and Martin Luther (1509–16) in the Context of Their Theological Thought* (Leiden, 1969) p. 94. On the basis of these remarks I think that Wolfhart Pannenberg is clearly mistaken in his *Basic Questions in Theology* (London, 1967) Vol. 2, pp. 55–57, when he equates Luther's model with an Aristotelian-Thomistic conception of reason, one which distinguishes between the coordination of reason *(ratio)* and intellect *(intellectus).* (One other interesting feature of his examination of Luther's faith/reason understanding is his erroneous claim that "Luther's evaluation of reason easily lends itself to being carried over to the Kantian understanding of reason." The overall issue of epistemology however will be discussed in detail below.) Hereafter intellect will be cited when synonymous with reason, otherwise it should be understood more generally as "comprehension" or "understanding." See Lewis and Short *A Dictionary of Latin* (Oxford, 1989), *intellectus* p. 974.

[40] See for example Luther's discussion WA XLII 46–49, especially 47.8–11; and conversely WA XLII 86.18–25 and XLII 124.11–12.

[41] Lewis and Short define *ratio* as "that faculty of the mind which forms the basis of computation and calculation, and hence mental action in general, i.e., judgment, understanding, reason" in *A Latin*

reason's *primary* function in the garden, while the latter are simply assumed as
the more obvious operations of reason. Accordingly, then, the former is rated
higher in importance. Adam's will, on the other hand, trusted in God's mercy,
and equally importantly, feared God and was concerned with the Word and will
of God.[42] Though Luther often makes a distinction between reason and will, it is
clear that these taken together constitute man's total nature. Thus the will necessarily affects reason, and vice versa; we cannot properly speak of one as totally
distinct from the other. Olsson seems to me correct when he states the following:
"Es besteht folglich eine innere Wechselwirkung zwischen Vernunft und Willen.
Damit ist auch gegeben, dass die Vernunft auf den Willen einwirkt und der Wille
auf die Vernunft."[43]

The significance of this observation in Eden is that reason and will were in
perfect harmony and *together* constituted Adam's righteous nature. This means
that Adam's intellect not only understood God but also *desired* what God desired.[44] The intimate, even inseparable relation between reason and will cannot
be overemphasized, as it appears to form the basis of Luther's understanding of
"right reason." "Sed Dialecticus facile deprehendet facum: videt enim, deesse
causam formalem, hoc est, rectam rationem, quia Deus non agnoscitur, nec est
recta voluntas erga Deum."[45] Significantly then, right reason consists both of the
knowledge of God *and* a right will toward God; Luther thereby acknowledges
the fact that reason does not somehow operate unaffected and completely distinct
from the will. As we will see, much of Luther's criticism of reason echoes this
position with the result that man's entire nature is condemned under the one word
ratio.

As already indicated, Luther believed that Adam possessed a natural, immediate, knowledge of his Creator. Coupled however with that instinctive knowledge
according to Luther was Adam's instinctive trust in God's command: "Non enim
Deus hominem malum condidit, sed integrum, sanum, sanctum, agnoscentem
Deum, cum recta ratione et bona voluntate erga Deum."[46] Thus Luther will maintain that Adam's simple faith in God's Word and will was his greatest strength,[47]

Dictionary (Oxford, 1989) p. 1526.

[42] WA XLII 86.21–23; 124.11–12.

[43] Herbert Olsson, *Schöpfung, Vernunft und Gesetz in Luthers Theologie* (Uppsala, 1971) p. 504. See
Olsson's extended discussion of the will and its relation to reason pp. 502ff.

[44] WA XLII 248.9–13.

[45] WA XLII 351.1–3.

[46] WA XLII 349.4–5.

[47] "Atque hoc etiam Satanae astus ostendit. Neque enim Heuam statim sollicitat suavitate pomi. Summam virtutem hominis primum invadit, fidem in verbum." WA XLII 122.10–12.

a faith so straight-forward as to be no more complicated than honoring God as God and acknowledging that what he says is true. Here, as above, we see Luther refusing to separate Adam's right knowledge of God from his trust in God's Word. Importantly, Luther's understanding of original righteousness consisted of precisely these two factors, and given these factors he maintains that it was completely without compulsion that Adam loved, believed, and knew God: "Haec tam naturalia fuere in Adamo, quam naturale est, quod oculi lumen recipiunt."[48]

Moreover, original righteousness had as its effect an instinctive understanding of God's workings:

> Sed nos, si Mosen sequimur, definiemus, originalem iusticiam dici, quod homo fuit iustus, verax, rectus, non solum corpore, sed magis animo, quod agnovit deum, quod obedivit Deo cum summa voluptate, quod intellexit opera Dei, etiam non admonitus.[49]

Luther repeatedly emphasizes that Adam had *immediate* knowledge about efficient and final cause, about the beginning and ending of all things, about who created and for what purpose it was created.[50] He thus knew immediately not only of his own origin but also the origin of Eve, that she was bone from his bone and flesh from his flesh: "Hic an non excellens intellectus est, statim primo obtuitu intelligere et agnoscere opus Dei?"[51] Adam also had a perfect knowledge of all the creatures, the herbs, and the trees,[52] and it is this knowledge of efficient and final cause that separated man from the beasts of the field. They do not know their Creator, their origin, and their end; they therefore lack that similitude of God. This will enable Luther to say that even though there is now a great difference between man and beast, in the Garden it was far greater when Adam and Eve were completely engulfed in the goodness and justice of God.[53]

---

[48] WA XLII 124.6–7.

[49] WA XLII 86.3–6.

[50] WA XLII 94.3–8.

[51] WA XLII 86.7–10.

[52] "Fuit enim in Adam ratio illuminata, vera noticia Dei et voluntas rectissima ad diligendum Deum et proximum, sicut Adam Heuam suam complexus est et statim agnovit ut suam carnem. Ad haec accesserunt alia leviora sed longe maxima, si cum nostra infirmitate conferas, nempe cognitio naturae perfecta animalium, herbarum, fructuum, arborum et aliarum creaturarum." WA XLII 47.33–38. See also XLII 87.3–5.

[53] WA XLII 50.13–19. See also XLII 94.3–8.

Reason's Limits

As we have seen Adam was endowed with a very keen intellect, with extraordinary perception so that he immediately knew his Eve, but even more important for Luther's account is the fact that he possessed an upright will.[54] Yet even in this blissful state, his will was yet imperfect (perfection was postponed until the spiritual life after the physical one).[55] Due to the fact, therefore, that his will was not immutable, God imposed limits to keep him from physical and spiritual harm. "Sic necessarium fuit," says Luther, "ut animalis homo etiam cultum animalem seu externum haberet, quo secundum corpus exerceretur in obedienta erga Deum."[56]

Everything had already been entrusted to Adam to make use of according to his will, whether for pleasure or necessity. But the interesting feature of Luther's account is his following qualification: "Requirit tandem Deus ab Adamo, ut in hac arbore scientiae boni et mali reverentiam et obedientiam praestaret erga Deum, et hoc quasi exercitium cultus Dei retineret, ne ex ea quicquam gustaret."[57] Adam was bound to certain forms of worship and was not to move outside of those limits, and the tree is specifically mentioned as Adam's form of obedience to God. Even though Adam had innate knowledge of God, he was still commanded to bring his reason and will captive to the Word, visibly represented at the tree. This was Adam's temple, altar, and platform where he was to give God the obedience he owed, acknowledge the word and will of God, give thanks to God, and call upon him for help against temptation.[58]

For now, the point I wish to make is that even in Eden Luther sees reason constrained by limits, and since the beginning of time these limits have had visible signs attached to them. The signs themselves physically communicate God's goodness and mercy and come to perform an important function within Luther's overall theology. This function is most dramatically illustrated in Luther's insistence that reason be taken captive to the external means, namely, to Word and Sacrament. In this sense, reason moves to the center of Luther's thought, as it is through these physical signs that God continually reminds those in doubt and an-

---

[54] WA XLII 87.1–6. Thus concerning man's corruption Luther states: "Sed gravissima iactura in eo est, quod non solum ista amissa sunt, sed aversio quaedam voluntatis a Deo secuta est, ut homo nihil eorum velit aut faciat, quae Deus vult et praecipit." WA XLII 106.16–18. See also 106.11–15.

[55] WA XLII 87.5–6.

[56] WA XLII 72.10–12.

[57] WA XLII 71.35–38.

[58] WA XLII 72.20–23.

guish of his abundant mercy (more of this will be said later). Having made these preliminary remarks, then, we must now turn our attention to man's expulsion from Paradise.

The Fall

It was observed above that faith in God's Word was Adam's greatest strength, and Luther makes it clear that faith was essentially a confidence in God's Word, or we might say, a simple belief. Adam's reason and will had been created such that he naturally believed God's command. We have also observed that his will was not yet perfect, and the possibility existed that he would will against his Creator. The significance of the tree in this connection was that Adam had a visible Word to assure that his memory remained consistent.

Given these considerations, it is easy to understand the fall and its consequences. Briefly, Luther traces out the cause as follows: Satan's only endeavor was to attack Adam's faith in God's Word i.e., he staked everything on this one effort, to draw man away from the Word and faith, that is, from the true God to a false god.[59] After he had removed the Word, he made corrupt the upright will man once had, so that his intellect doubted God and man instantly became a rebel: "Ex his sequitur postea rebellis manus contra mandatum Dei extensa ad pomum carpendum: Deinde os et dentes rebelles. In summa, omnia mala sequuntur incredulitatem seu dubitationem de verbo et Deo. Quid enim potest esse peius quam inbedientem esse Deo et abedire Satanae?"[60] Hence, corruption of the intellect is seen to be equivalent to Adam's doubt of God's Word. Luther maintains consistency here by asserting that intellect, or reason, is "right" only as it trusts God's Word. Therefore the sheer doubt of the Word by reason and will is itself the very source of man's corruption. Nonetheless, it is a corruption so deeply implanted in our flesh, through the bones and marrow, in the will, reason, and intellect[61], that it is now not even recognized as sin.[62]

---

[59] "Eo enim respicit Satan, quomodo eis verbum eripiat et cognitionem Dei, ut statuant: non est haec voluntas Dei, Deus hoc non praecipit. Hanc enim sententiam sequentia quoque comprobant, ubi dicit: Non moriemini. In hoc enim Satanae posita sunt omnia, quomodo a verbo et fide, hoc est, a vero Deo abducat ad falsum Deum." WA XLII 115.5–9.

[60] WA XLII 111.21–25.

[61] It is apparent here that Luther's main concern is to point out man's total depravity, as reflected in his list of bodily organs, and not necessarily to make any philosophical distinction between *ratio* and *intellectus*.

[62] WA XLII 125.1–5.

Luther rejects the notion that man now retains the image and similitude of God, at least in the sense described above.[63] Therefore, Seth was not born after the image of God but after that of his father Adam. That is, he inherited the image and likeness of his father which included original sin and the punishment of eternal death.[64] "Quare fugiamus delyria ista tanquam veras pestes et corruptelam sacrarum literarum et sequamur potius experientiam, quae docet, quod nascimur ex immundo semine et contrahimus ex ipsa natura seminis ignorantiam Dei, securitatem, incredulitatem, odium erga Deum, inobedientiam, impacientiam et similia gravissima vitia."[65] Considering these tragic results Luther concludes that it would appear more correct if the schoolmen said that the image of God in man has disappeared *(periisse)*, just as the original world and Paradise have disappeared *(perierunt)*.[66]

At this point then two issues should be highlighted concerning reason and will: (1) the intellect, or reason, has been darkened so that we no longer know God and his will and no longer perceive his works and, (2) the will is extraordinarily depraved so that we no longer trust the mercy of God but disregard the Word and will of God.[67] To elaborate, Luther says the outstanding fact in the case of the soul is that the knowledge of God has been lost: "Est quidem furor libidinis pars quaedam peccati originalis. Sed maiora sunt illa animi vicia: incredulitas, ignorantia Dei, desperatio, odium, blasphemia."[68] For just as it is the nature of the eye to see, so it was the very nature of reason and will in Adam to know, trust, and fear God.[69] But Satan has corrupted these through sin: just as leprosy infects the flesh, so the will and reason are impaired through sin, and man not only does not love God but avoids him and desires to be and live without him. How much more disgrace is this, Luther asks, that the will is impaired, the intellect corrupt and reason completely defective and altogether changed? Is this what it is to have perfect natural endowments?[70]

---

[63] This must not be misunderstood to mean that he rejects the image wholesale. As David Cairns points out in his *The Image of God* (London and Glasgow, 1973) pp. 131–132, Luther still believes we retain a relic of the image. What Luther is here rejecting is the doctrine of Scholasticism, which suggests that man has retained some of the knowledge of God.

[64] WA XLII 249.31–250.4.

[65] WA XLII 124.39–125.1.

[66] WA XLII 68.31–34.

[67] WA XLII 86.21–23.

[68] WA XLII 86.39–41.

[69] WA XLII 124.11–12

[70] WA XLII 124.19–21, 29–31.

It can safely be concluded from our first point that Luther has an overarching emphasis on Adam's *knowledge* of God. Thus despite Gerrish's assertion to the contrary, the epistemological issue is very strong within Luther's understanding of reason. In fact, one could say that the problem of knowledge becomes central-ized in many instances, especially considering Luther's insistence that reason has completely lost any specific knowledge of God – a knowledge, as previously noted, necessary for reason to be "right." The second point associates the will with reason in the fall, also the second element required for reason to be "right" as shown above. Consequently, Luther drives home the fact that man's total nature was involved in the fall, that depravity does not infest just part of man's nature, but his *entire* nature. Again it is very difficult to speak of reason as totally distinct from the will, as original sin means that human nature has completely fallen:[71] "Ostendunt autem haec, quam horribilis ruina Adae et Heuae fuerit, per quam amisimus pulcherrime illuminatam rationem et voluntatem conformem verbo et voluntati Dei."[72]

Before concluding we must note one final point. Adam's lack of confidence in the Word is an essential point in Luther's understanding of the fall. Luther points out that when this confidence was lost, there followed a terrible fright in the will and for the first time Adam's conscience was terrified by the "Law of God and the sight of its sins." Here it becomes manifest though just how depraved the intellect and will are after sin: the way that Adam thinks he is safe from God illustrates for Luther precisely how far reason has fallen. It is astonishing that Adam and Eve attempted to avoid God at all, but even more so that their attempt was carried out in such a ridiculously foolish manner as thinking they are safe among the trees. Luther maintains that when wisdom and understanding are lost, extreme stupidity follows, so that they attempt what is impossible by the most stupid means.[73] The main point of this illustration is to show that reason has not only lost its original prestige, but that it has also lost, in many ways, what in Paradise would have been considered common sense. But as can be clearly seen, this loss directly reflects the fact that man now improperly views God as judge rather than Savior.

Our goal up to this point has been mainly to clarify where Luther is coming from, so to speak. It should be evident by now that he had a particularly high view

---

[71] Thus concerning Cicero Luther comments: "Et tamen etsi haec statuat, tamen ceu fluctibus qui-busdam cogitationum obruitur, ut nonnunquam haec ipsa sententia tam firmiter apprehensa, manibus quasi elabi videatur. Nam illa de infinito diputatio violentissima est, et locus religionis a ratione nobis iterum excutitur, cum videmus tam variis calamitatibus naturam hanc oppressam esse." WA XLII 409.3–7.

[72] WA XLII 106.11–13.

[73] WA XLII 128.38–129.8.

of reason's created function, a fact that explains why he repeatedly assails reason's fallen state. Reason was created with the most majestic of functions, to know and to love God. With that knowledge came the immediate knowledge of all creatures, plants, etc. Through man's fall, however, that supreme gift was lost, with the most significant result that we no longer know or love God. Man is now faced with the most desperate of situations: he cannot answer *either* the question, "How do I know God?" *or* the question, "How am I saved?"[74] His reason has become entirely fragmentary and fleeting, not knowing the efficient and final cause of anything, much less of himself. When Luther points to reason's inadequacy these issues must be kept in mind, as they form the catalyst of his particularly severe criticisms. We conclude with Luther's own insightful summary of the fall:

> ...per quam amisimus pulcherrime illuminatem rationem et voluntate conformem verbo et voluntati Dei. Amisimus quoque illam dignitatem corporum, ut iam extrema turpitudo sit nudum conspici, quod tum fuit pulcherrimum et singularis praerogativa generis humani prae omnibus aliis bestiis. Sed gravissima iactura in eo est, quod non solum ista amissa sunt, sed aversio quaedam voluntatis a Deo secuta est, ut homo nihil eorum velit aut faciat, quae Deus vult et praecipit. Item, quod nescimus, quid Deus, quid gratia, quid iusticia, denique quid ipsum peccatum sit.[75]

---

[74] In reality, these should not be treated as though they are totally separate questions, a considerable mistake Gerrish makes in his study. Luther does not make a noticeable distinction between the two questions, as is evident from his understanding of the cross: For him, to know God is to know Him *as* Savior.

[75] WA XLII 106.12–19.

CHAPTER

THREE

Luther on Epistemology

The focus of the present chapter will be directed towards an examination of Luther's epistemology. An important part of this task is to consider his philosophical inheritance and deal with the whole question of possible forerunners in this regard. Though opinion varies somewhat concerning Ockham's influence on Luther's philosophy as a whole, there seems to be little question that at some level he did in fact have such an impact on the Reformer, particularly in reference to the issue of universals. However, minimal attention has been given to more specific epistemological connections between the two, and is therefore an issue that will occupy a major portion of the present section. Thus Ebeling's question — "What germs of the modern age are contained in Occamism or in late medieval mysticism and were transmitted from them to Luther?"[76] – though complex, requires special consideration here also if we are to effectively answer the question of Luther's relation to the epistemological theories at his disposal. But as Ebeling points out there is an inherent problem in this connection, namely, that we cannot be satisfied with "mere literary references," reasons for which should be more than obvious. Given our lack of references we are forced to examine the underlying, perhaps less apparent, influences that Ockham may have had on Luther. Oberman correctly warns that the problem is only compounded when we speak of causality in reference of one to the other because of its almost automatic connotation of a

---

[76]Gerhard Ebeling, "Luther and the Beginning of the Modern Age" in *Luther and the Dawn of the Modern Era* (ed.) Heiko A. Oberman (Leiden, 1974) p. 31.

"deterministic philosophy of history."[77] To be sure, Luther was his own man, and the attempts to define him solely in terms of Ockhamism have been rightly discredited as reductionistic.[78] On the other hand, it is difficult to understand Luther's philosophical development in complete separation from Ockham's considerable influence in this area. Unfortunately for our purpose, much of the research on this subject has been focused on the *initia Lutheri* and is consequently not immediately applicable to the topic at hand. Perhaps its non-relevance is also due to the narrow scope of our investigation, as the sole purpose here is to examine the problem of reason with associated questions concerning the origin and nature of knowledge. Thus, in order to stay clear of either a reductionist approach or one that completely disregards a particular philosophical influence, it will be one of the objectives of this chapter to detail some distinct *similarities* between Ockham's epistemology and Luther's, and similarly how those theories differ in some significant aspects. However, before examining the issues, some further remarks in support of our task and methodology are necessary.

G. J. Warnock has observed that the simple question "What can reason do?" is not in the least neutral, as its answer inevitably entails presuppositions of other, perhaps more central, questions. For however we may define reason, we are led thereby to distinguish this particular faculty as that by which we can arrive at a particular kind of truth. But this kind of truth will itself be distinguished from other kinds on logical or epistemological grounds. Thus Warnock concludes that "if this innocent-looking question unavoidably raises major philosophical issues concerning the logical and epistemological analysis and classification of propositions, it would probably be advantageous to raise those questions directly and overtly rather than as an only half-acknowledged corollary of a discussion that is ostensibly concerned with a faculty of the mind."[79] One's position as to the extent of reason's abilities seems explicable only in terms of these wider philosophical questions. Epistemological rationalism, for example, has traditionally given reason a much higher claim to fame than has empiricism. It therefore depends, to a large degree, on the epistemological position one adopts as to just how high reason may climb. Warnock, however, importantly points out that to dissent from rationalism is not thereby to disparage reason as such, for "the man who values, and shows that he values, reason is not he who merely pitches reason's claims exceptionally high but, rather, he who attempts, by painstaking reasoning, to determine how

---

[77] Heiko A. Oberman, "Headwaters of the Reformation" in his (ed.) *Luther and the Dawn of the Modern Era* p. 54.

[78] Oberman, "Headwaters of the Reformation" pp. 61ff.

[79] G. J. Warnock, "Reason" in *The Encyclopedia of Philosophy* (New York and London, 1967) (ed.) Paul Edwards Vol. 7, pp. 84–85.

high those claims may justifiably be pitched." Further, he who merely "sits" and "thinks" is prone to estimate highly the range and significance of reason's results. This propensity, Warnock says, "is scarcely an indication of devotion to reason; rather, it is an indication, if of anything, of pardonable self-importance."[80]

The inter-connectedness of the above issues with their potential for confusion can be shown, for example, in Gerrish's approach to Luther. "Occamism," he suggests, "manifested two fundamental characteristics: concerning everything that had to do with intelligence, it was pessimistic, sceptical, destructive; concerning all that is related to the will, it was optimistic and semi-rationalistic. Very roughly, it was the former characteristic which influenced Luther positively; against the latter he reacted violently..."[81] Two things however have to be demonstrated in order for this to be accurate: First, it must be shown that Ockham was indeed a "sceptic" concerning knowledge in general; second, and most importantly, that Luther was actually influenced by such a position (neither of which, incidentally, does Gerrish adequately demonstrate). He evidently fails to see the importance of dealing "directly," as Warnock put it, with the equally important issue of epistemology. He has thus neglected to distinguish the fundamental question, "What is Luther's *implicit* epistemology?" (subordinate or not) from, "*Did* Luther tend to subordinate the epistemological question to the soteriological?" The issue of reason is itself pregnant with epistemological presuppositions, and one cannot with any degree of accuracy avoid it and, at the same time, claim to provide a thorough definition. It is therefore difficult to see how one can come to an adequate position of such a highly fluctuating concept as "reason" without first coming to terms with the overall structure of that person's thought. Gerrish's failure to do so suggests an internal flaw in his approach.

In light, therefore, of the above warnings I propose a methodological shift in evaluating Luther. Rather than exegetically examining the various words for reason and Luther's use of those words, we will first examine Luther's epistemology in general and evaluate his understanding of reason in light of that overall structure. In so doing, we should be able to avoid the fallacy of *petitio principii* regarding those equally, perhaps more important, issues. In addition, the suggestion that Luther stands within the tradition of pessimism and fideism will be opposed; rather, it will be our contention that he stands squarely within an empiricist tradition which seeks, not to destroy reason, but to critically and reasonably analyze its scope of significance and make clearer its limitations. Though Luther

---

[80] Warnock, "Reason" Vol. 7, p, 85. Warnock points out that the current tendency has been to narrow the scope conceded to reason which in turn makes reason itself seem "less mysterious and grand" p. 85.

[81] Brian A. Gerrish, *Grace and Reason* (Oxford, 1962) p. 55.

was certainly no professional philosopher,[82] his general theological approach does imply an underlying philosophical method, a method which may indeed be one of those modern "germs" contained in Ockhamism but effectively refined by Luther. With that said we now turn our attention to Ockham.

A Brief Summary of Ockham's Position

In her impressive recent study, Marilyn Adams observes the following points concerning Ockham's theory of knowledge:[83] (1) The human mind begins its existence as a *tabula rasa* i.e., in order to engage in any activity at all (and, in particular, in order for it to know anything), it must first be furnished with concepts all of which have to be acquired after birth. Our mental activity therefore begins when mind-independent physical objects cause us to apprehend themselves by our senses.[84] (2) Ockham allows that we do apprehend our own mental acts, but insists that this would be causally impossible if we did not first apprehend physical objects. (3) Given acts of apprehending particulars, we can form abstract general principles. (4) Acts of apprehension are the acts in which the mind is aware of such objects immediately or directly – "By acts of apprehension Ockham does not mean to signify that they are voluntary or that the mind is not caused to have them by something other than itself. They are acts of the senses or intellect, not acts of will."[85] (5) Finally, Ockham speaks of acts of apprehension to indicate a condition in which the mind is actually, as opposed to potentially, aware of something.

As the above suggests, Adams says that "where awareness of sensible particulars is concerned, sensory intuitive cognition is a causally necessary condition of

---

[82] Though James MacKinnon notes in his "Martin Luther" in *Encyclopædia Britannica* Vol. 14 p. 491 that, "as a result of these four years [university training] of intensive study he had acquired a firm grasp of the current scholastic philosophy, and had developed a marked dialectic skill. He was an ornament of a circle of fellow-students, who met to discuss philosophy...." And Gordon Rupp observes that Luther was nicknamed "the philosopher" by friends in *Luther's Progress to the Diet of Worms* (London, 1951) p. 11.

[83] Marilyn McCord Adams, *William Ockham* (Indiana, 1987), pp. 495–500.

[84] Thus Ockham: "Circa secundum: Supposito quod quaestio intelligitur de cognotione propria singularis dico tunc primo: Quod singulare praedicto modo acceptum cognitione sibi propria et simplici est primo cognitum. Quod probatur sic: Quia res extra animam, quae non est signum, tali cognitione primo intelligitur; sed omnis res extra animam est sigularis; ergo, etc. Praeterea: Obiectum praecedit actum proprium et primum primitate generationis; nihil autem praecedit actum talem nisi singulare; ergo est." *Quodlibeta*, I, Q. xiii, in *Ockham: Philosophical Writings* (ed.) Philotheus Boehner (Indianapolis, 1990) p. 28.

[85] Adams, *William Ockham*, pp. 499–500.

intellectual intuitive cognition. As for our awareness of our own mental acts, Ockham says, '...likewise, an intuitive cognition of an act of intellect or an affection or delight etc. Nevertheless, if it were possible for love to exist in the will without any previous cognition, the intuitive cognition of that love would not presuppose another. But this is impossible in this life...'"[86] Adams therefore states that Ockham's position was such that, in this life, all intellectual cognition begins with the intuitive cognition of sensible particulars: "Thus, if we single out some awareness of a mental act, we will, if we trace the chain of awareness back to its starting point, eventually come to an act of whose object is a sensible particular."[87]

Consequently, Adams concludes that Ockham, with Locke, is best described a "conceptual empiricist." But she also makes the following important distinction regarding perception: for Ockham, the sensory intuitive cognition of Socrates and his whiteness cause an intellectual intuitive cognition of the same; and the latter act, which is the immediate proximate cause of the judgment that Socrates is white, is one in which the intellect is aware of Socrates and his whiteness, not indirectly, but directly.[88] Thus, says Ockham, in intuitive cognition "the thing itself is seen and apprehended immediately, without any intermediary between it and the act," and again that "in intuitive cognition nothing other than the object and the act is required to represent the object..." Adams sums up by noting that "Ockham clearly intends to endorse a direct realist position in the theory of knowledge."[89] Boehner agrees with this judgment, stating that "the intellect could not have an intuitive cognition of a sensible object without the help of sensory cognition, at least in the natural order; but the intellectual awareness relates to the sense-object as immediately as the sensory cognition does." Hence he also concludes that "both intuitive and abstractive cognition represent real objects outside or inside the mind. Ockham, therefore, is a realist in his epistemology."[90]

Given the general consensus concerning Ockham's theory of knowledge, can one viably maintain that Ockham was a "sceptic" concerning our knowledge of the external world? To arrive at a proper conclusion, we must first note what philosophical skepticism involves. Adams gives the following criteria:

---

[86] Adams, *William Ockham,* p. 514. See also Ockham, *Ord.* I, Prologue, q. 1, a.6; OTh I, 67.8–10.

[87] Adams, *William Ockham,* p. 515.

[88] See Adams, *William Ockham,* p. 550.

[89] Adams, *William Ockham,* p. 550. Adams quotes Ockham from *Ord.* I, d. 26, q. 3 (OTh IV, 241) and *Rep.* II, q. 12–13 (OTh V, 273–74).

[90] Philotheus Boehner (ed.) *Ockham: Philosophical Writings* p. xxv.

...a belief that p is true counts as knowledge of p, only if (i) p is true and (ii) the believer has some infallible sign by means of which he can distinguish, among instances of belief that p is true, genuine from merely apparent cases of true belief. And they have argued that while – for all we know – some of our beliefs may satisfy condition (i), it is impossible that any of our beliefs should satisfy condition (ii). These philosophers are known as sceptics, because they conclude that certain and infallible knowledge is impossible for human beings.[91]

Gilson and Pegis, Adams maintains, seem to assume that Ockham was interested in showing that we have certain knowledge of the physical world according to the above mentioned standards and that his failure to do so represents a serious defect in his epistemology. Adams has come to reject their view and maintains that Ockham was content to show how we can have knowledge that is "free from doubt and error."[92] Her conclusion is based on very convincing evidence, though it can only be highlighted here:[93] Ockham clearly regards evident cognition as the paradigm of certain knowledge and locates it as the source of all other certain knowledge. Further, according to Ockham's primary definition – as cognition of a true complex of terms (proposition) a sufficient mediate or immediate cause for which is a non-complex cognition of its terms – includes no stipulation that such a cognition must be distinguishable by infallible signs from mere beliefs. Moreover, the combination of this definition with his account of intuitive and abstractive cognition excludes the possibility that there *should* be any such infallible introspective signs.[94] Thus Ockham, as did Scotus, judged that no "reasonable" person would adopt the Academics' standard of certainty. And rejecting that standard as unreasonable, Ockham "proceeds to construct a theory according to which we can have knowledge that is free from doubt and error and that ultimately has its causal origin in sensory intuitive cognitions." His theory shows what he intended for it to show. Adams appropriately concludes therefore that

...it is no objection to a theory that attempts to show how we can have certain knowledge according to one standard, that it does not succeed in showing how we can have certain knowledge according to another standard – especially where the latter is a standard that no reasonable person would accept.[95]

[91] Adams, *William Ockham,* 551.

[92] Adams, *William Ockham,* p. 594.

[93] See also Philotheus Boehner, "In propria causa" in *Collected Articles on Ockham* (N.Y., 1958) edited by Eligius M. Buytaert pp. 301–319 for his reply to Professor Pegis.

[94] Adams, *William Ockham,* pp. 594–595 (emphasis mine).

[95] Adams, *William Ockham,* 601. See also Adams' insightful discussion concerning sensory illusion and the logical possibility that God can deceive us, pp. 597–601.

There is however one other charge of skepticism that appears to follow from Ockham's admission of the possibility of an intuitive knowledge of non-existents. Given this very possibility, how can we ever be certain whether or not we are being deceived? Boehner suggests that this so-called problem has been largely misunderstood by Ockham's critics.[96] Ockham merely asks if a *congnitio intuitiva* of non-existents is *possible*, not how propositions of non-existents are known to be true. Both the question and its answer are theological through and through, and its mere possibility was not intended to cast any doubt regarding the certainty of our everyday propositions about the world.

Specifically, Boehner replies with the following: First, it is impossible for God to cause in us a cognition by which a thing *evidently* appears to be present, while it is absent, because this includes a contradiction. He can, on the other hand, cause an act of belief, or an act of subjective conviction without factual evidence, that an absent thing is present. Thus, "the cognitive basis for this belief cannot be the *notitia intuitiva,* but only a *notitia abstractiva.*"[97] Second, although all knowledge which is based on intuitive knowledge is safe from any "intrusion" of natural or supernatural skepticism, assent itself is not. Ockham concedes that God can make an assent which is given to a proposition not based on intuitive knowledge, even if it does not correspond with the fact. But again, the assent is not an evident one, but only one of belief or conviction. Most importantly, then, there is an "epistemological distinction" between the two kinds of assent. The one is based on intuitive knowledge, which, if natural, implies the existence or presence of the object; the other is based on abstractive knowledge which does not imply the existence or presence of its object. Boehner concludes that, "in intuitive knowledge the reality is seen (or evidently not seen), and the assent is given to factual evidence, hence cannot fail. Our practical task, therefore, would be to test our conviction as regards contingent facts and to find out by experience whether factual evidence is really given or not. In any case, according to Ockham, if factual evidence is given, it is known by the intellect."[98]

To conclude, Boehner replies to the charge of skepticism by saying that "Ockham never doubted the infallibility of evident knowledge"[99] and thus "did not suf-

---

[96] Philotheus Boehner, "Notitia intuitiva of non-existents" in *Collected Articles on Ockham* (N.Y., 1958) edited by Eligius M. Buytaert pp. 274–292.

[97] Boehner, "Notitia intuitiva of non-existents" pp. 281–282. See also Andre Goddu, *The Physics of William of Ockham* (Leiden – Köln, 1984) pp. 27ff.

[98] Boehner, "Notitia intuitiva of non-existents" pp. 285–286. See esp. n. 28 for Boehner's reaction to Gilson.

[99] Boehner, *Ockham: Philosophical Writings,* p. xxvii.

fer under the philosophical experience of skepticism."[100] Adams, in general, agrees and maintains that Ockham's epistemology is neither self-consciously skeptical, nor does it have more skeptical consequences than other theories: "In my opinion, the attempt to identify Ockham as the chief of medieval sceptics is largely misguided and highly misleading and should, accordingly, be abandoned."[101]

Luther's Theory of Knowledge

Luther makes his position patently clear concerning the origin of knowledge in Paradise; simply put, it was immediate, or instinctive.[102] Having been cast out of the Garden, however, we are now confronted with an entirely different situation. One result of that situation is that the origin of human knowledge has been radically altered, so that Luther appears to concede with Ockham that we are born *tabula rasa*. With Ockham, then, Luther will say that in order for the mind to know anything it must be furnished with concepts after birth. Understood in this limited sense, Luther shares Ockham's empiricism.

At this juncture however an important point needs to be made before discussing the details of Luther's position; namely, comparison is here being drawn only between Ockham – Luther's philosophical predecessor – and Luther. This must be made clear in order that Luther's empiricism is not confused with its seventeenth and eighteenth century counterparts; such a comparison would not only be anachronistic but would also involve Luther in philosophical debates that he did not in fact engage himself. To be sure, Luther's empiricism is rather simplistic, and is no more than the general theory that experience rather than reason is the source of knowledge. This is significant because this thesis would later be shared by philosophers such as Locke and Hume – and in fact is shared by all empiricists to some extent – but with quite different emphases that were much more radical

---

[100] Boehner, "Notitia intuitiva of non-existents" p. 292.

[101] Adams, *William Ockham*, pp. 626, 629. Boehner also makes the important point that "Ockham, far from being an idealist, has not even a place in his system for the critical aporia from which idealism has started its subjective journey; for the problem, whether and how we can know anything of reality by conceptual knowledge, does not even enter Ockham's system, since in his system the immediacy of cognition and the firm causal nexus between object and thought does not admit of any separation between thought and reality." See "The Realistic Conceptualism of William Ockham" in *Collected Articles on Ockham* (N.Y. 1958) edited by Eligius M. Buytaert p. 158.

[102] "Si igitur volumus praedicare insignem Philosophum, praedicemus primos nostros Parentes, cum adhuc assent a peccato puri. Hi enim cognitionem Dei perfectissimam habuerunt, quomodo enim nescirent eum, cuius similitudinem in se habebant et sentiebant? Deinde etiam stellarum et totius Astronomiae rationem certissimam habuerunt." WA XLII 49.39–50.5.

than Luther's. Luther's insistence that we are born *tabula rasa* governs all that he says concerning the nature and extent of knowledge for humanity after the fall. For him, we can have no factual knowledge which is not derived from experience i.e., all knowledge of fact is *a posteriori* in nature. But this does not imply for Luther that all knowledge consists of sense experience alone. For instance, he was well aware on the basis of Romans 1:18ff. that we have a basic sense of morality and possess a natural knowledge of God. However, while these have been affected by sin (though not obliterated) we will see later, specifically concerning natural knowledge of God, that it is simply not saving knowledge.[103] So in this sense it is not true knowledge of God at all. True knowledge of God must be obtained through some external source; in Luther's case, that external source is Scripture alone. Thus Luther can be considered an empiricist (in the above general sense) concerning our knowledge of everyday objects, but he considered himself to be an *a posteriori* thinker in the case of theology for the obvious reason that theological concepts do not originate in the exact same way as our concepts of the external world i.e., our knowledge of tables and chairs arises through our experience of them, while theological knowledge comes *via* Holy Scripture. In theological matters Scripture alone is to speak the decisive word to the human conscience, and we will see later that he even pits Scriptural knowledge concerning the forgiveness of sins against what we perceive with the senses. So Luther's empiricism, in its strict sense, is limited to our knowledge of external objects, while theological knowledge is derived not from sense experience as such (as in the case of tables and chairs) but rather *a posteriori* through Scriptural revelation (though of course there is a distinct similarity between these two types of knowledge, the similarity being that they are both *a posteriori* in nature). Also, it seems for Luther that not only is our knowledge of everyday objects sensory knowledge, but our theological knowledge is also in some sense sensory knowledge as well; in that true knowledge of God (saving knowledge) is not innate and must be gained by hearing the external words of Scripture. That is, this type of knowledge does not come from within but must be gained, as all other factual knowledge, through the senses (in this case through the heard and written propositions of Scripture).

The above qualifications however bring up an important question. If all knowledge of fact is *a posteriori,* thus demanding an external source from which it is derived, is Scripture itself then an external object? It seems that for Luther such a question needs to be answered with a qualified Yes. On the one hand, he will insist that Scripture is the one and only external, objective, source for any and all knowledge of God (again in the saving sense, which for Luther really is the only

---

[103] Although even here we will see that Luther observes that it is just as easy for the fallen mind to conclude that God does not exist. Of course, this is also a result of man's sin and unbelief.

knowledge worthy of the name). That is, knowledge of this sort is revealed and brought down to the level of human language in the propositions of Holy Writ. Montgomery, for example, has noted that Luther's opposition to Erasmus was based on his convictions that whenever Scripture speaks, it speaks with absolute authority and clarity. In addition, propositional assertions of truth not only can be drawn from Scripture but in fact must be drawn. This view permeates Luther's writings both young and old, for example:

> The notion that in Scripture some things are recondite and all is not plain was spread by the godless Sophists (whom now you echo, Erasmus) – who have never yet cited a single item to prove their crazy view; nor can they. And Satan has used these unsubstantial spectres to scare men off reading the sacred text, and to destroy all sense of its value, so as to ensure that his own brand of poisonous philosophy reigns supreme in the church. I certainly grant that many passages in the Scriptures are obscure and hard to elucidate, but that is due, not to the exalted nature of their subject, but to our own linguistic and grammatical ignorance....Who will maintain that the town fountain does not stand in the light because the people down some alley cannot see it, while every one in the square can see it?[104]

Here Luther simply assumes that Scripture is a clear, external source of knowledge for the Spiritual Kingdom; a source that is truly objective and one which can be understood by all (we will have more to say about this later). In fact, we will see that Luther assumes that the objective content of Scripture is that which leads one to faith i.e., faith comes through the *fides historica*. So in this sense Scripture is indeed an external object of knowledge; thus its *a posteriori* nature. On the other hand, Luther makes equally clear that once committed to its truth, or once one has put his trust in its contents, Scripture now takes on a transcendent character for the believer. In other words, reason is now illumined by faith and rightly sees that spiritual life depends entirely upon a childlike trust in the words in which God has chosen to reveal himself (thus Luther's confidence in defending his eucharistic theology with the four words "This is my body").

Having made these preliminary qualifications then we can proceed to examine Luther's epistemological outlook. (Note: Although Luther did not engage in explicit discussions regarding epistemology, he does make several comments that, when compared to our previous remarks, give a fairly accurate picture of his *im-*

---

[104] WA XVIII, 606. Quoted in John Warwick Montgomery, *In Defense of Martin Luther* (Milwaukee, 1970) p. 71. See Montgomery's full discussion pp. 59–76.

plicit epistemology. Having said that, though, it is clear that Luther regarded the problem of knowledge as a crucial aspect to his theological methodology, which in itself provides us with important clues to his epistemological approach.)

We have briefly mentioned that, for Luther, knowledge is essentially material: "Sed qualis est haec vita, talis est definitio et cognitio hominis, hoc est, exigua, lubrica et nimio materialis."[105] By "material" Luther appears to invoke Aristotelian distinctions between the four causes as explained in the *Metaphysics*.[106] Our entire knowledge, according to Luther, is based solely on the material or formal cause, whereas the efficient and final cause we are presently unable to decipher.[107] As was noted above, knowledge of the latter two was extinguished through the fall, a fact which, significantly, Luther sees as a truly "wretched situation." For given his insistence that Adam's knowledge of these causes was immediate pre-fall, it is easy to see why Luther regards the present origin of knowledge as a direct result of original sin. Ockham makes a similar suggestion regarding the effect of the first sin when he observes that, in order to have an intellectual intuitive cognition of a sensible particular, one must now first have a sensory intuitive cognition. (He had, on the other hand, conceded that angels and souls separated from bodies can naturally have intellectual intuitive cognition without prior sensory intuitive cognitions.) Thus Ockham too seems to regard the present situation concerning knowledge as a result of sin.[108] Luther illustrates the severity of our present limitations by pointing to a familiar example; namely, that we have this man for a father and this woman for a mother is a fact that *in itself* cannot be known with absolute certainty because it falls outside of our own, severely limited, experience.[109] Ock-

---

[105] WA XXXIX, i, 176 proposition 19. Luther also says, "Ratio enim nata est ex muliere, et ad rationem pertinent sapienta, iura politica, disciplina, leges" WA XLIII 385.15–16.

[106] Frederick Copleston has a helpful discussion on the four causes in his *History of Philosophy* (London, 1976) Vol. 1, p. 313. Briefly, efficient cause is the source of movement, final cause is the ultimate cause why potentiality is actualized, material cause being that which is part of its nature, and the formal cause is normally equated with final cause: "Thus the formal cause of a horse is the specific form of horse, but this is also its final cause, since the individual of a species naturally strives to embody as perfectly as may be the specific form in question. This natural striving after the form means that the final, formal and efficient causes are often the same."

[107] Luther also points this out in *Die Disputation de homine* (propositions 13 and 14), "Nam Philosophia efficientem certe non novit, similiter nec finalem. Quia finalem nullam ponit aliam, quam pacem huius vitae, et efficientem nescit esse creatorem Deum." Regarding the formal cause which the philosophers call the soul, "nunquam conveniet inter Philosophos" (proposition 15). See WA XXXIX, i, 175.

[108] *Reportatio* IV, q. 14; OTh VII, 316. See also Adams, *William Ockham,* pp. 508–509.

[109] "Imo quid nos de nobis scimus? Videmus nos esse homines. Sed quod hunc patrem, hunc matrem habeamus, an non credi hoc debet, sciri autem nullo potest modo? Sic omnis nostra cognitio seu sapientia tantum est posita in noticia causae materialis et formalis..." WA XLII 93.16–20.

ham had himself used the illustration in the following manner: "Et sic sciuntur aliqua per fidem tantum. Sicut dicimus, nos scire quod Roma est magna civitas, quam tamen non vidimus; et similiter dico, quod scio istum esse patrem meum et istam esse matrem meam, et sic de aliis quae non sunt evidenter nota; quia tamen eis sine omni dubitatione adhaeremus et sunt vera, dicimur scire illa."[110] Although the two appear to use the illustration for different ends – Luther by pointing out inherent limitations and Ockham by showing its sufficiency as knowledge – they both arrive at the same conclusions i.e., the example demonstrates certain limitations regarding what we can evidently know; but it is, nevertheless, trustworthy knowledge.

Luther expands the theme of limitation by asking what sort of wisdom and knowledge it is that knows nothing about the final and efficient cause: "Nam quod formae noticiam habemus, sic vacca novit domum suam, sic (ut Germanico proverbio dicitur) intuetur et agnoscit ostium. Apparet itaque hic quoque, quam horribilis lapsus sit peccati originalis, quo amisimus eam noticiam, ut neque principium nec finem nostri videre possimus."[111] (We are reminded here of his assertion that this particular knowledge was that which truly separated man from beast[112]). Thus, as maintained above, Luther uses Paradise as a sort of measuring rod by which he demonstrates that man's problem concerning knowledge after the fall is a considerable one. In a similar fashion, he suggests that reason fails to make greater advances in understanding creation because the philosopher does not know from where it came or what is its aim.[113]

Luther however uses more precise philosophical terminology in *Die Disputation de homine* when he states that in spite of the fact that reason possesses a certain "majesty" and is something truly "divine," still, "nec ea ipsa ratio novit *a priore, sed tantum a posteriore*."[114] Reason no longer has that immediate knowledge of God, creature, or even *itself*. Luther's position here seems to be directly parallel to that of Ockham as noted above, namely, that in this life, all awareness of mental acts begin with the intuitive cognition of sensible particulars. Thus as a result of the fall, man knows nothing innately; rather knowledge, and even

---

[110] Ockham, *Prologus in Expositionem super viii libros Physicorum;* text quoted from Boehner, *Ockham: Philosophical Writings,* p. 4.

[111] WA XLII 93.30–34.

[112] Though it must again be stated that this separation still exists after the fall, but in a diminished state.

[113] WA XLII 93.15–16.

[114] WA XXXIX, i, 175 proposition 10 (emphasis mine).

more specifically, cognitive activity, obtains only through our experience of the external world. Luther's empiricism is therefore strongly parallel to Ockham's in this regard.

But, while we have observed that Ockham is not a philosophical skeptic, does Luther escape such a charge? His criticisms of reason alone seem to be much harsher than Ockham's; at the very least, Luther's language is far stronger. However, Gerrish's judgment (noted above) concerning Luther is, I think, as misplaced as Gilson's judgment concerning Ockham.[115]

Luther seems to operate under the simple assumption that we have direct contact with the physical world i.e., with Ockham he holds a direct realist epistemology. Furthermore, he appears to assume that our knowledge of the world is secure and doubt free. Although the difficulties are the same as above – that Luther does not explicitly discuss the issue – it can, nevertheless, be shown indirectly in several ways. First, he comments in the following: "Nec etiam utile est, Mosen in principio tam facere mysticum et allegoricum. Quia enim nos vult docere, non de creaturis allegoricis, et mundo allegorico, sed de creaturis essentialibus et mundo visibli ac exposito sensibus, appellat, ut Proverbio dicitur, Schapham scapham...."[116] Luther repeatedly rejects any methodology that would compromise our knowledge of the sensible world and consequently *in this context* rejects both mysticism and allegory – as each position throws us into a world that cannot possibly be known. As already shown, we can only come to know "real" things through the senses. There is, however, an unstated assumption in this line of argumentation that the knowledge we do have of the world is free from doubt. Luther here affirms not only confidence in our general knowledge but also confidence in our historical knowledge.[117] Second, Luther's healthy attitude toward the natural sciences would be completely groundless without a prior assumption that knowledge of the external world was both reliable *and* sufficient – sufficient enough, that is, on which to establish scientific knowledge. He rejected other so-

[115] One of the main reason's for Gerrish's view is that he sees Luther's condemnation of reason as subordinate to his condemnation of works-righteousness (see p. 98, n. 7). He can thus conclude that "the epistemological problem ('How do we know God') becomes subordinate to the soteriological problem ('What must I do to be saved?')." See *Grace and Reason* p. 55.

[116] WA XLII 4.33–37. Speaking of Moses' account in Genesis he similarly states: "Sic omnia haec sunt historica, Id quod diligenter admoneo, ne incautus lector offendatur autoritate Patrum, qui historiam relinquunt, et allegorias querunt. Ego Lyram ideo amo et inter optimos pono, quod ubique diligenter retinet et persequitur historiam...." WA XLII 71.15–19. See also Luther's criticism of Origen WA XLII 68.26–30.

[117] "Qui igitur Allegoriis volunt uti, hi fundamentum earum ex ipsa historia petent. Historia enim, quae, ceu Dialectica, vera et indubitata docet. Contra Allegoria quasi Rhetorica pingere historiam debet, ad probandum autem nihil valet." WA XLII 173.41–174.2.

called branches of knowledge because they could not meet the standards required for scientific inquiry. He would, for example, never be convinced that astrology should be numbered among the sciences simply because it does not admit of any plain demonstration *(nullam plane demonstrationem habet)*. He relates:

> Nam quod allegant experientiam, nihil me movet. Omnes enim astrologicae experientiae sunt mere particulares. Nam istas tantum artifices notarunt et retulerunt in literas, quae non fefellerunt; reliquas experientias, ubi falsi sunt nec secuti sunt effectus, quos praedixerunt certe futuros, non notarunt. Sucut autem Aristoteles dicit, unam hirundinem non facere ver, Ita ego ex talibus particularibus observationibus non puto scientiam constitui.[118]

Again, Luther cannot be convinced of astrological experience precisely because by nature they are not open to the objective standards of verification. But, of course, the notion of objectivity is itself based on the assumption that we have knowledge free from doubt concerning the world of particulars. Luther even suggests that our unrelenting quest for scientific knowledge points to an eschatological aspect of man's nature:

> Hic autem incipit se aperire et nobis ostendere immortalitas animorum, siquidem nulla creatura praeter hominem aut intelligere coeli motum aut metiri corpora coelestia potest. Sus, vacca et canis aquam, quam bibunt, non possunt metiri et homo coelum et omnia coeli corpora metitur. Quare hic emicat scintilla aeternae vitae, qoud homo naturaliter exercertur in illa naturae cognitione. Significat enim cura illa homines non eo conditos, ut in hac infima orbis parte semper vivant, sed ut coelum possideant, quod in hac vita admirantur et accupantur studio et cura coelestium rerum....Hoc enim est, quod non solum loqui et iudicare possit (quae ad Dialectician et Rhetorician pertinent), sed quod etiam Mathemata omnia perdiscit.[119]

To conclude, Luther seems to be no more "self-consciously" skeptical in his epistemology than was Ockham. He operated as if the knowledge we *do* have of the external world is secure from error and doubt. Furthermore, as Ockham rejected the contrived standards of the skeptical tradition, so Luther would certainly agree that they are, at best, unreasonable. Luther is not, therefore, open to the charge of skepticism. Consequently, Gerrish's triad Occamism-Luther-skepticism cannot be conceded. This will become even more evident concerning Luther's particular understanding of special revelation – an important subject to which we now turn.

---

[118] WA XLII 33.37–39; 34.5–10.
[119] WA XLII 34.22–29; 35.5–7.

Knowledge of God: Faith and Reason

It appears from the preceding discussion that Ockham and Luther have very similar approaches to knowledge in general. But do they differ with regard to the more specific question, "How do I know God?" Luther's break with Ockham, as a matter of fact, is shown nowhere more decisive than here, as his answer not only differs with Ockham in method, but also provides the key to his particular theological outlook.

Luther makes abundantly clear that our lack of knowledge concerning efficient and final cause is a result of sin. If we do not now have any more than material knowledge regarding the external world, how can we possibly know anything specific about an incomprehensible God? His reply is, in fact, rigidly consistent with his overall epistemology: As we are born *tabula rasa* as to knowledge of the world, so are we born *tabula rasa* as to any knowledge of God. Natural human reason is not only inadequate in forming correct judgments about God, but entirely paralyzed, simply because true knowledge of doctrine (*vera cognitio horum locorum*) – as all other knowledge – is not born, so to speak, in our home or in our hearts (*nec nascitur, ut sic dicam, domi nostrae, in cordibus nostris*).[120] Fortunately, we have reliable information concerning sensible particulars from which to draw proper conclusions about the external world. Regarding the nature of God, however, our information is not so easily accessible. If there is to be any clarity about God's nature, it is apparent that the information presented must be of a comprehensible, visible, nature. Otherwise it is evident from the above that we simply could not *know* Him with any degree of certainty. Perhaps, though, we must ask one prior question – did Luther consider knowledge in this sense important, or even possible? Regarding these and related questions, he answers with both philosophical (though implicit) and theological precision.

He would not concede, for example, that anyone can be saved *without* a proper knowledge of God e.g., it is senseless to speak as though the Turk or the Jew is truly redeemed apart from knowing Christ crucified.[121] Consequently he states that the first gift is knowledge of God[122] and that God justifies us by this knowledge.[123] Again, faith is nothing else but the truth of the heart, that is, the right

[120] WA XL, ii, 316.19–22.

[121] WA LIV 143.15–144.6.

[122] WA XLIII 608.3–4.

[123] WA XL, i, 579.14.

knowledge of the heart about God[124] and is therefore teaching or knowledge.[125] Conversely, endless sins proceed from the lack of knowledge of God.[126] Such statements can be found throughout Luther's works and show that proper knowledge is a dominant theme in his theology. This being the case, then, how do we obtain such knowledge? And, assuming that knowledge of this nature is even possible, what is the relation between general and special revelation? At this point, it may be helpful briefly to contrast Ockham's position with that of Luther's.

Resulting from Ockham's epistemology, natural reason is limited as to any precise knowledge of God's nature. Ockham will not admit, for example, that there is adequate proof that a first efficient cause is the first being. He did however think that the argument from efficiency, "in so far as it means that a thing continues in existence, it can well be proved."[127] That is, it can be proved from conservation, but even then it still only constitutes an abstract kind of knowledge. Specific knowledge that God is, on the other hand, a Trinity in persons is based solely on faith and incapable of demonstration. Such is the case also with doctrines such as the Personal union; Adams notes that "Ockham vigorously argues that unaided natural reason would find it easier to deny than to affirm the existence of relative things really distinct from absolute things."[128] In addition, Adams points out that motions or changes of material things cannot lead unaided reason to a provident governor of the universe who orders them to an end.[129] Thus natural reason is extremely limited as to its judgments on specific doctrinal matters.

---

[124] WA XL, i, 376.23–24: "Tunc autem homo recte de Deo cogitat, quando credit ipsius verbo. Cum autem extra verbum Deum ex ratione sua metiri et ei credere vult, non habet veritatem de Deo...." (376.24–27).

[125] WA XL, ii, 26.14–15: "Differunt ergo fides et spes primum subiecto, quia fides est in intellectu, spes in voluntate. Re tamen separari non possunt, sicut duo Cherubim Propiciatorii. Deinde officio, quia fides dictat et dirigit intellectum, non tamen sine voluntate, ac docet, quid crendendum sit" (26.11–14).

[126] WA XL, ii, 324.19–20: "Hinc nata sunt Monasteria, Regulae, Cuculli, Funes, Missae, peregrinationes et similes stulti cultus, quos natura destituta cognitione Dei sibi contra et praeter verbum finxit" (324.24–26).

[127] Thus Ockham: "...et ideo, quamvis posset poni processus in infinitum in productionibus sine infinitate actuali, non potest tamen poni processus in infinitum in conservantibus sine infinitate actuali." Ockham concludes: "Ad augmentum principale dico, quod per efficientiam secundum quod dicit rem immediate accipere esse post non esse, non potest probari primum efficiens esse, sed per efficientuam secundum quod dicit rem continuari in esse bene potest probari, hoc est per conservationem." *Quaestiones in lib. I Physicorum,* Q. cxxxvi, quoted from Boehner (ed.) *Ockham: Philosophical Writings* pp. 123, 124–125. See also Adams, *William Ockham,* p. 972.

[128] Adams, *William Ockham,* p. 981.

[129] Adams, *William Ockham,* p. 977.

How then does Ockham substantiate such religious claims? They are to be accepted on the basis of a threefold authority: No plurality should be assumed unless it can be proved by reason, or by experience, or by some infallible authority. Concerning doctrinal matters, Ockham takes these to be the Bible, the determinations of the Church, and certain sayings of the Saints. These authorities sometimes give pronouncements on doctrine that cannot be proved by natural reason or are even contrary to reason. Thus Adams states, "Ockham always allows the claims of reason and experience to be defeated by contrary pronouncements of the Church, which should lead 'every thought captive'. Ockham's method is thus to subordinate reason and experience to Church authority, while keeping violations of reason and experience to a minimum."[130]

Luther, not unlike Ockham, held that natural reason is unable to make specific conclusions about God's nature. The nature of God's oneness, to use our previous example, "rationi et sapientiae humanae est imperscrutabile," as such a judgment must be established on the basis of divine revelation.[131] Thus Luther thinks it generally "male arguunt" to argue from the natural working to the supernatural.[132] Cicero, Luther maintains, has omitted nothing that man is able to attain by means of human reason and all its powers, yet he is ignorant of God's will and attitude toward us. Instead of coming closer to the truth, his errors inevitably become progressively worse.[133] Luther here emphasizes the fact that Cicero cannot make greater advances because knowledge of God does not come from our innate reason. Plato too observes the government of God, but everything is merely objective (*obiectiva*) and is not yet the knowledge that Joseph has, that God cares, that he hears and helps the afflicted. This is something which Plato is not able to determine and thereby remains in his metaphysical thinking, just as a cow looks at a new door.[134] For although man has a general knowledge of God revealed in and through creation, and is therefore without excuse, he nevertheless suppresses the

---

[130] Adams, *William Ockham,* pp. 1008–1009; Ockham *Ord.* I, d. 2, q. 1 (OTh II, 17–18). See also Richard Marius, *Martin Luther: The Christian Between God and Death* (Cambridge, Massachustts, 1999) pp. 38–39.

[131] WA XLIII 478.30–34.

[132] WA XLII 28.25. See Luther's full discussion, 28.7–27.

[133] WA XLII 486.18–30: "Ratio huius ignorantiae est, quia non est rationis natae, videre Deum, sed spiritus Dei, illustrantis mentes nostras per verbum" (486.22–23).

[134] WA XLIV 591.34–39: "Haec igitur vera notitia Dei est, scire naturam et voluntatem eius esse, quam revelat in verbo, ubi promittit se fore Dominum et Deum meum, eamque fide apprehendere iubet, ibi enim certum et firmum fundamentum iactum est, quo acquiescunt animi." See XLIV 592.6–9.

knowledge he has. Therefore, natural reason cannot give us the specific knowledge required for salvation. But, in this position, Luther remains absolutely consistent in his epistemology, and, up to this point, is in general agreement with Ockham.

Luther and Ockham seem to agree that God's nature is unknowable through nature and natural reason alone. For Luther in particular, God is incomprehensible in His Majesty and unknowable as such. Therefore whatever is to be known about Him must be known by means of the senses. How then do we know God? The immediate tendency might be to answer our question by appealing to Luther's well-known axiom of *sola scriptura*. However, though such an answer is in the end accurate, it is nevertheless – regarding *this* question – indirect. Fortunately, Luther gives us a very direct response:

> Ordinatam potentiam, hoc est, filium incarnatum amplectemur, 'in quo reconditi sunt omnes thesauri divinitatis'. Ad puerum illum positum in gremio matris mariae, ad victimam illam pendentem in cruce nos conferemus, Ibi vere contemplabimur Deum, ibi in ipsum cor Dei introspiciemus, quod sit misericors, quod nolit mortem peccatoris: sed ut convertatur et vivat. Ex hac speculatione seu contemplatione nascitur vera pax, et verum gaudium cordis. Itaque Paulis dicit: 'Nihil iudico me scire praeter Christum' etc.[135]

Thus Luther is able to insist that the incarnation was foretold in order that "ut certam formam cognoscendi et appraehendendi Deum haberemus."[136] We must apprehend the incarnate Son and begin from the manger and the swaddling clothes in which He was wrapped.[137] Moreover, he demands that we consider the important fact that God has revealed Himself in the flesh through Christ and has given us a "imaginem visibilem" in order to satisfy our desire.[138] "Ideo ipse Deus se demittit ad captum infirmitatis nostrae, et sub similitudinibus ceu involucris puerili simplicitate se nobis offert, ut aliquo modo a nobis cognosci possit."[139]

---

[135] WA XLIII 73.3–10. See Luther's penetrating discussion pp. 71–73.

[136] WA XLIII 231.28–30.

[137] WA XLIV 194.6–9: "Vera autem speculatio, quae facit Israelitam, est mortificatio omnium virium, quae sunt sensuum et rationis nostrae, et haerere in sola fide et expectatione promissionis" (15–17).

[138] "Vere enim a Christo dictum est: 'Deum nemo vidit unquam', et tamen immensa bonitate revelavit se nobis Deus, ut desiderio nostra satis faceret, exhibuit nobis imaginem visibilem. En, habes filium meum, qui audit eum, et baptisatur, is in libro vitae scriptus est: hoc revelo per filium, quem potes manibus contrectare, et oculis intueri." WA XLIII 462.37–463.2. Note: "desiderio" denotes "desire for something lost or absent," see *Oxford Latin Dictionary* (ed.) P.G.W. Glare (Oxford, 1982) p. 525.

[139] WA XLII 294.3–5. Luther continues: "Et tamen hisce visibilibus formis se nobis offert, nobiscum agit, has formas proponit nobis, ne degeneremus in erraticos et vagos Spiritus de Deo quidem disputantes, sed eum penitus ignorantes, tanquam qui in nuda sua Maiestate non potest apprehendi. Hanc viam cognoscendi Dei videt Deus nobis esse impossibilem. Habitat enim, sicut Scriptura dicit, lucem

Luther's Christology is therefore such that apart from Christ there is no God.[140] The reason for this claim is that without God's self-revelation in Christ we could never truly know Him, that is, we would not know Him as Savior. What can be shown here is that Luther thoroughly considers the epistemological question, as it is inextricably bound to the soteriological question. For, in his estimation, we cannot love someone we do not know.[141] Hence Gerrish was mistaken with his claim that Luther subordinated the epistemological question to the soteriological.[142] It is evident that he holds them both as equally important; not so much that they are "side-by-side," but that both questions are in the truest sense intertwined and answered in the one person, Jesus Christ.

Given Luther's Christo-centric position, where does he direct the man in search of God? Certainly we do not have direct access to Christ – and He alone reveals the heart of the Father – so how do we come to know Him? We have seen that Ockham directs man to three sources; the Bible, the Church, and certain sayings of the Saints. Luther however clearly saw the difficulties in this view, difficulties that led him ultimately to reject it. For which source do we accept when one contradicts the other? Interestingly, Marius notes the presence of this question early on in Luther's mind at the Leipzig debate:

> On the one hand he pointed out that the fathers of the church had disagreed among themselves about a major doctrine – the primacy of Peter and the popes after him. This was hardly secret information. Abelard had collected patristic disagreements in his Sic et Non of the twelfth century. He had rankled people in the same way that Luther now did, for to call attention to the divisions and the lack of unity among the fathers of the church was to subvert one of the most treasured bastions of certainty in a time of religious doubt – that the grand unity of the church proved its divine infallibility. Luther suggested that the Bohemians had not been malicious in their heresy, and so in his way he was subverting another Catholic tenet. For to Catholic thinkers, part of the evil of heresy was its malice – the stubborn adhesion to error by those who knew better. The heretics "knew better" because an infallible church and their own consciences taught them so. To declare that heretics were not malicious – or else

---

inaccessibilem, et proposuit, quae possumus apprehendere et intelligere" (294.21–26).

[140] WA XXVI 332.19–20; 333.1–10.

[141] Nature itself no longer knows God, and it cannot love God whom it does not know: "Natura enim sic corrupta est, ut Deum non agnoscat amplius, nisi verbo et Spiritu Dei illuminetur; quomodo igitur sine Spiritu sancto amare Deum potest? Verum est enim, quod ignoti nulla sit cupido. Natura igitur Deum, quem nescit, amare non potest; Amat autem Idolum et somnium cordis sui. Deinde in creaturarum amore ita implicita tenetur, ut Deum, etiam postquam ex verbo agnovit, tamen negligat, et contemnat verbum eius: Sicut exempla nostrorum hominum ostendunt." WA XLII 349.29–36.

[142] Gerrish, *Grace and Reason*, p. 55.

fatally ignorant – was to assume that the teachings of the church about salvation were not clear and that, therefore, the chilly doubts rising around the knees of Christian society had no remedy.[143]

In the face of this important problem Luther sought a simpler, more direct answer – namely, by drawing a line directly from Christ to the apostles, and leaving tradition and sayings of the Saints open to critical appraisal. The apostles alone had the promise of the Holy Spirit, and they alone are called the foundation of the church, being the ones who must present the articles of faith. "Quare non sequitur, Apostoli hoc et hoc potuerunt, Ergo idem possunt eorum successores. Sed quidquid volunt docere aut statuere, debent autoritatem Apostolorum sequi et afferre."[144] Even more, the "authority" of the apostles can be found in no other place than that of Holy Scripture. Scripture alone, therefore, properly communicates information concerning Christ and thus the true knowledge of God.[145] God has bound Himself, so to speak, to the words of Scripture and He is to be sought nowhere else. Given all of the above considerations, then, it is entirely without surprise that Luther should declare that true knowledge of God is revealed by the Son of God, but "Primum externo verbo, deinde intus per spiritum:"

> Est itaque Evangelium verbum divinum quod de coelo descendit et per spiritum sanctum revelatur qui et ad hoc missus est, Sic tamen, ut verbum externum praecedat. Nam nec Paulus ipse habuit revelationem internam, nisi prius audis-

---

[143] Richard Marius, *Martin Luther: The Christian Between God and Death* (Harvard University Press: Cambridge, Mass., 1999) p. 176.

[144] *Die Disputation de potestate concilii*, WA, XXXIX, i, 184 propositions 4–5; 185 propositions 6–8.

[145] Hence I cannot agree with the judgment of Lohse that Luther's understanding of the authority of the divine Word "did not imply the authority of the Bible as a whole or of individual passages in a biblicistic sense" (aside from the inherent ambiguity of the word "biblicistic"). Lohse continues by saying that Luther ultimately "thinks of Christ in connection with the Word, that is, God's gracious promise to man." In light of the previous discussion regarding the problem of knowledge, it is difficult to accept his view precisely because "God's gracious promise to man," revealed in Christ, is found only in Holy Scripture. It cannot be *known* in any other way. It would also, on Lohse's account, be difficult to understand why Luther so emphatically demands that the Holy Spirit is given only through Scripture, whether written or spoken, if Scripture on the whole is not authoritative. For *what* the gospel is is only communicated through Scripture, and the need for this objective Word is easily seen given Luther's theory of knowledge. Lohse, as others, indirectly throw Luther back into the camp of skepticism, except that here it becomes a skepticism concerning our knowledge of God. Moreover, assuming his position is correct, what tool does Luther use to distinguish between authoritative and non-authoritative Scripture? The fact is that he provides no such tool. Knowledge of God comes only from Scripture as a whole, a position perfectly consistent with Luther's approach to epistemology. This must still follow even if Luther had genuine doubts concerning certain antiligomena books such as *James*. Lohse here quoted from "Conscience and Authority in Luther" in *Luther and the Dawn of the Modern Era*, p. 179.

set verbum externum e coelo, nempe hoc: "Saule, Saule, quid me persequeris?" etc. Primum ergo audivit verbum externum, deinde sequutae sunt revelationes, cognitio verbi, fides et spiritualia dona.[146]

We can therefore summarize Luther's progression as follows:

the cross —> Scripture (Apostolic testimony) —> knowledge of God

Though other facets of Luther's thought will later expand this, we must note the following preliminary points: First, Christ is the sole object of Scripture i.e., Scripture is the eyewitness accounts of Christ's ministry, death, and resurrection. Thus the historic Christ becomes Luther's methodological starting point, having both theological *and* philosophical implications. As such, Christ Himself is the epistemological link between God and man.[147] Second, knowledge of Christ comes only *via* the external – spoken or written – word of Holy Scripture.[148] Christ put His stamp of approval only on the Apostolic witness of Scripture, and we are not, therefore, justified in moving outside of that historic document. Once again, Marius notes that Luther makes this position public early on at the Leipzig debate:

> Both the Roman pope and the members of a council were men. Therefore they, too, were to be tested by the word of scripture. Everything stood under the judgment of scripture, and now Luther's bent was clear: Scripture could contradict the long-received traditions of the Catholic Church in major ways, and if such contradictions were manifest, the Catholic Church had erred. What happened then to the notion that God had been continuously with his church from the resurrection of Christ? Luther had yet to work out the answer to this fateful question....[149]

But answer the question, he did, and we will examine his mature position on this later.

Finally, because the authenticity of the Christian message rests on Christ's incarnation, death, and resurrection, one can be confident that his knowledge of such is based, not on something ultimately unknowable (e.g., mysticism), but on an historic event available to the senses of the eyewitnesses and thus open to the objective standards requisite for genuine factual knowledge.

---

[146] WA XL, i, 142.14–22.

[147] On this point see John Warwick Montgomery, "Lutheranism and the Defense of the Christian Faith," *Lutheran Synod Quarterly* vol. 11, no. 1, Special Issue (Fall, 1970) p. 27.

[148] "Atque in sanctis in hac vita aliqua Dei cognitio ex verbo et Spiritu sancto cernitur." WA XLII 49.35–36.

[149] Richard Marius, *Martin Luther* p. 178–179.

We can conclude by making the following observations: First, Luther – in a more characteristically modern fashion – highlights the problem of knowledge as he restricts reason's formal functions by shifting the emphasis from speculation to observation. In other words, he restricts the scope of reason's formal operations by insisting that our knowledge in general is contingent (*a posteriori*) and must therefore be measured against observational fact. In this narrow sense, he is implicitly part of a philosophical tradition that had its seed in Ockham and flourishes up to the present. Second, Luther's theological methodology is entirely consistent with his approach to knowledge in general. By requiring that we know God through the incarnation, with ultimate self-disclosure on the cross, Luther emphasizes the fact that knowledge of God must be of an *a posteriori* nature – thus providing a theological method with objectivity at its very heart.[150] The articles of faith, Luther typically states, are not subject to the judgment of human reason (=philosophy); "Hoc erat aliud nihil, quam coelum et terram includere in suo centro aut grano milii." On the contrary all thought, including philosophy, is to be taken captive to Christ. (Philosophy deals with matters subject to reason, but reason itself must be subject to experience). Therefore, the lofty matter of God cannot be enclosed in the narrow confines of reason or syllogisms. "Ut quae sit non quidem contra, sed extra, intra, supra, infra, citra, ultra omnem veritatem dialecticam."[151] We must not simply sit and speculate about God, but learn from our only secure source of knowledge, Christ. Luther thus characteristically brings the question "How do we know God?" into a much more narrow focus than Ockham or, for that matter, anyone else up to his era. Courtenay suggests that "perhaps the Christo-centric approach of Luther is the culmination of a long process away from a 'philosophic', natural theology that could serve apologetic ends."[152] His observation is no doubt partly true. Luther did indeed limit how far apologetics can go on the basis of natural theology alone, but he also anticipates an historically grounded, non-rationalistic, apologetic approach. To be sure, he is much less likely to bring upon himself charges of a philosophical nature simply because he starts with relatively few presuppositions, moving *from* the person and work of Christ to a knowledge

[150] J.W. Montgomery aptly remarks that "the investigation of the world of nature was, for Luther and his followers, in the final analysis a confrontation with the Christ of the Cross, who forms the center of all true theology. No greater incentive to scientific activity could be imagined." See *In Defense of Martin Luther* (Milwaukee, 1970) p. 94.

[151] *Die Disputation de sententia: Verbum caro factum est (Joh. 1, 14)* WA, XXXIX, ii, 4 propositions 7, 21.

[152] William J. Courtenay, "Nominalism and Late Medieval Religion" in *The Pursuit of Holiness in Late Medieval and Renaissance Religion: Papers from the University of Michigan Conference* (Leiden: Brill, 1974) ed. Charles Trinkaus and Heiko A. Oberman p. 58–9.

of God. By doing so he distinctively answers both the epistemological and soteriological questions in one sweep. In fact, to subordinate one of these questions to the other is ultimately to relinquish the force of Luther's theology as a whole.

CHAPTER

FOUR
───────

Logic Within Luther's
Epistemological Framework

Generally speaking, Luther believed that reason is sound concerning matters within its bounds e.g., it has an understanding of what is good as relates to the state.[153] God has given us reason to serve our uses, and it is a function within man that is absolutely indispensable.[154] Reason must, therefore, not be neglected and Luther criticizes those who think that what happens happens of necessity no matter what precautions we take: "Cum habeas scalam, non est, quod per fenestram te praecipites. Neque per albim medium incedas, cum habeas pontem. Sed quilibet hoc faciat, quod ratio monstrat, et reliqua commendet Deo, is dabit convenientes exitus."[155] Similarly, a tree must not be cut down with a blade of straw, but with an ax. For Luther, then, this is just one reason among many that God has given man reason, perception, and strength and we are to use these as means and gifts of God: "Haec semper repetenda et agitanda sunt in Ecclesia Dei, ut regia via incedamus, neque ad dextram, neque ad sinistram declinemus, neque enim dubitandum est de promissione, nec tentandus est Deus posthabitis aut neglectis mediis

---

[153] WA XLII 291.32–38.

[154] See Luther's discussion WA XLIV 17.10–41: "Ideo enim dedit Deus rationem et omnes creaturas omniaque bona temporalia, ut serviant nostris usibus" (32–33).

[155] WA XLIV 77.29–32: "Siquidem non dedit Deus rationem et rationis consilia et auxilia, ut ea contemnas" (21–22). See Luther's extended discussion of this, XLIV 77.15–80.14.

ordinatis divinitus."[156] So in his explanation of *Genesis* 31:19 Luther praises Jacob with "singulari prudentia et consilio" in seizing an appropriate opportunity[157] – Jacob uses *quod in se est* in the correct sense of the oft quoted phrase.[158]

Given these general considerations, what of the more particular topic of reason's inferential capabilities? How does Luther define logic and how significant is it within his epistemological framework? In what follows, I will examine Luther's particular views on the *nature* of logic and – for the sake of clarity – cite some examples of the way in which he actually uses logical analysis, ending the discussion with some preliminary remarks on the relation between logic and Luther's understanding of knowledge in general. So that my intentions are not misunderstood, however, I must emphasize that no attempt will be made to give a full description regarding the intricacies of Luther's logic. As our subject restricts itself to Luther's understanding of reason, the present section will be limited to examining the particular relation between logic and Luther's overall epistemology. Our attention will be drawn by such questions as, "What does Luther regard as a *reasonable* use of logical analysis?" and conversely, "When does our use of such analysis become *un*reasonable?" The importance of such issues will, I hope, become evident below. Having briefly laid the groundwork, then, let us turn to definition.

The Nature of Logic

Luther fortunately provides a fairly clear definition of logic, one in which it is "Non ut domina, sed ut ancilla et serva et pulcherrima ministra, quae docet definire et dividere:"[159] "Doctoris et Dialectici est primum omnium recte definire et dividere,

---

[156] WA XLIV 649.1–4.

[157] WA XLIV 17.31–32: "Sic pulcherrimam occasionem captavit Iacob singulari prudentia et consilio."

[158] WA XLIV 77.17–18: "Primum facit, quod in se est. Sicut usitate Papistae loquuntur, sed alio sensu. Non enim recte intelligunt, nec recte accommodant hanc phrasin." Elswhere Luther says, "Denn was frey ist, nemlich weder geboten noch verboten, darin man weder sundigen noch verdienen kan, das sol in unser macht stehen, als unser vernunfft unter worssen, das wirs mügen on alle sunde und sahr des Gewissens brauchen oder nicht brauchen, halten und saren lassen nach unserm gefallen und notturfft, Und wollen kurz umb hierin freie Herrn und nicht Knechte sein, die es mügen damit machen, wie, was, wo, und wenn die wollen." WA LIV 164.32–165.5.

[159] WA XXXIX, ii, 24.24–25 Argumentum vicesimum. Luther's above response is to the following argument: "Dialectica est instrumentum divinitus datum, inquirendae veritatis gratia. Ergo etiam in theologia.
Probo consequentiam, quia dialectica est ars artium, scientia scientiarum in omnibus professionibus" (20–23).

postea argumentari et concludere. Priora duo adversarii non faciunt. Sed ponunt propositiones et conclusionem sine ulla definitione et divisione."[160]

It seems that the best way of appreciating Luther's understanding of this is to observe his own practice of analysis. We see this in full force, for instance, when he maintains that the fanatics make a quality out of a substance by a faulty syllogism in which there are four terms, no universal premise, no essential predication, no distributed middle, and many other faults; for logicians know full well, he says, that under a substantial term an accidental term cannot be subsumed (*das sub termino substantiali non potest subsumi accidentalis*).[161] Accordingly, he maintains that people who fail to make proper logical distinctions cannot syllogize or draw valid logical conclusions. He uses Eutyches and Nestorius as prime examples of poor logicians. Eutyches forgets, Luther maintains, that he previously conceded that Christ is true God and man in one person and nevertheless refuses to admit the conclusion, or "consequens bonae consequentiae." He did not allow the human nature in Christ to remain *in consequenti*, though he confesses *in antecedenti* that the divine and human natures are one Christ, one person, and two natures.[162] Luther adds that in the schools this is called "Negare consequens antecedentis concessi in bona consequentia" and "destructo consequente retinere antecedens" – a dubious way of reasoning, and he says that those who make such errors should be called crude and ignorant people: "Zugleich ya und nein sagen in einerley sachen, das mus niemand thun, denn ein gar unverstendiger oder ein verzweivelter spotter."[163] It is interesting that he insists logical consistency actually compels us to believe that Christ is God and man in one person, and he warns that the idiomata, improperly defined, can take unthinking people and cause utmost confusion. Due to this very confusion Eutyches' position must be regarded *contradictory* because he regards Christ as God and man, but he refuses to ascribe the idiomata of the divine nature to the human nature.[164] Logically speaking, Luther

---

Luther comments in a similar manner as follows: "Quia unicum et optimum genus docendi est, bene dividere et definire." See WA XXVI 368.27–28.

[160] WA XLIII 257.9–11. He cites here, against promoters of works-righteousness, "fallacia compositionis et divisionis:" "Eiusmodi doctores digni odio sunt et reprobandi. Quia seducunt populum meris fallatiis: non distingunt inter argumenta et materias, de quibus disputatur" (see 4–8).

[161] WA XXVI 298.27–32: "Solchs heist aber dennoch schrifft und Gotts wort bey diesem geist."

[162] WA L 595.14–30: "Denn solche grobe Leute konnen nicht syllogisirn oder consequentias machen, Nemlich, das der solt die substanz oder natur verleugnet heissen, welcher die idiomata oder eigenschafft der natur verleugnet...." WA L 590.37–39–591.1.

[163] WA L 598.13–14; 599.2–4.

[164] "...so es doch die consequenz oder solge erzwingt aus dem, das wit Christum, Gott und Menschen, in einer person gleuben. Da sihestu, wie die idiomata unversehens unbedachte Leute fur den kopff stoffen und yrre machen. Luther continues: Darumb mus Eutyches kezerey widersinnisch also gethan

views this as uncritical and invalid. Consequently, he suggests that we would be better off if we retain the dialectic of St. Peter, St. Paul, and St. Augustine, "die des Heiligen Geists Dialectica ist, die es ganz gibt und nicht auss Nestorisch zestucket, oder eins allein wil lassen war sein und das ander, so aus demselben auch mus war sein, nicht wil lassen war sein."[165]

Likewise, Luther accuses Zwingli both with using bad logic, and then attempting to pass his faulty logic off as Scripture and Christian faith i.e., the fallacy of jumping right from a particular to a universal (*srisch a particulari ad universale*).[166] The principle of Zwinglian logic, says Luther, is "incertum per incertius, ignotum per ignotius probare."[167] In this connection he is particularly disappointed with Oecolapadius because he has not yet learned his schoolboy lessons, that is, common dialectics, such as rules of deduction, forms of syllogism, species of argumentation, etc.[168] – the fanatics, Luther exclaims, desperately need Peter of Spain's book on logic![169] Regarding their main issue of dispute, the Lord's supper, Luther asserts that we must not say without qualification, simply on the basis of our own deduction and opinion, that these two propositions are contrary to each other e.g., Christ's body is in heaven, and in the bread. If there are two different modes of presence there is no genuine contradiction. He points

sein, das er Christum auch fur Gott und Menschen helt, Uber die idiomata Gottlicher natur nicht wil geben dem Menschen..." See WA L 601.24–27; 602.20–23.

[165] WA L 620.30–33.

[166] WA XXVI 301.21–28: "sondern es ist Zwingelsche Logica, substantiam pro accidente, Quod pro qualiter zu brauchen...." Luther illustrates the fallacy as follows: "Der Schultheis ist nicht mit roten hosen ym bade, drumb ist er nicht ym bade. Der könig sizt nicht gekrönet uber tische, drumb sizt er nicht uber tische, kinderspiel und gauckelwerck ist das, wie die schulen wol wissen, Uber bey den geistern mus solchs schrifft und Christlicher glaube sein." Luther's charge of bad logic is repeated at the Marburg Colloquy: "Vos habetis malam dialecticam a baculo ad angulum" WA XXX, iii, 123.7. He also accuses Zwingli as "unreasonable" and insists that the fanatics in general have left behind their brains and reason with their unfounded arguments. See WA XXVI 277.29–32; 278.27–29; 285.38–40; 286.1–2.

[167] WA XXVI 323.22–24.

[168] WA XXVI 405.17–26.

[169] WA XXVI 414.30–31. Joseph P. Mullally notes that "the Summulae is a detailed analysis of terms, the logical characteristics of terms, the combination of terms into significant discourse, the conditions required for legitimate combinations of terms, and the constitutive elements of terms with the formal properties of these elements being distinctly labeled. All this is related to the legitimate mental process of discursive thinking. The end of this methodology is definitely practical because in resolving the principles which govern our rational procedure the principles which must be obeyed in developing all other sciences, speculative or practical, are determined....From the very nature of things, the study of logic should be prior to the study of the other sciences and not concomitant with them, since the rules of logic involve the primary principles of all reasoning." See *The Summulae Logicales of Peter of Spain* (Notre Dame, Indiana, 1945) p. xxii.

out to his opponents that elementary dialectics teaches that contradictories must have the same object of reference, in the same terms, and in the same context (*die kinder Dialectica leret, das contradictoria debent sieri ad idem, secundum idem, circa idem*).[170] Accordingly, he thinks that they have misunderstood *De predicatione Identica*.[171] Without a doubt, says Luther, it as undeniable that two diverse substances cannot be one substance – an ass, for example, cannot be an ox, or a man a stone: "Solchs alles mus alle vernunfft ynn allen Creaturn bekennen, da wird nicht anders aus."[172] However, he adds the point that if the fanatics were not such unskilled logicians, they would know how to handle this issue[173] – i.e., that it is inadmissible both in Scripture and in reason for two substances to be one, or one substance to be another. Luther maintains that it is not contrary to Scripture, indeed, he seems to think that it is not even contrary to reason or logic (given grammatical considerations, as we will shortly see); "sondern es dunckt sie widder die schrifft, vernunfft und Logica sein, Denn sie haltens nicht recht zu samen."[174]

Thus Luther holds against all hairsplitting logic that in the sacrament two diverse substances *may well be,* in reality and in name, one substance. He holds this position for the following reasons: (1) when we are dealing with the works and words of God, reason and all human wisdom must submit to being taken captive i.e., taught, instructed, lest we presume to judge God's words (2) because it is God who has uttered these words "Das ist mein leib" – distinct and clear, common, definite words – we must simply use his words as he has pronounced them.[175] Thus even if the doctrine seems to be contradictory, it is to be believed because the words are clear and unambiguous. Up to this point then we can say that, for Luther, it is not the place of logic to determine the *content* of truth; logic is rather a tool for clarification and making necessary distinctions. In the case of the natural sciences it is not judge over actual experience, and in theology it is not judge over the clear propositions of Scripture. We see this view in action when Luther, critiquing a Jewish argument, says that the historical account "cogit ex universali particularem facere." In other words, the major premise in the syl-

---

[170] WA XXVI 414.29–30.

[171] "Uber dis stucke bewegt billich alle redliche vernunfft." See WA XXVI 437.30ff.

[172] WA XXVI 439.6–12.

[173] WA XXVI 439.2–3.

[174] WA XXVI 440.15–18.

[175] WA XXVI 439.29– 40; 440.1–9.

logism is subject to the historical account and is, therefore, itself contingent.[176] Logic in his view is a servant, not a master, which nevertheless (and this must be emphasized) maintains its servitude even in theology,[177] for without its help endless confusion would inevitably result.

Logic and Language

This brings us to perhaps the most significant aspect of Luther's logic. He maintains that when we attempt to describe a supernatural union, say that of Christ, the way in which we use the language must first be taken into account so that we do not end up making errors due to a *premature* use of logic: "Denn wo man wil Logica wissen, ehe man die Grammatica kan, und ehe leren denn hören, ehe richten denn reden, da sol nichts rechts aussolgen."[178] Logic, on this account, is interdependent with our actual use of language. It appears that Luther follows a continuing trend to analyze the actual use of language as a means to determining the logical relation between terms within propositions.[179] (For Ockham, it may be observed, logic concerns the correct manipulation of natural and conventional signs within propositions and syllogisms.[180]) Mullally also notes (with Trendelenburg) of the widely used *Summulae* of Peter of Spain that it "carries on the trend toward the synthesis of grammar and logic and it emphasizes the close relationship which exists between the linguistic structure of grammar and the logical content of thought."[181] We can see many instances in Luther where this general approach has a marked influence on the way he argues. He insists, for example, that Wycliffe was deceived by a premature application of logic and did not first take into account the rules of grammar or the science of words. Logic rightly teaches, he

---

[176] "Maior igitur in primo syllogismo falsa est: omnes, qui sunt semen, sunt haeredes Abrahae, hoc enim in Ismaele non verum est. Historia igitur cogit ex universali particularem facere, si modo consistere argumentum debet." See WA XLIII 154.13–16.

[177] WA XXXIX, ii, 24.25 Argumentum vicesimum: "Sed usque ad theologiam."

[178] WA XXVI 443.10–12. See Luther's important discussion regarding grammar and logic in its entirety 443.8–445.17.

[179] Gerrish also notes this aspect of Luther's thought in his "Martin Luther" in the *Encyclopedia of Philosophy* (New York, 1967) V. 5, p. 112.

[180] William J. Courtenay, "Nominalism and Late Medieval Religion" in *The Pursuit of Holiness in Late Medieval and Renaissance Religion: Papers from the University of Michigan Conference* (Leiden: Brill, 1974) p. 37.

[181] Mullally, *The Summulae Logicales of Peter of Spain* p. xi. Mullally also points out that the "object of the Summulae was to prepare the minds of beginners for the dialectical tournaments and disputational examinations of university life" p. lxxviii.

points out, that bread and body, dove and Spirit, God and man are diverse beings. But we should first seek the aid of grammar, which lays down an important rule of expression for all languages: "Das wo zmey unterschiedliche wesen ynn ein wesen komen, da sasset sie auch solche zmey wesen ynn einerley rede, Und wie sie die einickeit beider wesens ansihet, so redet sie auch von beiden mit *einer rede.*" Luther concludes that this circumstance has deceived Wycliffe and the sophists who syllogize on total unity by means of partial unities, and vice versa (*quod de unitate totali per unitates partiales et econtra syllogisant*).[182] He illustrates the potentially misleading grammatical considerations as follows: If I point to or hand over a bag or purse and say, "Das sind hundert gülden," both the gesture and the word "das" refer to the purse. But since the purse and the money in some degree constitute one object, one lump, my words apply at the same time to the money.[183] We could indeed break down this complex and separate the money from the leather and distinguish the two constituents. But as a matter of course we use language in such a way that describes the matter in terms of the whole. "Denn man mus nicht achten, was solche spize Sophisten gauckeln, sondern auss die sprache sehen, was da fur eine weise, brauch und gewonheit ist zu reden."[184] So it is that the fanatics have misunderstood the words "This is my body" by their premature application of logic. They insisted that – in view of the Law of Identical Predication – *either* the bread remains, *or* the body. Luther almost gleefully points out that to resolve the difficulty the wiseacres have had to invent a miracle to show how the bread disappears, allowing its substance to be annihilated! Here is precisely, for Luther, where they have disregarded grammatical considerations. As the two substances are united they are called and designated one object. Luther does not consider it necessary that one of the two disappear or be annihilated, but both bread and body remain. Thus the one word "das" refers to the bread and, therefore, to the sacramental union of the two substances. On Luther's account, no *identical* predication obtains.[185] The important point here, whether Luther was justified in his position or not, is that he gave due attention to the concealed grammatical intricacies by examining the mode and use of language.[186] Without first unpacking how we actually use language, application of logic can be entirely misleading. Luther's insistence on such analysis only highlights further the fact that his actual

---

[182] WA XXVI 443.13–34 (emphasis mine).

[183] WA XXVI 444.3–7.

[184] WA XXVI 444.31–38.

[185] See Luther's important discussion WA XXIV 437.30–445.17.

[186] See especially Luther's penetrating critique of Zwingli's argument regarding representation in the Lord's Supper – e.g., a significant aspect of his critique shows how metaphors originate, and that the trope is not in the verb "ist." WA XXVI 269–280.

examination of propositions, with their inevitable consequences, moves in a characteristically more modern direction. (I do not wish to overstate this, however, as modern logicians would doubtless disagree with Luther on many issues, not the least of which is the fact that he actually takes "God-talk" seriously.)

A significant (and certainly not uncommon) example of Luther's attention to detail brings him to reject the following syllogism in *Die Disputation de sententia: Verbum caro factum est (Joh. 1, 14):*[187] "Omnis homo est creatura. Christus est homo. Ergo Christus est creatura." Luther points out here that where there is neither a major nor a minor premise there can be no syllogism. His contention runs as follows: the minor premise is denied because "homo" is used equivocally which results in four syllogistic terms. In other words, it is used in one way in the major premise and another in the minor, and for a syllogism to be valid a term must be used univocally.[188] But here in the major premise it designates physical man, and in the minor it designates both the divine and the incarnate God: "Nihil valet argumentatio, quia ambigua non debent poni in syllogismo, ut et rhetores dicunt, quod status debet esse simplex." But the Parisians disunite by uniting by means of their "immediatas suppositiones." Luther maintains that if a distinction in a word's meaning has to be made between the major and minor premise, "ergo non est idem." He effectively shows here that by their own artificial distinction in the one word "homo" the Parisians have undermined the logical relation between the major and minor premise.[189] We have already seen that Luther clearly recognizes that for a valid logical relation to exist, the respective terms must have the same meaning and the same reference. Thus I think he would undoubtedly second Waismann's recent contention that the "known relations of logic can only hold between statements which belong to a *homogeneous* domain; or that

---

[187] See WA XXXIX, ii, 10.4–5; 11.1–20; 12.1–10 Argumentum 4.

[188] "Dialectici veteres sic dicebant: Aequivoca non intrabunt disputationes. Disputationes sint univocorum, non aequivocorum. Item: Erroris mater est aequivocatio semper. Nam aequivocationes pariunt sophistica argumenta inepta et insulsa de verbis et non de rebus litigantia." See *Die zweite Disputation gegen die Antinomer* (1538) WA XXXIX, i, 446.18–20; 447.1 Octavum Argumentum. Luther makes a similar criticism in his response to the following argument: "Quod Pater est, Filius non est. Sed Pater est Deus. Ergo Filius non est Deus.
Respondeo: Est aequivocatio in verbo, 'est', quia in maiore respicit relationem, in minore substantiam." See *Die Promotionsdisputation von Georg Maior und Johannes Faber* (1544) WA XXXIX, ii, 329.10–11 Argumentum octavum.

[189] Dennis Bielfeldt notes in this connection that by "equivocating the middle term in the example, four terms result which disallow application of the syllogistic form. Instead of the form 'if A then B', 'A', therefore 'B'; by equivocating the actual logical form of the expression becomes 'if A then B', 'C', therefore 'B'." See Bielfeldt's unpublished Ph.D. dissertation *Luther, Logic, and Language: An Inquiry into the Semantics of Theological Language in the Writings of Martin Luther* (1987, University of Iowa) pp. 293–294.

the deductive nexus never extends beyond the limits of such a domain."[190] The content of Waismann's remark is, in my opinion, Luther's impetus for rejecting the syllogism. From Luther's perspective there is no *logical* connection between the major and minor premise, and if that is so, there can be no valid inference. Philosophy, he argues here, because of its limited domain of information i.e., being restricted to general revelation, cannot say that man is God; theology, on the other hand says that man is God apart from philosophy and any syllogism, for "philosophia nihil in grammatica nostra." "Homo," according to Luther, should mean something beyond what is meant in the tree of Porphyry, for in Christ it means something greater and more comprehensive (thus the basic fallacy of the above inference). Luther's response to such questions have prompted much debate on how he understands the relation between philosophical and theological grammar.[191] Because, however, we must keep our focus narrow we will not enter into

[190] Friedrich Waismann, "Verifiability" in *Logic and Language* (Oxford, 1963) (ed.) A. G. N. Flew, first series p. 128. Waismann continues on the same page to note that, "So long as we move only among the statements of a single stratum, all the relations provided by logic remain valid. The real problem arises where two such strata make contact...."

[191] One recent attempt was made by Dennis Bielfeldt in his unpublished Ph.D. dissertation *Luther, Logic, and Language: An Inquiry into the Semantics of Theological Language in the Writings of Martin Luther*. He puts forth what he calls the "theological interaction metaphor model" based in part on Max Black's interaction metaphor in his *Models and Metaphors* (Ithaca, New York, 1962) pp. 25–47. Briefly, Bielfeldt holds that to allow commensurability between theology and philosophy – to allow the "same thing to be true" in both through proper linguistic distinctions – is tantamount to collapsing the distinction between the earthly and heavenly realities (p. 298). Like Gerrish, Bielfeldt's thesis rests on the incommensurability of the "earthly" and "heavenly" kingdoms with the consequence there can be no ontological similarity between the two domains because there exist no senses through which to univocally "slice" the domains (p. 330). Bielfeldt observes that the "theological metaphor we constructed differs from a literary interaction metaphor in holding that there is no common essence between its terms, yet through the interaction of unlikes, a sense is established which allows reference to a divine reality" (p. 357). He continues by saying that "According to our modified interaction metaphor, human thinking retains the conceptual apparatus of 'earthly philosophy', yet thinks truths of the 'heavenly realm' through the 'new tongue' established by the interactive relationships between finite categories. Opposition in the finite creates a theological sense which cannot be reduced to a set of philosophical senses. It is this sense which points to a theological referent. We emphasize that this model of theological language retains the referential dimension of Luther's theological language. The conditions of the meaningfulness of theological language includes reference to divine reality" (p. 357). Bielfeldt's "modified" model seems problematic to me on several levels, the most obvious of those are as follows: First, it is difficult to see just how "philosophical contradiction" can be the "vehicle" for the establishment of a "heavenly" sense (a problem which Bielfeldt himself explicitly states). He responds by saying that theological "ways of thinking" for Luther must be grounded in scripture and the Fathers, and that these determine which "earthly" contradictions are philosophically significant and which are not (p. 342-3). Further, according to his model the theological "sense" references the "true theological world, the paradoxically nature of reality lying beyond the earthly realm of being" (see 360-2). I think, however, that Ronald W. Hepburn was correct when he said that it would be more honest to call such a language (here one ultimately

this highly debatable issue. My purpose in mentioning Luther's response is to demonstrate that he took great pains to show the connection between the relations of terms and the logical relations of propositions. Even more significant is the fact that he consistently employs rigorous analysis of terms and their relations in his *theological* disputes. Here his analysis leads him to reject a syllogism based on an equivocation of terms; an equivocation which he clearly recognized as being fraught with logical inconsistencies.

To note one final example, Luther's strength in analysis also plays a crucial role in his *Bon den Konziliis und Kirchen,* where he observes that Nestorius interpreted the word "Geborn" literally according to grammar or philosophy when he objected to the phrase "Gott geborn von Maria."[192] Luther replies by noting that it is true God did not derive his divinity from Mary; but it does not follow that it is wrong to say God was born of Mary. He illustrates his point with a plain example: if a woman bears a child, we are entitled to say that she is that child's mother. However, Nestorius may object by noting that the woman has given birth but she is not the child's mother because his soul is not derived from her nature or blood, but from somewhere else – for instance, God. Luther then points to the consequences of such reasoning – we might say the *reductio ad absurdum* – by observing that if this objection holds, no woman is the mother of any child and the fourth commandment "Du solt Pater und Mutter ehren" would have to be abolished. Consequently, whoever admits that a mother has borne a child of body and soul should admit that the mother has born the whole child, and that she is the child's mother. In the same way, Luther concludes, since God and man are one person in Christ, it must be said that Mary is the mother of God.[193] Generally

created by philosophical contradiction) a language of contradiction, "one which therefore delineates no possible being at all." Hepburn rightly points out that one cannot evade the linguistic problem by first admitting the breakdown in meaning within the language he uses, while still insisting that it is a vehicle used by God: "These moves rely on untenable theories of meaning." See *Christianity and Paradox* (London, 1958) pp. 16, 88. Second, it seems that Bielfeldt's use of Black's interaction metaphor runs the risk that Black himself points out, that is, the risk that the theory in question will be "permanently insulated from empirical disproof." How the grammars of philosophy and theology can be incommensurable, yet theological grammar somehow presupposing philosophical meaning in its "transfer" to the theological realm, is not sufficiently accounted for in Bielfeldt's thesis. In short, I reject his particular use of Black's model and I do not think that the model takes sufficient account of Luther's Christology – this seems to me an inevitable outcome of using the two-kingdom theory as a guide to Luther's overall thought (regarding this issue see the next chapter).

[192] WA L 586.3–8.

[193] WA L 586.12–35; 587.1–18.

speaking, Luther's opinion of Nestorius was that his entire position was logically inconsistent, and his overall conception of Christ's person must therefore
be rejected.[194]

Summary and Conclusion

Having made these brief observations, then, we can sum up our present discussion by noting the following points: First, for Luther, philosophy in general deals
with visible matters subject to the senses,[195] a position that follows from his epistemology. Philosophers in fact deal with almost every issue within the bounds of
human awareness, issues ranging from the natural sciences to those of ethics. The
common denominator of all these is that they are all within the scope of what we
can know apart from the aid of special revelation. Within this framework, logic
plays an indispensable role as that which accurately defines and distinguishes
between terms and propositions to make them intelligible. Second, logic exercises no less an essential role for the theologian. Without it, propositions would
become needlessly confounded and eventually contradictory.[196] The faith cannot
be properly understood or taught without its constant help. We must therefore,
Luther maintains, use our reason or else give way to the fanatics,[197] and he even
concedes that he is willing to change his position if anyone will show a good
reason for doing so.[198]

---

[194] WA L 589.13–20: "Denn der grobe ungelerte Man sahe das nicht, das er unmuglich ding surgab,
das er zugleich Christum ernstlich fur Gott und mensch in einer Person hielt, und doch die Idiomata
der naturn nicht wolt derselben Person Christi zugeben, Das erst wil er fur war halten, und das sol
nicht war sein, das doch aus dem ersten solget, damit er anzeigt, das er selbs nicht verstehet, was er
verneinet." See a similar illustration regarding the Personal union WA L 596.11–17.

[195] WA XXXIX, ii, 15.8–9 Argumentum septimum: "In summa, supra dixi hoc sic: Philosophia habet
visibilia, theologia vero invisibilia."

[196] "Caeterum opus est diligenti distinctione et Dialectica accurata, ne confundamus haec [first and
second table], aut sicut Papa et fanatici faciunt, abutamur hac distinctione" WA XLIV 21.11–13. See
also WA XXVI 368.19–36; 369.18–34; 370.19–24; WA XLIII 28.9–19. Teachers who fail to make
proper logical distinctions should be disregarded: "Illa confusione nihil sani docent. Sed turbant et
seducunt simplices animos." WA XLIII 257.12. Luther also maintains that the fanatics must show
him how his interpretation of Scripture is contradictory and uncertain if they are to establish their
position, WA XXVI 265.36–266.25.

[197] WA XXVI 337.14–15. I think this is what Luther had in mind when he warned against "absurdi-
missimas allegorias:" "Ac sane quod ad praesentem locum attinet, Quomodo, queso, possibile est sex
dies fuisse aut horam aut momentum unum? Nec ratio, nec fides, quae verbo nititur, admittunt hoc.
Ergo sentiamus, fuisse intervalla quaedam temporis...." See WA XLII 91.36–92.5.

[198] WA XXVI 373.22–24.

Given these factors then, let us attempt a more precise answer to our original question as to just how significant logic is within the confines of Luther's epistemological framework. As was noted above, his definition of logic was stated in response to the following argument: "Dialectica est instrumentum divinitus datum, inquirendae veritatis gratia. Ergo etiam in theologia. Probo consequentiam, quia dialectica est ars artium, scientia scientiarum in omnibus professionibus."[199] Mullally notes that, according to Peter of Spain, the subject matter of the *Summulae* – a widely used textbook for such disputations – constitutes an "art." He goes on to say that "since logic has significant speech for its object and significant speech is a necessary prerequisite for the formulation of any rules whatsoever, logic is prior to all the arts. It may truly be called the 'art of arts'."[200] For Peter of Spain, says Mullally, "dialectic was the science which held the key to the principles of all methods. Knowledge of it was acquired prior to the knowledge of any of the other sciences, for dialectic discussed with probability the principles of all the other sciences." The argument posed to Luther above appears to be in general agreement with Peter of Spain's position in the *Summulae*. However, Luther's response to the argument, combined with his comments on the nature of logic elsewhere, seem to suggest that he does not regard logic as the "science of all sciences." as for him logic is a "maidservant" and not "mistress."[201] As such it is subordinated to observation as a "serva et pulcherrima ministra, quae docet definire et dividere." And given the fact that knowledge of a factual nature comes only through sense-experience, Luther will argue that we must first take into account the subject matter, and only *then* is the role of logic properly fulfilled as it seeks to explain that subject matter with clarity and without contradiction. It is within this general context, I think, that his potentially misleading assertion, "In qua, si cessat dialectica, iacet et haec ancilla" is to be understood.[202] For Luther the subject matter must be our first concern: "Re igitur non cognita impossibile est, ut verba possint recte intelligi. Etsi enim verborum cognitio ordine prior est, tamen rerum cognitio est potior. Nam mutatis rebus etiam verba mutantur in alium sensum et fit plane

[199] WA XXXIX, ii, 24.20–23 Argumentum vicesimum.

[200] Mullally, *The Summulae Logicales of Peter of Spain* p. xxi. See also Etienne Gilson, *History of Christian Philosophy in the Middle Ages* (London, 1955) pp. 318–319. Gilson notes that the "Summulae of Peter soon became what we would call a best-seller in mediaeval universities, and it kept its place on the list for about three centuries, which modern best-sellers seldom do."

[201] Having said that we cannot forget that Luther himself used the *Summulae* as a textbook on logic and strongly recommend his opponents to do the same. The *Summulae* was a valuable tool precisely because, overall, "its use did not depend on any particular school of thought." See Mullally *The Summulae Logicales of Peter of Spain* p. lxxix.

[202] WA XXXIX, ii, 24.25–26 Argumentum vicesimum.

nova Grammatica."[203] If we do not completely understand the how of the subject matter – say, for example the Lord's Supper – with the result that it *appears* contradictory (though Luther did not think it is), we must in that case simply reassert the matter because it is stated in unambiguous language and, most importantly (in this instance), grounded on the authority of the God-man.[204]

This account seems to be consistent with the structure of Luther's overall thought, a general structure within which logic is limited to the extent that he accepts no necessary, metaphysical, relation between diverse and unrelated concepts. Oberman's observations concerning Ockham's possible influence on Luther may be instructive here in connection with my own regarding Luther's actual use of logic. Oberman notes three important points:[205] (1) Epistemologically speaking, nominalism relates experience and experiment in such a way that the individual is understood in its own context as potentially new, original, and unique before it is identified by classification into *species*. (2) This epistemological position was born out of a hunger for reality, and in particular it is a revolt against the *meta*-world of heteronomous authority and canonized speculation which overlays and distorts reality. So against the implication that our world is a mere reflection or shadow of higher levels of being, the nominalist insists on the full reality of the experienced world. And what is often called Ockham's razor is precisely the "slashing away" of the hierarchy of being, that is, of ideas and concepts, which had been invented

---

[203] WA XLII 195.18–21: "Quam magna igitur absurditas est in sancta Lingua, ubi theologicae et spirituales res tractantur, omissa rerum proprietate sentientias ex Regulis grammaticis colligere?" WA XLII 272.16–18.

[204] "Wir wissen aber, das diese wort 'Das ist mein leib ect.' klar und helle sind, Denn es höre sie gleich ein Christ odder Heide, Jüde odder Turcke, so mus er bekennen, das da werde gered von dem leibe Christi, der ym brod fey, Wie kondten sonst die Heiden und Jüden unser spotten und fagen, das die Christen fressen yhren Gott, wo sie nicht diesen text hell und klerlich verstunden?" WA XXVI 406.27–32. Luther criticizes Oecolampadius in this context as follows: "Uber (wie gesagt) Es mangelt Ecolampad und diesem geist an der puerili Dialectica, das er ex difficultate vel obscuritate intelligendi in re infert obscuritatem significandi in vocabulis, Hoc est male dividere, tertiam partem scilicet Dialectice ignorare" WA XXVI 407.24–27. Luther concludes: "Da Moses das Osterlamb einsezt, welchs doch ia ein bilde und figur war Christi, braucht er gar keins figurlichen worts, sondern durre, klare, einseltige wort, wie sie ym gemeinen brauch giengen, Und alle figurn des alten testaments sind mit durren, einseltigen, klaren worten gered, und ist nicht eines ynn allen, das da figurlich gered werde, Das man wol Ecolampads regel mus umbkeren und fagen, Man konne von keinen sacrament odder figur reden, es sey denn, das man durre, einseltige, gemeine wort dazu brauche" WA XXVI 409.17–24.

[205] See Oberman's two articles "Headwaters of the Reformation" in his (ed.) *Luther and the Dawn of the Modern Era* p. 57, and "Shape of Late Medieval Thought" in *The Pursuit of Holiness in Late Medieval and Renaissance Religion* (Leiden, 1974) edited by Charles Trinkaus and Heiko Oberman pp.13–14.

by sheer speculation.[206] It is highly significant to point out that it is a revolt against *a priori meta*-physics so as to provide freedom for a genuine *a posteriori* physics. It follows that in nominalist thought, we encounter the sternest opposition to the claims of intellect and reason when those claims are not verified by the tests of experience:

> On this basis, nominalism provided the setting for modern science, replacing the authority-based deductive method with the empirical method. The combination of *experientia* and *experimentum* allowed for a fresh investigation, by trial and error, of such basic phenomena as movement and retardation. In this way the chain of causation is reduced to observable second causes, a major advance in the transition from *the* speculative law of nature to the observable *laws* of nature.[207]

(3) In the same ways just mentioned, this epistemological position was a revolt against *meta*-theology to provide freedom for genuine theology. Here lies the interest in the antispeculative distinction between *potentia absoluta* and *potentia ordinata*. Oberman states that contingency is perhaps the best one-word summary of the nominalist program in this regard. What this means is that creation and salvation are not ontologically necessary. "The point is that in the vertical dimension our reality is not the lowest emanation and level in a hierarchy of being which ascends in ever more real steps to the highest reality, God."[208] It seems to me that Luther, on this account, maintains a position within an epistemologically engendered movement that begins to reject a metaphysical world view; a view that places a great deal of emphasis on an almost mystical "logical" nexus between the observed and unobserved. Consequently, Luther's epistemological outlook in general, and his understanding regarding the contingent nature of logic in particular, suggests that he too carries on the movement to examine the individual in its own, logically distinct, context. The tendency to run amuck with deductive inference is to Luther nothing more than returning to that dangerous metaphysical speculation which, if we may use Oberman's words, overlays and distorts reality. As we will shortly see, this is precisely why Luther so emphatically insists on his own particular distinction between the revealed and unrevealed God – to check our impulsive yearning to bring within the range of deductive certainty theological propositions which by nature do not offer mathematical-like precision. For the

---

[206] Oberman claims that "hunger for reality is so much the mark of nominalism, that it is a perhaps humorous but certainly a misleading tradition that bequeathed upon its opponents the name 'realists'." See "Shape of Late Medieval Thought" p. 13.

[207] Oberman, "Shape of Late Medieval Thought" p. 14.

[208] Oberman, "Shape of Late Medieval Thought" p.13.

premises in the syllogism are themselves contingent and subject to the observable (in this case the historical narrative). In his views, Luther again appears to move toward a more modern conception regarding the relation between the purely deductive and inductive inference.[209] This too may be one of those elements within his theological approach that forces Luther's legacy right to the doorstep of the modern era. Montgomery's following observations are especially relevant here:

> ...[Luther's] *inductive* methodology (Luther's requirement that one discover what Scripture is actually saying and not force it into alien categories – e.g., Zwingli's metaphysical speculations about the nature of "bodies" – made possible the defense of the faith in a world about to recognize the necessity of open, inductive, scientific procedure in the discovery of truth; those who followed Luther's hermeneutic, as opposed to the deductive model of Ramist Calvinism, were thus – as in the case of Brahe and Kepler – at the forefront of both scientific advance and the apologetic reconciliation of Scripture and scientific discovery.[210]

Given the above factors, then, it seems to me that Luther was dissatisfied with the reasoning of his opponents precisely because they did not give due credit to the primacy of what he calls the subject matter, while at the same time failing to note important connections between our actual use of language and the way in which we draw logical inference. The fanatics failed to take these considerations into account and, failing to do so, drew conclusions which do not in fact follow

---

[209] Goddu's comments on Ockham at this point highlight both Luther's continuity and discontinuity with Ockham and the medievalists: "In effect, Ockham developed a conception which corresponds to the model of deductive-nomological explanation; he developed no conception corresponding to the probabalistic-statistical form of explanation....Anneliese Maier has suggested that the reason for the prejudice against measurement is the medieval bias against approximation or rather the bias in favor of exact measurement, which is impossible, and the reason for this bias is the fundamental Aristotelico-mediaeval notion of scientia which yields necessary and evident knowledge and which discounts the possibility of knowledge of that which is below the level of form. In Ockham's view even induction can arrive at necessary and evident knowledge, and since its effects are not specifically different from those of demonstration, there is no specific difference between deduction and induction. Nevertheless, this conclusion also marks a movement away from Aristotle. If there is no essential difference between the knowledge of a proposition obtained by experience and the same knowledge obtained by demonstration, Ockham's rigorous interpretation of the conditions for demonstration shifted the emphasis to knowledge obtained by experience. Such knowledge rests on the principle that a natural cause under the same conditions always produces the same effect with physical necessity...The certitude of such conclusions is not metaphysical, because although the uniformity of the laws of nature is a necessary principle, the contingency of events permits only a physical certitude with respect to inductive conclusions." Andre Goddu, *The Physics of William of Ockham* (Leiden – Köln, 1984) pp. 90–91.

[210] John Warwick Montgomery, "Lutheranism and the Defense of the Christian Faith," *Lutheran Synod Quarterly* vol. 11, no. 1, Special Issue (Fall, 1970) pp. 29–30.

from the subject matter, objectively considered.[211] Logic here is not to be supreme judge over the clear pronouncements of Holy Scripture – i.e., as logic in itself does not determine our observation of the natural world, neither should it determine our data for theology. It is to be used as a tool for making clear the doctrines presented in Scripture but it is not to determine what that doctrine itself is. For Luther, then, the data for the theologian comes not from bare logic or mathematics but from God's self-revelation in Christ documented only in Holy Scripture.[212] This view is consistent with Luther's notion that theological knowledge is derived *a posteriori* through Scripture. I think that Luther was not dissatisfied with logic or philosophy in itself, as the above makes abundantly clear, but with its use as the primary teacher (in theology *or* the natural sciences) rather than as a tool for clarity and noting fallacies, contradictions, etc.

Thus Luther appropriately observes – within this conceptual framework – that such things as the forgiveness of sins and the mystery of the incarnation cannot be *deduced* by logic. It is true as philosophy teaches that all men know by nature that theft is unlawful, "Quod vero haec summa, propter quae vel sola data est scriptura, theologica, videlicet de iustificatione, de remissione peccatorum, de liberatione a morte aeterna tribuerunt philosophiae et viribus humanis, hoc non possumus nec debemus ferre." "Hoc dicimus, quod non contradicit theologia philosophiae, quia tantum loquitur de matrimonio, obedientia, castitate, liberalitate et aliis virtutibus. Sed longe aliud est credere in filium Dei, habere et expectare vitam aeternam, quam esse castum, coniugare, honeste vivere in mundo, liberalem, mansuetum, obedientum, benignum esse et placidum."[213] Thus Luther's criticism of reason, and specifically that of philosophy and logic, spring from the same source i.e., the articles of faith are not innately known: "Facessant, dixit recte S. Ambrosius, dialectici, ubi credendum est piscatoribus apostolis."[214] Or, to say it from a dif-

---

[211] Thus Luther responds to the following: "Quicunque tollit rationem syllogizandi, concedit occasionem haereticis interpretandi pro libidine. Vos haec facitis. Ergo facitis accasionem haereticos esse.

Response: Imo haeretici magis, qui hoc peccarunt, qui irruerunt hac forma syllogistica in theologiam, per rationem omnia conciliare et concludere syllogizando contra scripturam sinunt. Nam hac forma et ratione confisi intulerunt multas molestias et vitiosas consequentias in scripturam etiam reclamente aliquando aperto textu. Sic itaque dicimus: Taceat mulier in Ecclesia." See WA XXXIX, ii, 26.8–16 Argumentum 25.

[212] "Wer nicht schrifft hat, der mus seine gedancken haben, Wer nicht kalck hat, der mauret mit dreck." WA XXIII 159.24–26. From the data of Scripture however Luther concedes that doctrines, such as that of the resurrection, can be deduced. See WA XLIII 479.17–30.

[213] WA XXXIX, ii, 14.3–13 Sextum argumentum.

[214] WA XXXIX, ii, 4 proposition 9.

ferent angle, all of Luther's criticisms follow from his implicit epistemological framework, within which logic in and of itself knows nothing of God and is to give way to Scripture for its subject matter.[215]

---

[215] Within this general context, Luther wants nothing whatever to do with mathematical reasons and he excludes and rejects completely from the words of the Lord's Supper the adverb of space: "...verba sic sonare: Hoc, non ibi, est corpus meum. An vero in loco vel extra locum sit, hoc se nescire malle quam scire, siquidem deus nondum revelaverit, nec quisquam mortalium probare possit." See *Das Marburger Gespräch* (1529) WA XXX, iii, 137.17–23.

PART TWO

Reason Brought Captive

CHAPTER

FIVE

Reason and Speculation:
Luther's Connection

We are now at an appropriate place to examine the nature of Luther's attacks on reason. As shown above, he had a very high view of logic in general which retains its function even in the theological enterprise. That being the case then, what has dismayed Luther so much that he is willing to say that reason is by its nature a "schedliche hure?"[216] And even more shocking is his retort that reason is the "Teuffels Braut"[217] and his recommendation that his hearers say to it, "du versluchte hure, wilt du mich versüren, das ich mit dem Teuffel hurerey treiben solte?"[218]: "Und was ich von der brunft, so ein grobe fünde ist, rede, solchs ist auch von der vernunfft zuverstehen, denn dieselbige schendet unnd beleidiget Gott in Geistlichen gaben, hat auch viel ein greulicher huren übel denn ein Hure."[219]

In *Vom abendmal Christi, Bekendnis* Luther states that it is reasons he demands from Scripture and not cleverness out of the fanatics' "imagination."[220] His view of the imagination and speculation is key to understanding is vehement attacks on reason, as we will show presently. Luther's understanding of these becomes particularly relevant here because be believes that the very formation of man's thinking is evil: "Usus enim hic est singulari Phrasi certo consilo, quod non simpliciter

---

[216] WA LI 129.19–21.
[217] WA LI 126.29.
[218] WA LI 130.25–26.
[219] WA LI 127.24–27.
[220] WA XXVI 342.28–31.

dicit Cogitationes hominis esse malas, sed ipsum figmentum cogitationum."[221] This "formation" involves the sum of man (i.e., consisting of reason and will), and he not only creates it but also regards its results as most glorious: "Sic vocat hoc, quod homo potest in suis cogitationibus, seu cum ratione et libero arbitrio, etiam in summo gradu. Ideo enim figmentum vocat, quod homo summo studio excogitat, deligit, facit, sicut fagulus, et putat pulcherrimum esse." Thus the *figmentum* of the human heart is evil from its youth.[222] Luther immediately defines this "formation" as reason itself, together with intellect and will: "Vocat autem figmentum, sicut aliquoties supra dixi, ipsam rationem cum voluntate et intellectu, etiam tum, cum Deo cogitat, cum honestissimis operibus exercetur sive politicis sive oeconomicis." Consequently, he maintains that out of the heart flows idolatry, by which the glory of God is changed into a calf: "Hoc peccatum si alio nomine appellare voles, vere est blasphemia nominis Dei, et violatio Sabbati, est foeda idolatria qua gloria Dei vivi mutatur in vitulum, hoc est, in idolum cordis."[223]

Luther's understanding of the imagination is closely linked to his view of the natural inquisitiveness and speculation of man's reason. Inquisitiveness, he says, is original sin itself by which we are impelled to strive for a way to God through speculation.[224] He has made clear earlier that, in the fall, reason was not satisfied and wanted to rise higher and know God in a different manner than provided for in his Word. After men have disregarded the Word they turn to their own thoughts, and can only then form false notions about God, salvation, and ultimately about themselves.[225] When, however, one approaches God through such speculation there can be no knowledge gained, for he is by nature invisible. And it is precisely here that the speculation of reason becomes a terrible disease of the human situation.[226] For by nature we lack knowledge of God, but human nature

---

[221] WA XLII 291.22–28.

[222] WA XLII 348.29–33. "Heart," "reason," and "intellect" take on similar, if not identical, characteristics: "Non enim exiguum aliquid dicit, qui sensus et cogitationem humani cordis ab adolescentia ad malum pronam esse dicit. Praesertim cum supra sexto capite dixerit Moses: Cunctam cogitationem cordis intentam esse ad malum omni tempore, hoc est, studere malo, at esse in intentione, studio et conatu ad malum." WA XLII 348.8–13.

[223] WA XLII 412.35–38.

[224] WA XLIII 459.9–11: "Est enim curiositas ista ipsum peccatum originis, quo impellimur, ut ad Deum adfectemus viam naturali speculatione. Sed est ingens peccatum, et conatus inutilis et irritus."

[225] WA XLII 121.24–27: "Radix igitur et fons peccati est incredulitas et aversio a Deo, Sicut e contra fons iusticiae et radix est fides" (122.12–13).

[226] "Alias cogitationes et vias rationis aut carnis occidito, quia Deus eas detestatur. Id unum age, ut suscipias filium, ut placeat in corde tuo Christus in sua nativitate, miraculis et cruce. Ibi enim est liber vitae, in quo scriptus es. Idque unicum et praesentissimum remedium est istius horribilis morbi, quo homines in inquisitione Dei procedere volunt speculative, et ruunt tandem in desperationem aut

is such that it cannot be *without* the worship of God, and if it does not have the Word, it invents services and fabricates traditions.[227] Althaus similarly observes that in Luther there is a "contrast between man's attempt to find and know God on his own and the knowledge and encounter which God gives through His Word, and this contrast is of decisive importance," and adds the point that this motif "runs through Luther's entire theology, in all phases of development, and Luther repeatedly discusses it."[228]

Deus absconditus

An important theme in this connection is Luther's concept of the *Deus absconditus*. We have seen that his theory of knowledge drives him to the conclusion that we do not know anything specific about the nature of God apart from his self-revelation. He grants the consequences of such an epistemological position and consistently warns against vain speculation into God's divine majesty apart from ordained coverings. He observes, to take but one example, that philosophers cannot even come into agreement over a subject matter as basic as the soul. That being the case, then, how much less concerning the nature of God?[229] The people of Israel, he argues, did not have a God whom they viewed "absolute," the way the monks try to rise into heaven itself with their speculations, thinking about God as he is in himself: "Hunc Deum absolutum debent omnes fugere, qui non volunt perire, quia humana natura et Deus absolutus (docendi causa hac appellatione nota utimur) sunt inter se infestissimi inimici..."[230] God by nature is invisible and we by nature are unable to recognize spirits when presented as such – and this situation is intensified by the more severe problem that human weakness cannot help being crushed by God's majesty.[231] Luther further urges us not to interpret David as though he were speaking with the absolute, uncovered, God. David is speaking to God as he is dressed and clothed in his Word and promises and we must take hold of this God, not naked, but clothed and revealed in his Word: "Hic Deus tam clementi specie et, ut sic dicam, tam iucunda larva indutus, nempe promissionibus suis, potest apprehendi et cum gaudio ac fiducia a nobis conspici, ubi econtra

contemptum." See WA XLIII 459.35–40.

[227] WA XL, ii, 324.19–30; WA XLII 221.20–29.

[228] Paul Althaus, *The Theology of Martin Luther* (Philadelphia, 1981) p. 20.

[229] See WA XLII 11.11–12.25.

[230] WA XL, ii, 329.22–25.

[231] WA XLII 294.1–2, 16–17; WA XL, ii, 329.25–26.

Deus absolutus est ceu ahaeneus murus, in quem non possumus impingere sine nostro exitio." Consequently, he makes a distinction between the Prophets, who speak to a revealed God, and the Gentiles, who attempt to know God outside of his promises according to the thoughts of their own hearts. "Ideo Sathan hoc dies noctesque satagit, ut nos ponat in occursum nudi Dei, ut obliti promissionum et beneficentiae in Christo ostensae cogitemus de Deo ac iudicio Dei. Id cum fit, periimus illico, prolapsi in desperationem."[232]

Luther therefore maintains that he follows this general rule: "quantum potest, tales questiones vitem, quae nos protrahunt ad solium summae maiestatis. Melius autem et tutius est consistere ad praesepe Christi hominis."[233] When God reveals himself to us it is necessary for our sakes that he does so through a veil or a wrapper. Thus Luther appeals to the account of Isaiah, that he saw the Lord in a wide garment for the simple reason that God cannot be portrayed or shown by direct perception, or by an absolute vision (*Deus in absoluta seu intuitiva visione non potest pingi nec cerni*).[234] God sees that this way of knowing him is literally impossible for us, for he dwells in unapproachable light, and has made known what we can grasp and understand. Those who approach the revealed God have a true understanding, while those who boast of visions and revelations are either overwhelmed by God's majesty or remain in utter ignorance.[235] For it is certain that a human being cannot find God through his own wisdom. But here where one tries, there is an additional danger that Satan is able to transform himself into an angel of light, surrounding himself with divine majesty while producing signs and wonders to confirm his errors.[236] Consequently, the epistemological problem within the category of speculative reason surfaces as a major theme.

One of the main reasons for man's inquisitiveness, Luther suggests, is that from the beginning he was prone to ask of God the fatal question "why?" Because Adam turns from the command which God had given him and discusses the reasons why God has forbidden him to touch the tree, he is hurled into sin

---

[232] WA XL, ii, 329.35; 330.16–21.

[233] WA XLII 293.29–32.

[234] WA XLII 12.35–37: "Necesse enim est, ut Deus, cum se nobis revelat, id faciat per velamen et involucrum quoddam et dicat: Ecce sub hoc involucro me certo apprehendes. Id involucrum cum amplectimur, cum ibi adoramus, invocamus, sacrificamus, Deum invocasse, Deo sacrificasse recte dicimur" (21–25).

[235] WA XLII 294.18–35: "'Non videbit me homo et vivet', inquit in Exodo. Ergo imaginem sui proponit, quia se nobis ita ostendit, ut apprehendere eum possimus."

[236] WA XLII 624.40–625.2, 30–34: "Certum enim est, quod homo per suam sapientiam non potest Deum invenire, et ex ea quoque parte ingens periculum est, quod Satan se transformat in Angelum lucis, et sibi circundat maiestatem divinam, dum signa et prodigia ad errores suos confirmandos facit."

and death: "Non enim quaerendae erant rationes praecepti divini. Hoc enim est iudicare divinam voluntatem, et pervestigare vias eius, quae sunt impervestiga-biles, et compraehendere iudicia eius, quae sunt incompraehensibilia."[237] God, says Luther, wanted us to walk on the earth, not on the clouds, and we should therefore restrain our curiosity and remain within the definite bounds that he has placed before us: "...voluit verbum revelatum studiose disci, non voluit cogitari de iis, quae altiora sunt nobis: Voluit verbum et mandatum suum nos sequi, non voluit scrupulosius mandatorum suorum causas inquiri." Adam and Eve attempted precisely this and perished as a result, for they put themselves in the place of the Creator and forgot that they are mere creatures. For Luther, their attempt was nothing less than to become a god.[238] But just as Adam and Eve inquired as to the why, so our reason hampers and deceives us too. We are not, as a result, sat-isfied with knowing that God has given a command, but in our anxiety we want to know the cause for the command. God hates this inquisitiveness and wants us rather to obey his command and be satisfied with the simple fact that he himself has given the decree.[239]

Interestingly, Luther highlights a certain similarity between Adam's inference that there was some secret reason why God had forbidden the fruit of the tree (and wanting to know the reason for the prohibition) and our questions about the nature of predestination. Both inquiries stem from the same attempt to know the unrevealed God i.e., the wish to penetrate the depth of the divinity.[240] Noting our sinful concerns, Luther elaborates: "Oportet fieri, quod Deus praefinivit. Igitur incerta et inanis est omnis cura de religione aut de salute animarum."[241] Yet such speculation only serves to make one unsure of God's sure promises, and more importantly, it has not been given to us to render a verdict that is in itself *imper-vestigabilis*. On the contrary, God has most sternly forbidden investigation of the divinity. Thus when the apostles ask in Acts 1:6, "Has it not been predestined that at this time the kingdom should be restored?" Christ says to them: "It is not for you to know the times" (Acts 1:7). Here, significantly, Luther expands God's words to include, "Sine, me esse absconditum, ubi me non revelavi tibi: aut tibi ipsi causa exitii eris. Sicut Adam horribiliter lapsus est. Quia scrutator maiestatis opprimetur a gloria." He continues in this context and says that God wanted to meet this curiosity at the very beginning:

[237] WA XLII 646.36–647.2.

[238] WA XLII 647.15–21.

[239] WA XLIII 77.3–9.

[240] David Steinmetz also makes this observation regarding predestination in his *Luther in Context* (Bloomington, 1986) p. 26.

[241] WA XLIII 458.3–11.

Ego tibi praescientiam et praedestinationem egregie manifestabo, sed non ista via rationis et sapientiae carnalis, sicut tu imaginaris. Sic faciam: Ex Deo non revelato fiam revelatus, et tamen idem Deus manebo. Ego incarnabor vel mittam filium meum, hic morietur pro tuis peccatis, et resurget a mortuis. Atque ita implebo desiderium tuum, ut possis scire, an sis praedestinatus, an non. "Ecce, hic est filius meus: Hunc audito," hunc aspice iacentem in praesepio, in matris gremio, pendentem in cruce. Vide, quid is faciat, quid loquatur. Ibi me certo appraehendes. "Qui enim me videt, inquit Christus, videt et patrem ipsum."[242]

For, according to Luther, one must debate either about the hidden God or the revealed God. And as we have already noted above, there can be no knowledge or understanding of God insofar as he is hidden and unrevealed. With these speculative thoughts nothing is achieved, for they present an object (the hidden God) that is absolutely unknowable: "Ideo quando ad Deum non revelatum accedimus, ibi nulla fides, nullum verbum, neque ulla cognitio est, quia est invisibilis Deus, quem tu non facies visibilem."[243] The problem of speculation is largely an epistemological one, for God's judgments are beyond our comprehension and reason is unable to grasp them. Consequently, if reason does argue about them, it not only deceives itself but also falls into utter blasphemy. "Satis igitur nobis sit, qoud audimus verbum, et intelligimus, quid praecipiat, etsi causam non intelligamus, cur praecipiat."[244]

As we have seen, Luther calls reason a whore, and it is in the context of its speculative endeavor to know God unrevealed that this comment should be understood. Reason in this sense is an idolater running after an idol, or a whorechaser who runs after a harlot.[245] In its whoredom, reason creates self-chosen works and shrines for worship, which of course is nothing short of idolatry. Very little pleases a man, Luther insists, so much as self-love (*philautia*), when he has a passion for his own wisdom: "Die begirde der geizigen ist nichts dar gegen, wenn einem sein eigen dünckel herzlich gefelt."[246] Reason wants to flatter itself whatever the situ-

---

[242] WA XLIII 459.15–31.

[243] WA XLIII 458.37–459.14. See Luther's insightful discussion in its entirety 458.37–463.17. He makes a similar comment in the following: "Pernitiosa igitur et pestilens cogitatio est de Quare, ac certum affert interitum, praesertim cum ascendimus altius, et de praedestinatione volumus Philosophari....Qui autem scrutare se altiora non desinit, et solicite disputat: Quare hoc praecipit? is per illud Quare eiicietur ex Paradyso, sicut Adam. Est enim divinae maiestati prorsus intolerabile et nobis impossibile." See WA XLII 670.26–28; 671.6–8.

[244] WA XLII 672.24–28: "Crucifigamus igitur hanc pestem Quare: et dicamus soli sapienti Deo gloria: nobis autem confusio" (12–13).

[245] WA LI 127.27–29.

[246] WA LI 130.34–36.

ation, and to this extent man is his own worst sycophant.[247] As a result, reason is not content to stay within the limits that God has placed on it, and also wants such idols for veneration as Mary and St. Christopher. Yet you must not serve God, Luther warns, on the mountains or in the valleys or under the trees, but in Jerusalem, which is the place that God appointed for his worship and where his Word is.[248] God *could* have said, "If you say a Paternoster to this saint you will saved." But he has not said this; in fact, he has sternly forbidden it.[249] People who speculate about God as such are the ones who put the cart before the horse and will not stay on the road which God himself has shown, but always have to have and do something special. "Ei, es stehet sein, wenn das Ey wil kluger sein denn die Henne, Ein schöne Meisterschafft mus das sein, wo die Kinder yren Pater und Mutter die narren und thoren weise Leute regieren wollen."[250] Luther would rather we cling only to Christ's Word and come to him, as he invites us, and say: "Du bist allein mein lieber Herr und Meister, ich bin dein Schüler."[251]

To conclude, speculative reason within Luther's thought should be seen as that innate desire to know God apart from his chosen medium, the incarnate Son of God revealed in the writings of the Apostles. As will be shown later, speculation is no less problematic for the Christian than it is for the unbeliever. Luther warns Christians to keep their own ideas in check and to beware of their own thoughts and wisdom: "Der Teuffel wirt das liecht der vernunfft anzünden und euch brengen vom glauben."[252] To leave the manger is to separate oneself from the one true God. He suggests that this is precisely what happened to the Anabaptists and antisacramentarians who have done nothing but instigate heresy, and adds that he has had more than thirty fanatics approach and attempt to teach him, but that he has refuted them all with this uncomplicated phrase: "Dis ist mein lieber Son, an welchem ich ein wolgefallen hab, den höret."[253] Importantly, he claims that he has literally been sustained by this simple passage, otherwise he would have had to accept thirty different faiths. In fact, this unrelenting conviction leads us now to the most significant aspect of Luther's thought, the one aspect that gives cohesion to every other facet of his theological perspective: the historic person of Jesus Christ.

---

[247] WA XLIII 406.1–3: "Adeo ratio nostra sui amans est: et quicquid boni dicitur, ad se trahit. Ut, si quis laudatur, putat id verissime de se dici. Adeo est homo adulator pessimus, et gnato sui ipsius."

[248] WA LI 127.34–36; 128.32–35.

[249] WA LI 134.29–31.

[250] WA LI 188.24–36.

[251] WA LI 194.31–35.

[252] WA LI 131.22–25; 132.29–37.

[253] WA LI 131.23–29.

CHAPTER
SIX

Luther's Christology Reexamined

The present reexamination of Luther's christology can be considered a central part of this thesis. We have already alluded to the fact that the later Luther finds God only in the person of Jesus Christ, a revelation that is consistently put in opposition to the *Deus absconditus*. At this juncture however it is necessary to evaluate in some detail how Luther's later position on the issue of the *Deus absconditus*, so essential to his interpretation of Christ's passion, differs from that in his early works. That is, in order to fully develop our thesis it will be necessary to sketch briefly the young Luther's position and note the evolution which takes place to form his later view. In my judgment, there was a significant shift of emphasis which occurred in his later life that has a direct bearing on the issue of reason, and one that has been overlooked by previous approaches on the subject. We will then attempt to examine in more detail the peculiar elements in Luther's later christology, noting especially those features which directly relate to our present subject. With that said, let us turn to the young Luther.

The Relevance of Luther's Theology of the Cross

Luther's Heidelberg Disputation – especially theses 19–20 – has been one of the main focal points for his early view on the *theologia crucis*.[254] McGrath notes in

[254] WA 1 354.17–20. The propositions read as follows: "19. Non ille digne Theologus dicitur, qui invisibilia Dei per ea, quae facta sunt, intellecta conspicit, 20. Sed qui visibilia et posteriora Dei per passiones et crucem conspecta intelligit."

his recent study on the subject that, for the early Luther, the sole place of man's knowledge of God is the cross of Christ. Here God is to be found revealed, yet he is paradoxically hidden in that same revelation. While the cross truly reveals God, Luther emphasizes that this revelation is of the *posteriora Dei*. As such the revelation of God must be regarded as indirect, but Luther underscores the fact that it is a genuine revelation nonetheless. His insistence upon the *posteriora Dei* is based on his understanding of *Exodus* 33:23 where Moses is only allowed to see God from the rear, as a direct revelation of God in his majesty would most certainly crush human nature. Consequently, we are similarly denied a direct knowledge of God and must seek him only in his hidden revelation in Jesus of Nazareth.[255]

McGrath summarizes the important features of Luther's early thought as developed in the Heidelberg Disputation (1518) and the *Operationes* (1518–21) neatly in the following:[256] (1) The *theologia crucis* is a theology of revelation which stands in sharp contrast to speculation. (2) It is a revelation that is indirect and concealed. That is, it is God who is revealed on the cross, but he is not immediately recognizable *as God*. Thus because it is truly God who is made known on the cross, it is revelation, but this revelation can only be discerned by the eye of faith and is therefore concealed. Thus McGrath observes that the "'friends of the cross' know that beneath the humility and shame of the cross lie concealed the power and the glory of God – but to others, this insight is denied." (3) This revelation is to be recognized in the sufferings and the cross of Christ. Importantly, McGrath points out here that only in Christ crucified can theology or knowledge of God obtain – i.e., the cross truly "shatters human illusions concerning the capacity of human reason to discern God in this manner." The moralist and the rationalist wrongly attempt to find God through reflection upon the nature of man's moral sense or the created order. (4) Knowledge of God hidden in his revelation is a matter of faith. The theologian of the cross is he who discerns the presence of the hidden God in his revelation in Christ and his passion and cross through faith. Thus the concept of the hidden God lies at the center of the theology of the cross. (5) God is known through suffering. Specifically, God is not merely known *through* suffering, but God *makes himself known* through suffering. The significance of suffering on this account is that it represents the *opus alienum* through which God works out his *opus proprium*.[257] The most crucial point for our present study, however,

---

[255] Alister E. McGrath, *Luther's Theology of the Cross* (Basil Blackwell, Oxford, 1985) p. 148–149. See McGrath's full discussion pp. 148–181.

[256] McGrath, *Luther's Theology of the Cross* pp. 149–152.

[257] McGrath also notes in this regard the significance of suffering on the personal dimension: "Far from regarding suffering or evil as a nonsensical intrusion into the world (which Luther regards as the opinion of a 'theologian of glory'), the 'theologian of the cross' regards such sufferings as his

is McGrath's conclusion that for Luther God's revelation in the cross of Christ must be regarded as hidden, thereby defying the attempts of reason to master it. Human wisdom thus takes offense at the cross, which stands in contradiction to what reason would otherwise expect. As such, human reason cannot understand the ways of God and is therefore driven to despair.[258]

It is evident from this that the early Luther often brings the notion of human reason into direct confrontation with the suffering of Jesus, illustrating by it the fact that reason truly knows nothing of God or his ways. The question for us is how much of it do we find in the writings of the mature Luther? But before we attempt to answer that question, it might be advantageous first to give a more precise definition to the term *Deus absconditus* as Luther understands it. This, as McGrath has pointed out, is central to his notion of the *theologia crucis* and a brief examination of it will provide us with the proper background for the following remarks.

McGrath points out that the *Deus absonditus* has been improperly understood and utilized by many Luther scholars.[259] He suggests that Luther uses the term in two different ways which have little in common, except for the very general idea of "hiddenness:" (1) *Deus absconditus* is the God hidden *in* his revelation. Thus, and very importantly, the *Deus absonditus* and the *Deus revelatus* are identical. (2) *Deus absconditus* is the God who is hidden *behind* his revelation. Thus defined, the *Deus absconditus* is the God who will forever remain unknown to us. McGrath notes that this second meaning is virtually non-existent until Luther's 1525 treatise *De servo arbitrio*. Here we find an inescapable tension between the *Deus incarnatus* and the *Deus absconditus*. No longer are they identical, as there is reason to believe that the hidden and inscrutable will of God may stand in contradiction to his revealed will. If this is in fact what Luther intended to convey, McGrath seems correct in his judgment that the argument "inevitably makes theology an irrelevancy, if any statements which can be made on the basis of divine revelation may be refuted by appealing to a hidden and inscrutable God, whose will probably contradicts that of the revealed God."[260] Lienhard has attempted to view Luther's difficult remarks within the overall pattern of his thought. Interpreted thus Luther is emphasizing the freedom of God e.g., God is not obliged to become incarnate or to save human beings as *Deus praedicatus*. He determines

most precious treasure, for revealed and yet hidden in precisely such sufferings is none other than the living God, working out the salvation of those whom he loves." See *Luther's Theology of the Cross* p. 151.

[258] See especially McGrath's remarks in *Luther's Theology of the Cross* pp. 167–169.

[259] McGrath, *Luther's Theology of the Cross* pp. 164–166.

[260] McGrath, *Luther's Theology of the Cross* pp. 166–167.

faith by placing it in tension between love and fear. According to Lienhard's analysis, it is therefore necessary to speak of a double hiddenness of God. For one, there is the revelation of God hidden and yet revealed in the cross of Christ. But there is also the hiddenness that is part of God's being. It is this hiddenness which attracts human speculation, but it is also the hiddenness which consumes those who try to penetrate it.[261] Whatever interpretation is accepted, it cannot be denied that Luther's remarks in *De servo arbitrio* are troubling to say the least and have always somewhat perplexed Luther scholars. It is not my intention here to offer an explanation to these problematic passages, but only to note the change in Luther's notion of God's hiddenness which takes place in this treatise. Fortunately for our study, *De servo arbitrio* is not his final word on the subject.

As was noted above our focus is primarily on Luther's later views, roughly from the years 1527 to 1546, and it is my opinion that he is much clearer in these later writings on the whole notion of the *Deus absconditus*. Specifically, we see a shift of emphasis towards the idea that the *Deus absconditus* is the God found in and through creation, and the only God we will meet outside of the man Jesus Christ.[262] This is, in short, the God men meet through vain speculation, an all consuming fire. We have already noted that Luther did not believe we can actu-

---

[261] Marc Lienhard, *Luther: Witness to Jesus Christ* (Minneapolis, 1982) pp. 255–262.

[262] The comments of Siggins in this regard are interesting yet (in my estimation) philosophically obscure: "The 'back parts' are now the rational knowledge of God from creation and law. This contrast strikingly demonstrates the way in which Luther has changed his mind. It remains true that God is utterly incomprehensible in His essence and majesty; but in Christ, God is not hidden but revealed – revealed not *sub contraria* but as He truly is. Of course, to reason this revelation is still hidden *sub contraria*, but strictly speaking, the revelation is not offered or available to reason. Whereas earlier, however, the revelation was hidden *sub contraria* even (perhaps especially) for faith, now Luther insists that faith in Christ is the right, proper, open, enlightening, and unobscured knowledge of God's true mind and heart." Passing over for a moment his cryptic remark about reason, it might be valuable to ask how Luther's later view has actually clarified anything on the above reading. What actual difference is there, for instance, in saying that faith is now the right and unobscured knowledge of God's heart, as opposed to the earlier view that God's revelation was hidden *sub contraria* even for faith? Philosophically speaking, I fail to see how such a distinction makes matters clearer. What the distinction rather accomplishes, it seems to me, is to make out of an *extremely* confusing notion simply a *confusing* notion i.e., stripping one thin layer off of an essentially problematic view. It is apparent that Siggins presupposes some of the same tenets about Luther's view of reason that Gerrish does, as evident in the following: "Here reason is out of its depth; but God takes pity on our estate and preaches the gospel of Christ to us, declaring His true will and heart of love and favor toward us in spite of our bondage. This goes against all human reason: only faith is competent here. The true knowledge of God yielded in faith is genuine and true – 'right-handed' – in a way in which rational knowledge can never be." As we will detail criticism of this position in the final chapter, it is only important to point out here that Siggins merely echoes Gerrish's sentiments and, in so doing, robs Luther's position of what I see as a major part of its richness. See Ian D. Kingston Siggins, *Martin Luther's Doctrine of Christ* (New Haven and London, 1970) pp. 80–84.

ally come to know anything of significance about the hidden God. Thus we can say that Luther's notion of the naked or hidden God tends to coalesce more or less with his notion of general revelation within his later writings i.e., the hidden or uncovered God is all that is found through the natural created order, whether through the rationalizations of reason alone or creation in general. Lienhard seems to present a similar position when he discerns a certain evolution in Luther's later thought. He notes that Luther came to criticize strongly the concept of the *Deus absconditus,* not in the sense that the concept is rejected, but in the sense that he unambiguously rejects any search for God beyond or outside of Jesus Christ. Such a search can only end in destruction. Significantly, Lienhard says that Luther does not thereby deny the hiddenness of God as found in *De servo arbitrio.* What he does reject, however, is any hint of a dualism which would set an incomprehensible God in opposition to a Savior God. Such a dualism, as McGrath also points out, would undermine all assurance. It becomes essential for Luther that it is the real God himself whom we meet in Christ. In other words, the saving act of God reflects the very being of God in himself (this will be clearly seen below), while this fact does not exhaust the mystery of God. Here Lienhard underlines the fact that this is Luther's later reaction against any attempt to penetrate the *Deus absconditus* apart from revelation. Does the theology of the cross then, with his insistence on the *Deus absconditus,* remain at the forefront of Luther's later theology? Lienhard replies in the following:

> It remains understood that, for Luther, God, Jesus Christ, and the realities which they determine, such as the church, salvation, the Christian life, are placed under the cross, offered to us *sub contraria specie.* They are hidden, and they require faith. At the same time that this orientation remains, there seems to appear a new emphasis which insists on the reality of the revelation of Jesus Christ as revelation. The early Luther insisted above all on the hiddenness as such, at the same time as he insisted on the judgment directed to natural human beings, a judgment under which was hidden grace. Now, it seems it is affirmed more clearly that we know God and his saving intentions truly in Jesus Christ, that the announcement of the gospel is forgiveness, not judgments hiding forgiveness.[263]

It is Lienhard's opinion that a certain shift of emphasis occurs from the young to the mature Luther in that he no longer fixes his attention only on the dialectic *sub contraria specie* of the revelation of Jesus Christ, but now insists more on the Law as an instrument by which God brings death and hides himself. In Jesus Christ on the other hand he brings life and fully reveals himself. Accordingly the *posteriora Dei* are now the law and creation. The conclusion Lienhard draws is

---

[263] Lienhard, *Luther: Witness to Jesus Christ* p. 263.

that the revelation of Christ is now emphasized more as revelation. The hidden-ness of God is essentially placed outside of Christ, in the law, while in Christ God genuinely reveals himself and effects our salvation. The principle accent, Lienhard maintains, is placed on the revelation by Christ of the saving intentions of God.[264]

I am in general agreement with Lienhard's analysis and must also second his objection that the theology of the cross has been too often limited to the earlier works of Luther. However, Luther's later view of the cross undoubtedly changes in emphasis, and we find God's *hidden* presence in Christ much less pronounced as his christology develops. In fact we find God's *immediate* presence in Christ surfacing as a major theme in direct proportion to his formal development of the two natures, beginning with the great sacramental debates (1526 onward). Lien-hard notes that Luther even criticizes his earlier position in which he sought for a way to rise from the human toward God; this seemed to him to be in danger of separating God from the humanity.[265] No longer in these later years are the *Deus absconditus* and the *Deus revelatus* identical i.e., knowledge of the hidden God is now set in direct opposition to knowledge of the revealed God.[266] This of course must not be understood to mean that there are two opposed wills within the one God as appears to be the case in *De servo arbitrio*. Generally speaking, Luther is now adamant that the will of the hidden God is truly the same as that of the revealed God. That is to say, if we have the revealed God we also have the hidden God.[267] Thus he will later assert for instance that if you cling to the revealed God

---

[264] Lienhard, *Luther: Witness to Jesus Christ* pp. 264–265. Lienhard sees a certain continuity how-ever with the young Luther regarding these aspects, and says that this should rather be viewed as a change of emphasis.

[265] Thus Luther states: "We cannot touch or grasp the divine majesty, any more than we would wish to touch or grasp a devouring fire....That is why he has presented his flesh to us, in order that we may attach ourselves to it and to a certain extent be able to touch and comprehend it...Therefore do not listen to those who say that the flesh avails nothing. Reverse this word and say that God without the flesh avails nothing. For it is on the flesh of Christ from the Virgin's womb that your eyes must be fixed, so that you may take courage and say: 'I have known nothing of God, neither in heaven nor on earth, apart from the flesh, sleeping in the Virgin's womb'....For otherwise God is in all ways incomprehensible, it is only in the flesh of Christ that he can be grasped." WA XXV 106.33–107, 11. Quoted in Lienhard, *Luther: Witness to Jesus Christ* pp. 341–342.

[266] Luther does, of course, still say that God is hidden in Christ. However he says this now only to emphasize the fact that, because of our infirmity, God has hidden his majesty in Christ such that we are able to understand. We are therefore not to seek him on high but only in the Man Jesus Christ i.e., we must now seek and acknowledge God only in this Man. See for example WA XXXVI 570.33–39; 571.15–29.

[267] See WA XL, i, 572.24–26. It is interesting that in his evaluation of Luther's doctrine of the Trinity Lienhard observes this same theme at work. Because of Luther's later understanding of revelation, everything depends on the fact that the accomplishment of salvation is determined by the eternity

with a firm faith, so that you are determined not to lose Christ even if you are deprived of everything, then you are most assuredly predestined and you will also understand the hidden God. Indeed for Luther you will understand Him right now if you acknowledge Christ and his will, namely, that He wants to reveal Himself to you and wishes to be your Lord and Savior. You are therefore sure that God is also your Lord and Father.[268]

Yet insofar as the hidden God alone is concerned, there can never be any true knowledge. In fact, throughout Luther's later writings, thoughts which investigate the hidden God are considered utterly destructive because they present an object that is entirely inscrutable i.e., God is by nature invisible and we cannot know him as such. Luther often returns to that familiar verse particularly connected with his early theology of the cross, *Exodus* 33:23, but now sets it within the context of man's natural inquisitiveness. Commenting on *Genesis* 26:9, for instance, he notes that reason's inquisitiveness is rooted in original sin itself and is that by which we attempt to know God through natural speculation alone (thus Moses' inquisitive desire to see God's face). He immediately sets the *Exodus* verse in juxtaposition with Christ's statement "No one comes to the Father but by Me," thereby affirming that God is utterly hidden and unknown outside the historic person of Christ. It therefore seems to me that the primary emphasis of the mature Luther is placed on the correlation between the hidden God and man's attempt to know him by means of natural human wisdom. Interestingly, Luther remarks that this is precisely the distinction taught in *De servo arbitrio*. This might suggest that his numerous later references to that earlier work are rooted in a satisfaction with his initial discovery of the *Deus absconditus* and *Deus revelatus* in terms of religious epistemology – i.e., the impossibility of knowing the hidden God given human frailty, thereby *demanding* the revealed God in the person of Jesus Christ – while now categorically denying a two-fold will within the one Godhead.[269] At any rate, Luther never tires of repeating in his later years that man has no vice equal to

---

of God, realized by the Father, Son, and Holy Spirit. In this sense it is necessary to speak of the "immanent" Trinity. If there are two "Gods", says Lienhard, the God who saves and God in himself, assurance is definitely put into question – in fact, Luther believed that this is where modalism ultimately leads. It appears, on the other hand, that Luther held in his later years that the saving act of God in history only translates what God is from all eternity, that is to say, action between the Father, Son, and Holy Spirit. See *Luther: Witness to Jesus Christ* (Minneapolis, 1982) p. 319.

[268] WA XLIII 460.23–35.

[269] See for instance WA XLIII 458.35–459.34. Luther's following remarks are extremely important. He insists that he wanted to transmit this epistemological distinction carefully and accurately because after his death many will publish his books and attempt to prove their errors from some of his previous statements. He acknowledges that elsewhere he has written that everything is absolute and unavoidable: "sed simul addidi, quod aspiciendus sit Deus revelatus, sicut in Psalmo canimus: Er heist Jesu Christ, der Herr Zebaoth, und ist kein ander Gott." But people will, Luther says, skip over all

his own self-love, or a love for his own ideas and rationalizations. To know God revealed however, according to Luther, is the only remedy for reason's horrible innate disease of speculation.[270]

As we will shortly see, Luther consistently offsets man's speculative attempts to penetrate God's majesty with the sacrificial victim Jesus Christ, in whom we truly perceive the heart of God himself. What is significant for the mature Luther is that he becomes more outspoken concerning the certainty of knowing God in and through the humanity of Christ. Doubtless this change of emphasis occurs as a partial result of the famous sacramental debates with his Protestant opponents. In fact it was in response to his opponents on the sacraments in these later years, thereby developing in detail his understanding of the two natures, that Luther was forced to deal with religious epistemology. But it is nonetheless an important change of emphasis for his view of human reason. Having made these remarks then let us move to examine Luther's mature christology in more detail as it relates to the subject of reason.

Luther's Theological Starting Point

Our present discussion about Christ would prove incomplete had we not already observed the dangers Luther saw in reason's attempt to know God through its own speculative endeavor. The theme of the *Deus absconditus* provides the necessary background for our particular reevaluation of Luther's doctrine of Christ. We have noted above that Luther saw a particular danger, even futility, in trying to know God without what Luther calls his "coverings" or his "wrapper." Without such coverings man could not make any advances as to the true knowledge of God and would therefore remain in utter darkness, and most importantly, would remain dead in sin. It might be helpful to recall Luther's peculiar emphasis on man's fall from Paradise. On his account, the most devastating effect of the Fall was man's complete loss of his once glorious immediate communion with the Creator. What we now possess is a reason and will turned hopelessly inward without that internal knowledge it once possessed. This situation, of course (previously noted), produces nothing but self-chosen and self-pleasing works, monasteries, shrines,

these places and take only the passages that deal with the unrevealed God – but he asks his hearers to remember he has clearly taught that one should *not* seek to understand the hidden God and should be satisfied with what is revealed in the Word. See WA XLIII 463.3–17.

[270] WA XLIII 459.35–460.2.

etc., all as a result of man's perverted view of God. Thus men cannot know God's true character outside of his self-revelation. Steinmetz comments on this aspect of Luther's thought in the following:

> Because God is hidden outside his revelation, Luther is adamantly opposed to any attempt to uncover the naked being of God through speculative reason or religious ecstasy. The dazzling glory of the being of the hidden God would blind and terrify us if we could uncover it. God must hide his glory in his revelation; he must accommodate himself to our finitude and sin. The gospel is the good news that we are not required to ascend to God through prayer, self-denial, and the discipline of reason and desire. God has descended to us as a child on its mother's lap. He has met us at the bottom rung of the ladder, on our level rather than on his. Holiness may alarm and terrify us, but no one is frightened of a child.[271]

It can be accurately asserted that Luther's entire theological system revolves around the person of Jesus Christ. We are therefore not to begin with metaphysical presuppositions as to what God and man are, but from the humanity and cross of Christ.[272] Thus we find Luther's remarks on human reason continually taking their departure from the lap and breast of the Virgin, Christ's death, and his triumphal resurrection. It is not surprising then that Luther thinks reason's presuppositions directly contradict the very notion of the personal union itself. Here at this historic union, our thoughts which we deem to be infinitely wise are stripped away from us. In the face of this Luther claims that we should run to Bethlehem, to the stable and manger where the babe lies, or to Mary's lap: "Das heisst die vernunfft doch gar gedempfft, Denn das vorige stück ist uber alle mas hoch, das die vernunfft selbs möcht dencken: Quae supra nos nihil ad nos, Was dir zuhoch ist, das lasse ungeforschet, Und leichter daran verzweivelt und sich gefangen gibt, Uber hie kompt es herunter mir für die augen, das ich das kindlin sehe ynn der mutter schos." For Luther, reason must bow before the cross and confess that its speculative attempts to rise and know God in his divinity are utterly futile.[273]

As he has effectively shown elsewhere, philosophers with the most admirable use of their reasoning abilities have not been able to come into agreement on any issue of much significance e.g., his above illustration of the soul. Luther therefore firmly believed that God's incarnation was foretold in order that we might have a definite pattern for recognizing and taking hold of him,[274] as God has once and for

---

[271] David C. Steinmetz, *Luther in Context* (Bloomington, 1986) p. 25.

[272] H. R. Mackintosh, *The Doctrine of the Person of Jesus Christ* (Edinburgh, 1956) pp. 230–231.

[273] WA XXXVII 42.33–40; 43.6–25. Quoted in Steinmetz, *Luther in Context* pp. 25–26.

[274] WA XLIII 231.28–30.

all condescended to speak with us in human fashion.[275] Consequently, he claims that the true speculation of the godly is precisely where reason and imagination fail to produce there intended effects. To properly understand Luther at this point we must recall that in his later writings reason is consistently equated with man's fertile imagination. That is, reason in his view is always "imagining" something or other about the nature of God outside of the God-man, and not only does it create these concepts but it also regards them as most glorious and holy inventions. It is against this background that we must understand Luther's insistence that we are to apprehend God only in the incarnate Son and begin from the manger and the swaddling clothes in which he was wrapped.[276] Steinmetz is therefore correct in saying that, for Luther, Christian theology must begin with the God revealed in the humanity of Jesus Christ: "It must resist all temptation to speculate about the nature and being of God apart from Christ and must focus on the self-disclosure of God in this man."[277]

This pivotal theme is also strongly present in the famous *Galatians* commentary of 1535. Here Luther insists that St. Paul teaches us that the Christian religion does not begin at the top, as all other religions do, but at the bottom. According to Luther Paul commands us to ascend on Jacob's ladder, at the top of which God himself is resting and the feet of which touch the earth next to the head of Jacob. Luther once again warns against the speculative endeavor to understand God's majesty and says that we should rather hasten to the stable and lap of the mother and apprehend this infant Son of the Virgin. We must look only at him being born, nursed, growing up, teaching, dying, rising again, ascending into heaven, and having authority over all things – only this view of God can keep us on the right path.[278]

---

[275] "Ideo discamus Deum appraehendendum esse non nostra ratione. Sed sicut ipse se revelavit, et dignatus est nobiscum loqui, et agere humano more: adeoque cum gaudio amplectamur divinam maiestatem dimittentem se ad nos tam humiliter, ut non simpliciter promissionibus ad se invitet, sed etiam iureiurando interposito cogat ad amplectendum ea, quae in verbo offeruntur." WA XLIII 239.20–25.

[276] WA XLIV 194.4–17.

[277] Steinmetz, *Luther in Context* p. 27.

[278] WA XL, i, 79.24–32; 80.11–16. After citing this passage John Warwick Montgomery makes the following important remarks: "Luther insists that the search for God begin at the connecting link between earth and heaven which exists at the point of the incarnation. There we find a genuine human being ("nursed and growing up," "dying") but also Very God of Very God ("returning from the dead and being exalted above all the heavens"). "Philosophy," which starts elsewhere, must be forgotten; absolute truth is available only here. Why does Luther concentrate relatively little on traditional proofs for God's existence (even though he considered such argumentation valid)? Because for him it did not constitute the proper point of departure...." See "Lutheranism and the Defense of the Christian Faith," *Lutheran Synod Quarterly* vol. 11, no. 1, Special Issue (Fall, 1970) p. 27. Mackintosh

The Significance of the Hypostatic Union

The theme of Jacob's ladder is an integral part of Luther's particular notion of the hypostatic union. His exposition of *Genesis* 28:12–14 succinctly illustrates his position as follows: The incarnation, he says, is the article by which the whole world, reason, and Satan are offended. For in one and the same Person there are things that are to the highest degree contrary: "Is, qui est summus, ut Angeli non capiant, non modo compraehenditur, sed ita compraehensus, ita finitus est, ut nihil magis sit finitum et conclusum: et contra." Luther stresses that "Ibi est Deus et Homo: summus et infimus, infinitus et finitus in una persona, evacuans et implens omnia."[279] Jacob's ladder therefore signified the wondrous mystery of the incarnation, and the ascent and descent is the mystery that in one and the same Person there is true God and man.[280] This ascent and descent is thus nothing less than to see the highest and lowest forever united in the same Person, "Summum Deum iacentem in praesepi." Thus, in Luther's view, the union of the divine and human nature is such that the humanity has been made subject to death and hell, yet in that very humiliation it has devoured both the devil and hell in itself. This is, says Luther, the *communio idiomatum*. As such we must say "Ille homo, qui flagris caesus, qui sub morte, sub ira Dei, sub peccato et omnia genere malorum, denique sub inferno est infimus, est summus Deus," a proposition that must be affirmed because it is one and the same Person: "Duplex quidem est natura, sed persona non est divisa."[281] Consequently, the angels descend as though there were no God up in heaven and come to Bethlehem adoring and worshipping him as he lies in the manger at his mother's breasts. "Imo in cruce, descendentem ad inferos, subiectum peccato, inferno, portantem omnia peccata totius mundi adorant, et submittunt se perpetuo huic infimo."[282]

---

similarly states of Luther that the "foundations of faith are to be laid in the recorded facts of our Lord's career as man, and anything else would be to start building from the roof." See *The Doctrine of the Person of Jesus Christ* p. 232.

[279] WA XLIII 580.13–24.

[280] WA XLIII 578.19–30; 579.7–9.

[281] WA XLIII 579.24–29; 579.39–580.12: "Utrunque igitur verum est, summa divinitas est infima creatura, serva facta omnium hominum, imo ipsi Diabolo subiecta. Et econtra infima creatura, humanitas vel homo sedet ad dexteram patris, summa facta, et subiicit sibi Angelos, non propter humanum naturam, sed mirabilem coniunctionem et unionem, quae constituta est ex duabus naturis contrariis et inconiungibilibus in una persona."

[282] WA XLIII 580.25–33: "Ambrose et inprimis Bernardus admodum delectantur hoc loco prae omnibus dulcissimo, et opere isto incarnationis, et quidem recte et pie. Nam talis delectatio erit gaudium supra omne gaudium, et beatitudo aeterna, cum illic vere intuebimur nostram carnem per omnia similem nobis, et in summo pariter et infimo loco. Haec enim omnia fecit pro nobis, descendit ad inferos, et ascendit ad coelos. Hoc conspectu Angeli perpetuo fruuntur in coelis, et hoc illud est, quod

Steinmetz suggests that, historically speaking, Luther does not say anything very new in his exposition of the passage, although he does explain the text at a greater length in terms of Christ being the ladder that links heaven and earth.[283] Granted that this is probably true in terms of its historical significance, I think that Luther's exposition combined with his christology in general proves to be extremely significant with respect to our present subject. His explanation does, in fact, betray the very heart of his christological formulation. For here in one Person we truly behold our own flesh which is like us in every respect, but *for our sake* he is in the highest and lowest place, as he descended into hell and then ascended into heaven.[284] Noting the centrality of this in Luther's thought, Steinmetz says that the "angels who ascend and descend are real angels who marvel at the communication of attributes between the two natures of Christ and the condescension of a God who can be found in dust."[285]

It has been argued that the peculiar accents of Luther's christology can only be understood in relation to the *communicatio idiomatum,* as this aspect of his thought proves to be one of the most important expressions of that historic reality. Nilsson, for instance, argues that the heart of Luther's theology is the communication of attributes. It expresses the very relation between the human and the divine, and is of fundamental importance for the Christian faith lest we improperly understand Christ as a perfect super-man or a terrifying God-judge. His following comments deserve special mention:

> It is the *communicatio idiomatum* by which Luther's whole system of theological thought stands or falls. The *communicatio* must not be understood as an accessory, more or less important, to the main theological structure. This is a matter of the utmost importance in understanding Luther. The *communicatio* is not a doctrine in itself which one might derive by careful and diligent study from the thought of Luther about the unity of Christ's person and work. The

ait Christus: 'Angeli eorum vident faciem patris, qui in coelis est', assiduo intuentur divinitatem, et nunc descendunt de coelo, postquam homo factus est, et intuentur Christum, admirantur opus incarnationis, vident hominem factum, humiliatum, positum in gremio matris: et crucifixum et abiectum hominem adorant, et agnoscunt filium Dei." WA XLIII 580.41–581.10.

[283] Steinmetz notes that Luther's exegesis is not merely analytic: "He is not merely interested in the bird on the dissecting table; he wants to see and hear the bird on the wing. Analysis can clarify the text, but only synthesis can create the illusion of three-dimensionality which belongs to the text as a living narrative." Luther's contribution, he says (and without a doubt true), is that Jacob can only be an inspiration to the church because he has "precisely the same defects all Christians have. The triumph of God is a triumph in the midst of human frailty." See David C. Steinmetz, "Luther and the Ascent of Jacob's Ladder" in *Church History* 55, 1986 pp. 189–192.

[284] WA XLIII 581.1–4.

[285] Steinmetz, "Luther and the Ascent of Jacob's Ladder" p. 189.

doctrine of the *communicatio idiomatum* is not merely a consequence of the unity in Christ, but an expression of this unity itself and the whole basis on which, according to Luther, life and happiness rests.[286]

Whether one agrees with Nilsson's contention or not, he is right about the fact that the mature Luther places a great deal of emphasis on it himself. I think he is also accurate in his judgment that the *communicatio* must not be seen as an accessory to Luther's thought, but should rather be seen as the expression of his christological focus. That the mature Luther's attention is continually focused on preserving the unity of the God-man cannot be denied, and he sees the whole notion of the communication of attributes as achieving more or less that goal.

As it is Luther's concern that the *communicatio* expresses the reality that God is found only in the person and work of Christ, it is an important implication for our study that the communication of attributes reduces to ashes all metaphysical conceptions of fallen man about God. In direct contradiction to a Platonic tradition which sees God as impassable and epistemologically out of reach, Luther believes that the world's Creator himself has literally bridged the gap between heaven and earth in the unity of this person who was crucified, and then ascended to heaven. The *communicatio* thus expresses the fundamental truth that there is no valid relationship with God which is not found in the historic union of the God-man.[287]

Although Luther expresses himself in various ways, we can summarize the main features of his christology as follows: To begin with he rejects Augustine's formulation, "The divine Person assumes a man," for what he sees as more precise, "The divine Person assumes the human nature."[288] Accordingly, he holds that the human nature of Christ is without personality of its own (*anhypostasis*), thereby committing himself to the fundamental belief that the Logos assumes to himself human nature. On this account, the personality of Jesus subsists in the Logos (*enhypostasis*), and Luther therefore sees the natures themselves in reciprocal communion, yet retaining their respective properties – all within the unity of the one person. Thus Althaus can correctly say that Luther affirms "the full unity of the deity and the humanity in the person of Christ, the full participation of the humanity in the deity and of the deity in the humanity. 'God has suffered; a man created heaven and earth; a man died; God who is from all eternity died;

---

[286] K. O. Nilsson, *Simul: Das Miteinander von Göttlichem und Menschlichem in Luthers Theologie.* Forschungen zur Kirchen und Dogmengeschichte 17. Göttingen: 1966 p. 228. Cited in Lienhard, *Luther: Witness to Jesus Christ* p. 355 n. 100.

[287] Lienhard, *Luther: Witness to Jesus Christ* pp. 341–343.

[288] Paul Althaus, *The Theology of Martin Luther* (Philadelphia, 1981) p. 194, n. 33. See WA XXXIX, ii, 93f (thesis 11f., 116ff.).

the boy who nurses at the breast of the Virgin Mary is the creator of all things'."[289] Luther's emphasis is on the unity of the two natures in order that the person is not divided, while still affirming the distinction between the natures. Althaus remarks that Luther "teaches that Jesus Christ, according to his human nature, also possessed the attributes of the divine majesty, that is, that even the child Jesus was omniscient, omnipotent, and omnipresent. Luther thus does not understand Christ's emptying himself in the incarnation to mean that he left his deity or essential characteristics of it in heaven."[290]

Luther will consequently argue that because Christ is a man who is supernaturally one person with God it must follow that he is wherever God is, and that everything is full of Christ even according to his humanity. He insists this does not imply that Christ's body is itself infinitely extended in a circumscribed mode – as he makes clear with his distinction between the three modes of presence[291] – but it is rather his purpose to emphasize the fact that the two natures are forever united in the one person. He could hardly be more clear; wherever you place God, you must also place the humanity: "Sie lassen sich nicht sondern und von einander trennen, Es ist eine person worden und scheidet die menscheit nicht so von sich, wie meister Hans seinen rock aus zeucht und von sich legt, wenn er

---

[289] Althaus, *The Theology of Martin Luther* pp. 193–194. Althaus cites Luther from *Die Promotionsdisputation von Theodor Fabricius und Stanislaus Rapagelanus* 1544 WA XXXIX, ii, 280.16–22. The full passage reads as follows: "Unio humanitatis et divinitatis in Christo est una vera persona, non duae, et quod uni tribuitur, alteri quoque recte assignatur. Impugnare personam Christi est negare eius naturam. Deus est passus, homo creavit coelum et terram, homo est mortuus, Deus, qui fuit ab aeterno, est mortuus, puer ille sugens ubera Mariae virginis est conditor omnium rerum. Haec sunt discenda christiano, ut nunquam divellat divinitatem Christi ab humanitate seu incarnatione, alias fierent duo Christi."

[290] Althaus, *The Theology of Martin Luther* p. 194.

[291] "Nach deinem alten dunckel, der nichts mehr denn die erste leiblichen begreifflichen weise vernympt, wirftu dis nicht verstehen, wie die schwermer thun, Welche dencken nicht anders, denn als sey die Gottheit leiblicher begreifflicher weise allenthalben, als were Gott so ein gros ausgebreitet ding, das durch und uberaus alle creatur reichet, Das mercke dabey, weil sie uns schuld geben, wir breiten und denen die menscheit aus und umbzeunen die Gottheit damit, welche wort klerlich von der leiblichen begreifflichen weise reden, wie ein bawr ynn wammes und hosen steckt, da wammes und hosen ausgedenet werden, das sie den leib und die schenkel umbgeben." WA XXVI 333.31–39. Steinmetz notes that since the "right hand of God is found everywhere, and since the body of Christ is at the right hand of God (Luther is in these circumstances prepared to concede that point), then the body of Christ is ubiquitous. It is not limited by space and time but is present wherever God rules." Because of the communication of attributes the humanity has taken on certain divine attributes such as the property of ubiquity. "The important thing for Luther, however, is to see the doctrine of the ubiquity of the body of Christ in the context of the divine will and Word." See Steinmetz, *Luther in Context* pp. 80–81.

schlaffen gehet."[292] For Luther then, apart from Christ there is no God,[293] as he takes most seriously St. Paul's assertion that "in him the fullness of the Godhead dwells *bodily.*" Christ indeed walks on earth, but the entire Godhead is in him in person and in essence on earth. God is therefore entirely present, personally and essentially, in Christ on earth in his mother's womb, in the crib, on the cross, and in the grave. Yet he is also in heaven in the Father's bosom. Luther concludes from this that Christ is at the same time everywhere and essentially, personally filling heaven and earth with his own nature and majesty.[294] For in Christ, God is not present as he is in all other creatures, but he dwells bodily in him in such a way that the one person is God and man: "Und wie wol ich sagen kan von allen Creaturn: Da ist Gott odder Gott ist ynn dem, so kan ich doch nicht sagen: Das ist Gott selbs." We can and must, however, say of Christ that this is God himself.[295] Observing the connection with Christ's ascension, Steinmetz summarizes this feature of Luther's thought nicely in the following:

> Once having come to us in the incarnation, Christ does not go away. He remains in our space and time. What changes in the ascension is not the fact of Christ's presence but solely the mode of that presence. Prior to the ascension, he was accessible in a circumscriptive way to sight; after the ascension, he is invisibly accessible to us in the means of grace. Before, he could be arrested by his enemies and flogged; after, he can only be found where he has bound himself by his Word to be: in bread and wine and water. The ascension does not point to the absence of the humanity of Christ at the right hand of God. Rather, it celebrates the ubiquitous presence of the God-man, Jesus Christ, and the universal accessibility of that saving presence through preaching and the sacraments.[296]

Three Interrelated Observations

At this point we can make three observations regarding Luther's mature christology: First, Luther's constant warnings against speculation, together with the associated epistemological problems, come into sharp focus within his mature

---

[292] WA XXVI 333.7–10.

[293] WA XXVI 332.18–21.

[294] WA XXIII 139.25–33; 141.1–10.

[295] WA XXIII 141.23–32. Luther emphasizes his position here by noting that anyone who kills a man may be called a murderer of one in whom God is present, but he who kills Christ has killed the Lord of Glory.

[296] Steinmetz, *Luther in Context* p. 81.

christological formulation. For him, if Christ were present at one single place only, as a divine and human person, then at all other places he would have to be nothing more than a mere "isolated" God without the humanity.[297] Luther wholly rejected Zwingli's position on the hypostatic union partly due to this very problem. Steinmetz' comments on Zwingli's view will serve to illustrate my point:

> While the human nature remains finite in the hypostatic union, the divine nature remains in that same union infinite and unbounded. Christ can be present with the Church in the power of his divine nature. Indeed, it is the presence of Christ by his Spirit and in the power of his divine nature which transforms a congregation of individual believers into the eucharistic body of Christ. The divine nature which is present is hypostatically united to a finite human nature which must be absent. Both the presence of the divine nature and the absence of the human nature are soteriologically essential to the being and well-being of the Church.[298]

Luther rejects this position because he firmly believes that Christ is the one Person who truly links the earthly and heavenly kingdoms. It is evident that he sees such a Zwinglian attempt to separate the two natures as casting the entire Christian faith into the deep mire of uncertainty. Without a real union of the human and divine natures, all we are left with is precisely that epistemologically bankrupt speculation about God's majesty that he had spent so much effort in debunking. As we have seen, Luther virtually rejects any proposition about God disconnected from his self-revelation in Christ – thus his view of the two natures reflects his continuing concern over the issue of reason's innate speculative impulse. Consequently, he urges that we take a stand and insist that wherever Christ is according to his divinity, he is there naturally and personally, as his conception in his mother's womb conclusively proves. And if he is present naturally and personally wherever he is, then he must be man there as well, since he is not two separate persons but a single person: "Wo sie ist, da ist sie die einige unzurtrennete person, Und wo du kanst sagen: Hie ist Gott, da mustu auch sagen: So ist Christus der mensch auch da."[299]

---

[297] WA XXVI 333.2–6. Lienhard also very briefly notes this connection in his *Luther: Witness to Jesus Christ* pp. 215–216.

[298] Steinmetz, *Luther in Context* p. 79.

[299] WA XXVI 332.30–32. Luther continues here with one of his most famous declarations: "Und wo du einen ort zeigen wurdest, da Gott were und nicht der mensch, so were die person schön zurtrennet, weil ich als denn mit der warheit kund sagen: Hie ist Gott, der nicht mensch ist und noch nie mensch ward, Mir aber des Gottes nicht. Denn hieraus wolt folgen, das raum und stette die zwo naturn von einander sonderten und die person zurtrenneten, so doch der tod und alle teuffel sie nicht kundten trennen noch von einander reissen." See 332.33–333.2.

Within this context, Luther frequently warns against the monastic contemplative life so pleasing to speculative reason i.e., attempting to understand things that are categorically beyond its capacity.[300] No one, he says, will obtain salvation through spiritual speculations without external means.[301] He often recalls with favor a story regarding a father in the desert who rebuked monks given to such speculations: "Si, inquit, videris tibi ascendere in coelum, et iam unum pedem figere supra limen coeli, statim eum retrahe, nec sequaris altero pede."[302] Luther clearly has his own monastic experiences in mind and declares that he paid a terrible price for these speculations before being freed; "Placet enim rationi, et, ut Paulus appellat, videtur esse Angelorum religio." Witzel once objected, Luther claims, that spiritual things are being completely overshadowed by his incessant emphasis on externals. But his view regarding reason's central role in the contemplative life remains crystal clear in his response: reason simply wants to move above and beyond what it is capable of understanding. Reason by its very nature cannot discern "spiritual" things and must have an external source of information brought down to the level of human comprehension. The bulk of the devil's efforts, in fact, are focused on drawing men toward the contemplative life and away from knowing nothing "except Christ and him crucified" (1 Cor. 2:2). Accordingly, the man Christ is the only profitable object of contemplation and one must beware of forsaking him; for those who give up the human nature or the flesh of Christ and speculate about God as such are driven into the depths of despair and swallowed by the divine majesty.[303] We however do not want to deal with the uncovered God,

---

[300] "Ante hoc tempus, priusquam Deus lucem Euangelii ostenderet, multa scripta et dicta sunt de vita speculativa et activa: ac in monasteriis utriusque sexus, qui fere fuerunt optimi, occupati sunt hoc studio, ut offerrentur eis visiones et revelationes. Hinc etiam factum est, ut quidam omnia sua somnia annotarent: hi scilicet omnes expectaverunt illuminationes singulares sine externis rebus: sed hoc quid aliud est, quam sine scalis velle ascendere in coelum? Igitur praestigiis diabolicis saepissime delusi sunt." WA XLIII 71.38–72.3. See Luther's full discussion 71.17–73.23.

[301] Luther says here that attention must be paid to the Word, Baptism, and the Eucharist, as apart from these the Holy Spirit works nothing: "Nemo igitur consequetur salutem spiritualibus, ut vocant, speculationibus, sine externis rebus. Verbo attendendum est, Baptismus petendus. sumenda Eucharistia, absolutio requirenda. Haec quidem omnia externa sunt, sed in verbum inclusa. Igitur sine eis spiritus sanctus nihil operatur." WA XLIII 71.33–37.

[302] "Hic damnavit speculationes, seu vitae genus speculativum, quod indocta et imperita posteritas tantis laudibus evexit. Qui enim recte speculari volet, intueatur Baptismum suum: legat Biblia sua, audiat conciones, honoret patrem et matrem, fratri laboranti subveniat, non concludat se, ut sordidum monachorum et monacharum vulgus solet, in angulum, et delectetur ibi suis devotionibus, ac sic putet se in Dei sinu sedere, et commertium habere cum Deo sine Christo, sine verbo, sine Sacramentis etc." See WA XLIII 72.4–14.

[303] WA XLIII 72.15–30: "Gerson quoque scripsit de vita speculativa, ac ornat eam magnis titulis, ac imperiti cum legunt talia, amplectuntur ea pro divinis oraculis, sed revera, Ut in Proverbio dicitur: Thesaurus carbones. Igitur seu externum, seu civilem te appellent vani speculatores isti, nihil te hic

Luther concludes, whose ways are inscrutable, but should direct our attention to the ordered power of God. That is, the incarnate Son in whom are hidden all the treasures of the Godhead:

> Ad puerum illum positum in gremio matris mariae, ad victimam illam pen-
> dentem in cruce nos conferemus, Ibi vere contemplabimur Deum, ibi in ipsum
> cor Dei introspiciemus, quod sit misericors, quod nolit mortem peccatoris: sed
> ut convertatur et vivat. Ex hac speculatione seu contemplatione nascitur vera
> pax, et verum gaudium cordis. Itaque Paulus dicit: 'Nihil iudico me scire praeter
> Christum' etc. Huic speculationi cum fructu vacamus."[304]

Elsewhere Luther highlights Christ's statement, "No one has ever seen God" (*John* 1:18), in order to add one of his most frequented motifs, that in his boundless mercy God has revealed himself to us in order to satisfy our desire – he has shown us a *imaginem visibilem:*: "En, habes filium meum, qui audit eum, et baptisatur, is in libro vitae scriptus est: hoc revelo per filium, quem potes manibus contrectare, et oculis intueri."[305] He stresses here our need for epistemological clarification – just as he has said above that one cannot love someone of whom he has no knowledge – and in effect once again emphasizes the fact that apart from Christ there is no knowledge of God. Our first point simply illustrates that, for Luther, Christ is the connection between heaven and earth, visibly making known to us the heart of the Father. The incarnate Son is, in other words, the "covering" in which the Divine Majesty presents himself to us with the gift of salvation; we must come to the Father only through him.[306]

Our second point switches gears slightly toward Luther's philosophical rejection of the axiom *finitum non capax infiniti*. This aspect of his thought is of importance for two main reasons. First, it is the foundation upon which Luther is able to affirm the *genus majestaticum,* an element that has become one of the hallmarks of his christology. Second, it becomes the central subject in the great sacramental debates of Luther's later years. He clearly recognized that the real issue of contention lay in the nature of the hypostatic union itself. Thus this issue

---

moveat, age tu Deo gratias pro verbo et externis istis, et relinque istas ampullosas speculationes aliis" (lines 31–36).

[304] WA XLIII 73.4–10. Luther later cites once again a certain hermit in "vitis patrum" advising saintly neophytes against vain speculation. Here predictably Luther adds the following: "Caveant igitur pii, et id unum agant, et discant adhaerere puero et filio, Iesu, qui est Deus tuus, propter te incarnatus. Hunc agnosce et audi, ac delectare in eo et age gratias. Si hunc habes, tunc etiam Deum absconditum pariter cum revelato habes. Et illa est unica via, veritas et vita, extra quam nihil praeter exitium et mortem invenies." See WA XLIII 461.17–28.

[305] WA XLIII 462.37–463.2.

[306] WA XLII 296.21–34.

is not only important for the outcome of Luther's christology, but will also serve to illustrate Luther's own methodological principles of discovery. (It will, consequently, add slightly to our prior discussion of Luther's logic.)

Briefly then, Luther rejects the fanatics' arguments concerning the Personal union and thus their understanding of the Lord's Supper because they are based on a closed system of inference i.e., grounded in epistemological rationalism.[307] This comes to light in two ways. For one, Luther could not accept the axiomatic assumption that Christ's human body was limited in such a way as his opponents envisaged. His own procedure as we have noted above is essentially inductive in nature – an open-ended, non-Cartesian method of drawing inferences about the unknown. He simply did not believe we are able to say anything *a priori* about the external world (i.e., concerning matters of a factual nature), much less concerning God's ability to offer his body and blood in the Supper. Second, Luther believed that this form of rationalization affected the fanatics' judgment of other Scripture passages that seem to suggest the contrary of their position. As he saw it, the solution should be sought by adducing individual passages from Scripture to settle the problem, *a posteriori*, rather than deducing axioms from *a priori* principles.[308]

In fact we find both of these elements clearly argued at *Das Marburger Gespräch*, when Luther makes the following three observations concerning the Zwinglian methodology: (1) Zwingli wishes to prove his case by way of logical conclusions (2) he holds that a body cannot be in two places at the same time,

---

[307] Luther argues that in no passage of Scripture is one nature taken for the other. Zwingli, Luther maintains, has committed this error with his *Alleosi*. This method, he says, will eventually entail a kind of Christ who is and does no more in his passion and his life than any other "schlechter" saint. "Denn wenn ich das gleube, das allein die menschliche natur fur mich gelidden hat, so ist mir der Christus ein schlechter heiland, so bedarff er wol selbs eines heilands." See WA XXVI 319.27–40. Luther sees this controversy then as at the heart of the Christian message – if it is not properly understood, the entire Christian faith is at risk. On this see Lienhard, *Luther: Witness to Jesus Christ* pp. 214–215.

[308] Richard Cross has recently observed that it was important in Zwingli's understanding that the *meaning* of some christological propositions are not what they literally imply. Unless a proposition is *straightfowardly true* as it stands, then it will require interpretation that will reveal in what ways the proposition is true and in what ways it is not. As such the real meanings of these propositions will not be those suggested by their surface meaning. Thus Cross says that "Zwingli takes all non-straightforwardly true christological propositions to be examples of *alloiosis. Aloiosis,* or the communication of properties, occurs when there is a breakdown between the proposition and the reality it represents." Cross points out that *alloiosis* is therefore a *way of speaking* which does not have a true literal sense. Luther however – if I am correct – believed that Zwingli, instead allowing Scripture to inform us of that "reality," began rather with certain axioms e.g., that a body cannot be without limitation, thereby denying the reality of the *comunicatio idiomatum*. This situation forced Zwingli, according to Luther, to disregard the logical structure of the actual text. On Zwingli see Cross's article *"Alloiosis* in the Christology of Zwingli" in *The Journal of Theological Studies,* Vol. 47 Part 1, April 1996 pp. 114–122 (emphases his).

putting forward the argument that a body cannot be without limitation,[309] and
(3) he appeals to natural human reason.[310] These objections, in my opinion, all
stem from the same source – Luther would not allow a closed-system method to
determine the meaning of passages not otherwise logically related. Zwingli attempted, as he saw it, to connect diverse and unrelated passages by overstepping
the rules which govern and sustain valid logical relations.[311] Consequently (and
predictably), he rejects Oecolampadius' appeal to *John* 6 where Christ speaks of
spiritual eating, arguing on that basis that there is therefore no bodily eating in the
text of the Supper. Luther points out that Oecolampadius' argument is based on a
preconceived opinion and is question-begging, as it does not directly relate to the
text of the Lord's Supper i.e., there is no logical connection.[312] Intimately related is
Luther's objection to the simple assumption, prior to any specific scriptural data,
that Christ's body is limited (this is, I think, what he had in mind with his third
point). He had similarly objected a year earlier that the fanatics simply presuppose
that Christ's body has to be alone in a corporeal mode without giving a sufficient
reason, jumping directly from their lady *Alleosi*.[313]

In sum the fanatics' position, as Luther saw it, was based on certain axiomatic propositions that colored their interpretation of other non-related Scripture
passages[314] i.e., they did not allow the individual contexts of Scripture to speak

[309] For a recent critique of this *finitum* principle, see David Andersen's "A Critique of John Calvin's
Philosophical Axiom *finitum non capax infiniti*." Published on-line in *Global Journal of Classical
Theology* Vol. 3, No. 2 (11/02).

[310] WA XXX, iii, 112.7–10.

[311] See WA XXIII, 101.4–23. Luther here criticizes Zwingli's construction of syllogisms and hence
his invalid deductions: "das partibus er puris sequitur nil atque negatis."

[312] See for example XXX, iii, 114.1–6. Steinmetz observes the crucial point that Luther's opponents
have taken a firm hold of a double-edged sword. "One could as easily say of preaching as of the
eucharist: 'the flesh profits nothing'." If physical acts cannot impart spiritual nourishment to the soul,
there is no reason to hold the preaching office in high esteem. Thus the only Word that could matter
would be the inaudible Word spoken, without the medium of human language, by the Holy Spirit.
Steinmetz concludes that "to attack the eucharist as a physical act is to leave the Christian nothing but
mental prayer and wordless contemplation. The parishioner who hangs on the words of the preacher
stands in the same peril of idolatry as the communicant who relies on the visible elements of bread
and wine." See *Luther in Context* pp. 82–83.

[313] WA XXVI 331.30–32; 332.8–11. Thus Luther replies: "Item quod dicitis deum nihil proponere
incomprehensibile ...... vobis [non concedo]. Virgo Maria, remissio peccatorum, huiusmodi multa, ita
etiam: corpus meum hoc est. Semitae tuae in aquis multis et vestigia non cognoscentur. Si vias eius
sciremus, non esset incomprehensibilis, qui admirabilis." WA XXX, iii, 119.11–15.

[314] Luther therefore objects to their method of seeking the articles of faith: "Ich wuste nicht, das
man ynn artickeln des glaubens muste nichts nach Gotts wort fragen, sondern die leiblichen augen
auffthun und mit den selbigen der vernunfft nach urteilen, was zu gleuben fey...Wie werden wir
aber gewis, lieben herrn, das ein leib nicht müge durch Gotts gewalt zu gleich ym hymel und ym

for themselves.[315] These considerations become extremely important for our third point, as Luther saw little difficulty in affirming the ubiquity of Christ. He did not see any universal principle as necessarily valid which, from the outset, flatly denied the possibility of Christ's humanity participating in the attributes of the divinity. As we will shortly see, his formulation has a direct relation to the problem of fallen reason.

Finally, our third point will briefly highlight once again the *communicatio idiomatum* with a special emphasis on Luther's understanding of the so-called *genus majestaticum* i.e., that Jesus, according to his human nature, possessed all divine power and attributes at his birth.[316] On Luther's account, the personality of Jesus subsists in the Logos (*enhypostasis*), and because the two natures are now forever united in Christ such that the logos is nowhere beyond or outside the humanity, the divinity permeates the humanity.[317] He attempts to describe this reality in various ways, the most famous of which is the analogy of fire and iron: "Qui in ferro ignito attingit ignem, ferrum attingit. Ita qui tetigit cutem Christi, vere Deum tetigit."[318] Luther significantly expands on this elsewhere by saying that unheated iron is, of course, still iron. But when fire is added and it glows we can say that it no longer has the qualities of iron, as it is now like fire:

abendmal sein, wil Gotts gewalt kein mas noch zal hat und solche ding thut, die kein vernunfft begreyffen kan, sondern schlecht müssen gegleubt werden?" WA XXIII 117.6–16. See also WA XXIII 247.12–36; 249.1–12.

[315] Luther, for example, makes this clear in the following: "Ja auss das man sehe, wie gar weit sie seylen der warheit, sind sie nicht alleine das schüldig, das sie aus der schrifft beweisen, das 'leib' so viel als 'leibs zeichen', und das 'wesen' so viel als 'deuten' sei, sondern noch eines. Wenn sie gleich etwa an einem ort der schrifft solchs auffbrechten, welchs doch nicht müglich ist, so sind sie dennoch auch schuldig zu beweisen, das es hie ym abentmal auch so müsse sein, das 'leib' 'leibs zeichen' sey, und hülffe sie gar nichts, wenn gleich die ganze schrifft an andern ortern eitel leibs zeichen auffbrecht und brechts nicht auch an diesem ort ym abentmal auss. Denn wir haddern izt nicht furnemlich, ob etwa ynn der schrifft 'leib' 'leibs zeichen' heisse, sondern obs an diesem ort des abendsmal so heisse." WA XXIII 97.23–32.

[316] On this see Althaus, *The Theology of Martin Luther* p. 197. It has often been noted that we do not find this particular phrase in Luther's writings. However, the concept itself is clearly explicated within the later works and I will therefore follow the common practice of utilizing the phrase for the sake of brevity.

[317] Thus Lienhard says that "the saving work is not realized by the Word alone – occasionally united to the humanity – but by the Word and the humanity intimately linked. Luther carries this to the point of saying that only the suffering of God thus united to humanity guarantees the reality of our redemption." See *Luther: Witness to Jesus Christ* p. 233.

[318] WA XL, i, 417.17–18.

Es ist wohl Eisen, aber es ist so gahr durchfeuert, das, wen du es sihest oder
angreiffest, das dein auge nicht sagen kan: Es ist Eisen, Sondern du shulest eitel
feur, so gahr ist eitel feur fur augen. Wen du non wilt ein loch darmit durch
ein fas bohren oder ein zeichen auss etwas brennen oder machen, do thuts das
Eisen nicht, Sondern das feur thuts, dan wen ich ein ander eisen neme, das
nicht gluendt were, so wurde ist noch lange nicht ein Zeichen brennen, Sondern
Ich mus das Eisen nemen, dorinnen das feur ist, undt widerumb wil das feur
seine arbeit nirgendts thun dan in dem Eisen. Alfo ist hie gott in Christo auch
leibhafftig undt thut, wie ein gott thun sol, oder thut, wie das feur im eisen
thut, man sihet wohl nur fleisch undt blutt, aber der glaube sihet einen solchen
menschen, ein solch fleisch undt blutt, das do sei wie ein fuerig eisen, den es
ist durchgöttertt.[319]

Lienhard draws the conclusion from Luther's mature utterances on the hypostatic
union that the person of the Son indeed unites in itself the two natures. However,
in this personal union a history begins, one in which the divine nature participates in the human suffering, and reciprocally the human nature participates in
the divine ubiquity: "The divine hypostasis thus truly descends into the history
of human beings. It does not remain beyond them as an unchanging concept, but
participates entirely in the history of Jesus of Nazareth."[320] Luther's later insistence on the *genus majestaticum* emphasizes a fundamental reorientation in his
overall christology. That is, God is now immediately present in Christ for Luther
in a most real, visible, and active sense. Montgomery makes a similar observation when he states that "Luther declares that Jesus Christ, in His own person,
offers immediate access to the Divine. One begins with the earthly and finds the
heavenly."[321] Luther saw the reality of the personal union to be at the very core of
Christian assurance – epistemological and soteriological – as upon it alone rests
the sweet comfort that God has reconciled the world to himself. It is thus necessary to begin our search at the manger of Christ the man and find God only in him
(as the angels themselves bow to this lowest One) – anything less is foolish, futile,
and inherently dangerous. And if our own thoughts and reason lead us elsewhere,
we must shut our eyes and say, "Ich soll und wil von keinem andern Gott wissen
denn ynn meinem Herrn Christo."[322]
Luther's method of discovery cannot be underestimated as it bears on the issue
of reason. His christological focus demands that reason find the divinity only in
the humanity. Here Luther's direct link between the Father and the Son becomes

[319] WA XXXIII 191.3–31.

[320] Lienhard, *Luther: Witness to Jesus Christ* p. 234.

[321] John Warwick Montgomery, "Lutheranism and the Defense of the Christian Faith" pp. 25–26.

[322] WA XXVIII 101.24–28.

significant. Christ portrays for us the heart and will of the Father, that he does not want to be angry with sinners but shows mercy through the Son. For Luther, the foremost comfort about Christ's being in the Father is that we do not doubt that everything he says and does stands in direct relation to the will of the Father. Therefore Christ's word and work stands in heaven before the angels, in the world before all tyrants, in hell before all devils, and in our hearts before an evil conscience and our own thoughts.[323] Jesus does not therefore point us *to* God, but is presenting the eternal God himself *in* his very person. Althaus comments on this as follows:

> ...the decisive thing about Christ is that God has opened his heart to us in the person, activity, and history of Jesus Christ and thus gives us certainty about how he feels about us and what he intends to do with us. This is the new meaning and importance of the deity of Jesus Christ for Luther. Christ is "the mirror of God's fatherly heart," in whom God himself appears to us.[324]

He goes on to note that Luther finds the Father only in the person of Jesus Christ. Luther is interested in "recognizing the Father in his Son, in knowing God himself." We therefore "ascend from the viewing of Jesus to the Father, that is, 'through the heart of Christ to the heart of God'."[325] Mackintosh seems to me right on the mark when he says that theology and christology are no longer independent aspects of doctrine, as the "heresy of heresies for Luther is that which separates the mind and disposition of God from that of Jesus."[326] Luther saw the humanity of Christ as the entire content of the good news, a foundation upon which our hope for eternal life rests. The supreme evidence of God's mercy consists in the fact that he condescended not only to become man at the level of its joys, but to the very depths of its frailty and wretchedness.[327] Mackintosh states that for Luther, Christ could not have redeemed us by the cross except as a man. "Thus it is impossible," he says, "to draw Christ too deeply down into nature and the

---

[323] WA XLV 589.14–38.

[324] Althaus, *The Theology of Martin Luther* p. 182. Marc Lienhard notes that the "humanity of Jesus Christ is not a curtain, behind which is hidden an impersonal and immutable God, but it expresses truly the heart, the very being of God" (p. 228). See Lienhard's full discussion on Luther's notion of the hypostatic union in his *Luther: Witness to Jesus Christ* pp. 226–240. See also Siggins, *Martin Luther's Doctrine of Christ* pp. 84–87, 88–90: "That 'Christ is in the Father' (with the identity of will, word, and work this implies) is for Luther 'the chiefest article and cardinal point' of Christian faith" (p. 85).

[325] Althaus, *The Theology of Martin Luther* p. 182–183.

[326] H. R. Mackintosh, *The Doctrine of the Person of Jesus Christ* (New York, 1912) p. 230.

[327] Rod Rosenbladt's unpublished Ph.D. dissertation, *The Christology of Chemnitz and Contemporary English Philosophical Scepticism* (1980, University of Strasbourg) pp. 33–34.

flesh. We cannot make him too human. The mere juxtaposition of Godhead and manhood, as Luther never tires of repeating, is of no avail; we must have the Son of God fused and interwoven with humanity, and one person therewith."[328] For Luther, Christ has become flesh and blood like any other man for our sake, and it is this same man which sits at the right hand of God. Thus we may boldly defy the devil and anything else that assails us.[329] And if the weight of our treasure consists in the fact that Christ, true God and true man, suffered for us, and this same man also rose from the dead and ascended into heaven, then we know for sure that sin and death have been overthrown. We see and hear nothing but mercy in this very person.[330]

Luther's later procedure in knowing God is thus very clear, one in which we find the heart of the Father only through the visible, empirical, revelation of himself in the historic person of Christ. He in fact insists that no other god is to be worshipped or sought outside of Christ,[331] and maintains that among the ungodly God is absolutely silent as they have not one letter to prove that what they do is justified. Luther boldly asserts, however, that we have a God who has disclosed himself, "ut habeamus visibilem, sensibilem et appraehensibilem Deum."[332]

Does this mean then that reason can find the transcendent God in Christ? Or, is the deity of Christ *itself* a matter of knowledge? Here Luther's change of emphasis within his theology of the cross plays a crucial role in unpacking his mature view of reason. No longer is his emphasis on God's hiddenness in Christ. His later writings employ an abundance of tangible language concerning God's actual self-revelation in the humanity of this historic person. This means that there is ample *reason* to believe this man is truly who he claims to be, God-incarnate (more will be said on this later). It therefore seems to me that Rosenbladt is correct, contrary to most modern Protestant existential approaches, when he states that the reason one can be assured that Christ's heart and will toward us is the Father's is very simply because, for the mature Luther, Christ *can* be known to be God (e.g.,

[328] Mackintosh, *The Doctrine of the Person of Jesus Christ* p. 232. "It was among the rare excellencies of Luther's Christology that he fastened an indissoluble bond, as St. Paul had done, between the person of the Redeemer and His redemptive work. Any view of Christ, therefore, which may be developed in abstraction from what He actually did for men, in His life, death and resurrection, is but a formal and delusive play on words...These two, the person and the office, are an organic unity, neither being intelligible apart from the other" (p. 231).

[329] WA XLVI 631.27.

[330] WA XLV 559.19.

[331] WA XL, ii, 387.26–27.

[332] WA XLIII 404.30–36.

from his miracles, etc.).[333] God, according to Luther's later understanding, has in his boundless mercy revealed himself to us in order to satisfy our desire. He has shown us a visible image. "En, habes filium meum, qui audit eum, et baptisatur, is in libro vitae scriptus est: hoc revelo per filium, quem potes manibus contrectare, et oculis intueri."[334] Though we will examine it in detail later, we must conclude up to this point that the mature Luther does not see faith operating epistemologically. If he did, his repeated later declarations that *reason* come captive to Christ would make little sense, and even divest them of their vitality within his thought. For Luther, in other words, it is reason which must bow before the crucified Christ, and faith which must appropriate that suffering (for me!).

Summary

To summarize our present discussion we can note the following: Luther insists, unambiguously, that reason restrain itself and find God not through its own speculative endeavor – which always results in idolatry – but in and through the humanity of Christ. Lienhard has noted this same aspect of Luther's formulation when he states that Luther refuses all reflection on God apart from the incarnation, as this speculation would be to speak of God detached from the place where he wishes to be found, namely the humanity of Christ.[335] For as we have seen, the result of the Fall is such that we no longer have immediate knowledge of God and must now seek that knowledge through a comprehensible medium. Against this background it is easier to understand Luther's belief that Christ restores reason somewhat to its original state with a true knowledge and trust in its Creator.[336] This is entirely consistent with his position laid out above, that reason's primary created function consisted in its knowledge and love of God. Luther therefore demands that if anyone maintains that ignorance of God merits excuse, he completely overturns Holy Scripture and takes Christ from the world, who was revealed in order to remove

---

[333] See Rosenbladt, *The Christology of Chemnitz and Contemporary English Philosophical Scepticism* pp. 58–61.

[334] WA XLIII 462.37–463.2.

[335] Lienhard, *Luther: Witness to Jesus Christ* p. 233.

[336] Luther points out however the following: "Notum autem est, cum praedicatur noticia Dei, et hoc agitur, ut ratio restituatur, tunc, qui optimi sunt, et melioris, ut sic dicam, rationis ac voluntatis, hi tanto acerbius Euangelium oderunt." WA XLII 107.38–40.

our ignorance.[337] God, in his later view, has provided this knowledge in an empirical fashion through Christ's humanity, which meets our need for soteriological *and* epistemological clarification.[338]

This factor allows us to conclude that reason plays an absolutely central role for Luther in bringing a man to a knowledge of the crucified God. Indeed, it would be meaningless to speak otherwise. It is not insignificant then that Luther claims the resurrection was itself objective proof of God's wish to draw our hearts away from this troubled life and into true godliness and knowledge of him. He notes that though there are always those who regard such a claim as undeserving of belief, it is precisely why God has committed it to historical record: "Sunt itaque haec divina autoritate commendata literis, et scripta Sanctis ac fidelibus, ut ea legerent, intelligerent, crederent et sequerentur. Ostendunt enim manifestam victoriam mortis et peccati, ostendunt certam consolationem victae legis, irae et iudicii divini de Henoch. Quare piis his Historiis nihil potuit esse iucundius aut gratius."[339] On the basis of this certainty Luther urges us to call upon God, take hold of his Word, and cling to the sacrificial victim Jesus Christ.[340] For Luther God has made his historic descent and promises to meet us at the bottom rung of the ladder, the cross, where he publicly displays his heart and pours out mercy upon

---

[337] WA XLII 487.19–23. Luther's discussion on the topic of ignorance is very interesting; see WA XLII 485.33–488.9.

[338] Hence Wayne Gustave Johnson is mistaken in his unpublished Ph.D. dissertation *Martin Luther's Law-Gospel Distinction and Paul Tillich's Method of Correlation: A Study of Parallels* (University of Iowa, 1966) where he makes the following claims: "In the light of this analysis it seems clear that Luther's critique of reason is grounded not so much in epistemology as it is in soteriology. Luther is not primarily concerned about what is 'true', rather he is concerned about what is 'saving'. Or, to put this in another way, Luther is concerned about what is 'saving' because, in the area of ultimate matters, of ultimate concern, only that which is 'saving' can be 'true'" (p. 109; see also pp. 125–126). Johnson clearly relies on Gerrish's thesis e.g., p. 111, and that position virtually forces him to the following: "Luther would, of course, insist that a saving or 'evangelical' knowledge of God is not to be understood in any purely formal way, as if such knowledge were a matter of obtaining a clearer philosophic or doctrinal statement of what God is like. To know God revealed through Christ is not to receive new information about God, but to find oneself living in a new relationship with the divine. Such knowledge does not so much inform, as it transforms...Right knowledge, then, is an existential knowing which transforms human attitudes and existence" (p. 130). This position is, in my opinion, manifestly confused. Luther could not be any more clear concerning his overriding emphasis on knowing what is "true." According to Luther, we cannot have a knowledge of what is "saving" unless we first obtain a clear understanding of "what God is like." And contrary to Johnson's position, to know God through Christ *is* to receive "new" information about God according to Luther – new information in fact so important that without it one *cannot* live in a "new relationship" with the divine, as he could not possibly otherwise know what that relationship involves! It appears that Johnson views Luther through modern existentialist spectacles.

[339] WA XLII 257.36–258.17.

[340] WA XLIII 28.29–33.

a sinful and dying world. The good news for reason is that it no longer has to rely on the contradictory views of God propounded by an endless stream of senseless philosophizing, and can finally rest – holding itself in check – as it beholds the ominous spectacle of a God who poured out his own blood for a degenerate and hell-bound humanity. The epistemological and soteriological issues thus could not be any more intertwined as they are in Luther's thought. Without a consideration of both, certainty (an issue so important to Luther) could simply not be obtained. I will conclude here with Luther's own words:

> Itaque debemus assuefacere nos, ut in talibus conscientiae certaminibus relictis nobisipsis, lege et operibus quae tantum nos cogunt aspicere nos ipsos, simpliciter vertamus oculos in illum serpentem aeneum, Christum cruci affixum, in quo haerentes fixo intutu certo statuamus eum esse iustitiam et vitam nostram, nihil morantes minas et terrores legis, peccati, mortis, irae ac iudicii Dei. Nam Christus in quo intenti et fixi haeremus, in quo sumus quique vivit in nobis, est victor et dominus legis, peccati, mortis et omnium malorum in quo nobis proposita est certa consolatio et donata victoria.[341]

---

[341] WA XL, i, 282.33–35; 283.12–17.

Theoretical Touchstone:
Luther on 1 Corinthians 15

In the last chapter it was shown that, at the theoretical level, Luther believed God can be known in the humanity of Christ. However how are we to know, in light of Luther's own stipulations, that we have not simply arrived at a pseudo-knowledge of God through theoretical reasoning that has no connection to reality? What is the actual touchstone with reality for human reason in this matter? This is just one of the important issues dealt with in Luther's sermons on *1 Corinthians 15* – spanning from August of 1532 to April of 1533 – a series that in general proves to be highly significant for our study because reason is thoroughly analyzed. Luther's beginning remarks in fact set the tone for the entire series by offering a penetrating analysis of reason's impatience with the articles of faith. His comments here are not only slightly different in nature from the ones we have already discussed, but they also set the stage for our immediately following examination of reason and limits. We will thus consider the series in detail.

He began in the afternoon of 11 August, 1532. As was just noted, the tone for the entire collection is set in this first sermon and it is therefore important to discuss at some length. In it he claims that St. Paul continued to deliver a message so simple that human reason naturally imagined there must be something more complicated hidden below its outer surface. Drawing such an inference reason then moves to uncover the hidden aspects of God's character. According to Luther, this is a universal phenomenon not in the least peculiar to the situation at Corinth. Reason, he says, typically judges that the pastor can preach about nothing but Baptism, the Ten Commandments, the Lord's Prayer, and the Creed, with which even children are conversant. But why, it asks, does he constantly bombard us with the same message? Who is not able to do that? Reason judges rather that one should not always stick with the same thing, but *develop and move on.*[342] St. Paul however reminds the Corinthians of the oral message he had spoken and even assigns to it such claim that they who stand in it are saved by it alone. Mingling his exegesis with the contemporary situation, Luther claims that Paul says this in direct contrast to the fanatics who forsake the external Word and Sacrament and instead yield to their own imaginary spiritism.[343] As such he believes the entire force of Paul's following remarks is directed towards leading us away at the very outset from the tutelage of reason to the Word, which he had received from Christ himself and proclaimed to them. For human reason, by its very nature, cannot progress beyond judging and concluding based on what it sees with the eye or what it contemplates with the senses. We are asked in this letter for instance to believe in the resurrection of the dead. But reason can only conclude on the basis of what it sees, namely, that the only experience it presently has is that one person dies after another, remains dead, and decomposes, from which it appears no one has ever returned. When reason hears this article of faith it is entirely confused, and judging on the basis of the "facts" it concludes that there is no truth value to its claim. It judges the same way in everything.[344]

This is exactly, says Luther, what has happened to the fanatics regarding Baptism and the Sacrament; they refuse to believe the simplicity of the Word and insist on drawing conclusions from their own speculative reason. The motif of this sermon is that reason cannot and will not remain within the confines of the Word or be captive to it, but must always let its cleverness have a voice. Because reason sees the Word running counter to its understanding and to all the senses, it either denies the content of Scripture or forces it into agreement with human presuppositions. But if we insist on judging according to what we see and feel when God's Word is held before us, then we do not have it in our hearts; it has literally been suppressed and extinguished by our own ideas, reason, and reflections.[345] We must however, says Luther, rely on the Word alone and believe contrary to our experience, and must even feel what we do not feel. But how can that can be? Surely experience must come along and it must be perceived. Luther responds by saying that this is correct, except perception must follow later and faith must precede it, working above perception. Our consciences must therefore become lords and victors over

---

[342] WA XXXVI 489.25–35; 490.10–13 (emphasis mine). See Luther's full discussion 486ff.

[343] WA XXXVI 491.17–28.

[344] WA XXXVI 492.32–37; 493.4–26.

[345] WA XXXVI 493.33–35; 494.4–26.

sin and death *as* it feels sin and trembles.[346] What does Luther mean here? How exactly does faith *precede* perception, working above it? He makes himself clear in his (immediately following) exposition of verses 3–7.

Paul's remarks in these verses set the tone, claims Luther, for the entire chapter on the resurrection. Significantly, Luther asserts that Paul substantiates the doctrine of the resurrection forcefully in two ways. For one, it is proved in Scripture. Second, and most important in this context, Paul cites his own experience and points to the eyewitness accounts of many people still living concerning the resurrected Christ. It is the mark of a reasonable man, says Luther, to prove what he says, not only with words, but also with concrete examples both of himself and others. Accordingly Paul enumerates the eyewitnesses of Christ's resurrection: Peter and the Twelve to whom Christ showed himself alive so that they saw and heard him in his external physical body. He was then later seen by more than five hundred people, many of whom are still alive and will bear witness to the event. "Diese sind allezumal neben mir gewisse zeugen des, das wir gesehen und erfaren haben, also geschehen, wie es zuvor ynn der Schrifft verkündigt ist."[347]

Why does Luther see this portion of Paul's letter as so significant? Because according to him, reason is naturally prone to draw conclusions on the basis of its *own* experience, past and present. As Christ's resurrection is not an event that falls within our own experience, knowledge of it must be obtained through the eyewitness accounts recorded in the New Testament. Thus, given the fact that reason is so inclined to conclude on the basis of its own limited experience, Luther insists that we direct our attention to this recorded event of Christ's resurrection as proof to human reason that doctrines such as the forgiveness of sins, the resurrection of the body, and the life everlasting are true – even though we may not now see their effects. In fact, as we will see below, Luther claims that the resurrection provides the very foundation and reason for every other article of the Christian religion. According to him the real problem lies not with the fact of the resurrection, but with fallen human reason. Reason simply has a difficult time focusing on, and therefore remembering, Christ's resurrection because it is a past event that falls outside of its own purview. As we will see Ozment has pointed out that, for Luther, to forget the manifest past works of God is to forfeit confidence in the promised future works of God. This explains why Luther says

[346] WA XXXVI 495.29–36; 496.3–6.

[347] WA XXXVI 499.9–41; 500.3–20. After quoting verses 3–7 Luther states: "Mit diesen worten deutet er und widderholet, was sein Euangelium gewest fey, das er ynen gepredigt hatte, dadurch sie stehen und selig werden müsten, Und machet daher eine ganze predigt von der Aufferstehung Christi, welche man wol möchte auss den Ostertag lesen und handlen, denn daraus fleuffet grund und ursach dis Artikels, den er furgenomen hat von der todten aufferstehung" (499.9–14).

that in theological matters (or in matters pertaining to the Spiritual Kingdom) faith must often precede perception. This is to say that though we may not *now* see or feel the forgiveness of sins or the resurrection of the body, they are theological doctrines that derive their validity from the past event of Christ's resurrection, an event that Luther seems to think that we can be certain about. So in the face of anguish and a stricken conscience, faith is to precede perception in the sense that the forgiveness of sins is not always felt and the resurrection of the body will be realized only after death; nevertheless, we can be sure that such doctrines are a reality on the basis of the words uttered by the risen Christ.

At this point, one might ask Luther how it is that we can be sure that the resurrection was indeed the resurrection of the Son of God. That is, we certainly do not see that this is God himself; we see only a man who is despised and forsaken of men. How is it then that we can be sure that this is the resurrection of the Son of God, inasmuch as God is not visible? As this is more of a modern philosophical question, we must not expect Luther to have a precise answer that will be satisfactory to all. Having said this though we have seen that Luther believes we meet God himself in the flesh of Jesus. In Jesus we have direct access to God, and in touching his flesh we are touching God himself. It appears that Luther's proof of this is not only the fact that nature itself obeys Christ's every command, but that – more centrally – Christ predicted that he would raise himself up from the dead, and in fact did so. Thus Luther sees Christ's miracles, and most importantly his resurrection, as self-authenticating. The resurrection itself imposes the boundaries and determines the way we are to view Christ's ministry, suffering and death. While such an answer may seem over-simplistic to the modern mind, we must stress here as we did in our discussion of epistemology, that Luther could not benefit from debates that were not at issue during his lifetime.

Luther, having now hinted at the centrality of Christ's resurrection – an event that he will now develop in more detail – continues in the sermon by asking his hearers to consider once again how Paul appeals to the testimony of the external Word with his phrase, "in accordance with the Scripture." In his view, Paul does this to resist the spiritualists who disdain the external message and instead seek other secret revelation. For there is no other way of preserving proper doctrine and faith than the physical or written Word, poured into letters and preached orally. Scripture is not all spirit, as the fanatics maintain, asserting that the Spirit alone imparts life and that Scripture is a dead letter. But although the letter by itself is not life-giving, it must be present, as only through hearing the Word does the Spirit work salvation. The Spirit does not work apart from the Word, and if it is abandoned Christ and the Spirit will be lost completely. Luther makes this point stronger by maintaining that the Holy Spirit has in fact disclosed his very wisdom and council and all mysteries in the external Word of Holy Scripture.[348]

The importance of these remarks, claims Luther, is that they are stated by Paul in order that we resist the temptation to take counsel with reason concerning this or any other article of faith. This is precisely what happened to the Corinthians: They allowed reason and speculation to teach them doctrine and thereby crowded out proper faith. We must not consult reason but rather what Scripture teaches, by which the message was proclaimed and confirmed by public testimony. The factious spirit will never be able to prove his story irrefutably with Scripture and then with people who witnessed the events themselves. We may thus cheerfully defy his account and challenge him to step forth and produce such proof. Luther brings this situation into contact with a contemporary one and again levels the charge of rationalism against the fanatics' position on Baptism and the Lord's Supper. They are sure to come along with their own ideas, produced by reason, and though they may use Scripture to prove their case, they have brought their own thoughts in and forced Scripture to agree with their interpretation. For example, they observe with their reason and perception that Baptism is nothing but water and cannot see anything beyond that, concluding from this that externals cannot benefit the soul. They stretch Scripture to fit the case and seek to interpret contrary verses in accordance with their preconceived notions.[349]

Luther claims that he cites these as examples to warn the saints to be on guard and not raise many questions as to what reason says about doctrinal matters, but rather to look solely to Scripture. If we fail to cling to the Word of God, the factious spirits and reason will most assuredly lead us astray. To stress the universality of this phenomenon, Luther claims that as a doctor of Holy Scripture he has read and reread the Word, yet he also experiences the wayward thoughts of reason: "wenn ich nicht recht ynn meiner rustung stehe und damit wol geharnischt bin, das mir solche gedanken einfallen, das ich solt Christum und das Euangelium verlieren, und mus mich doch ymerdar an die Schrifft halten, das ich bestehen bleibe, Wie wil denn ein mensch thun, das gar on Scrifft und nach lauter vernunfft feret?"[350] One might for example ask how it was possible that the Virgin Mary became pregnant without a man. But this, Luther declares, must be the rule in such cases: The articles of faith are not based on human reason and understanding, but on Holy Scripture. It follows of necessity that they must not be sought anywhere but Scripture or explained otherwise than with Scripture.

---

[348] WA XXXVI 500.21–35; 501.6–16.

[349] WA XXXVI 501.17–36; 502.6–36.

[350] WA XXXVI 503.35; 504.12–20.

To reemphasize his point and assure that no one will misunderstand him, Luther insists that factious spirits base their faith on visions and the worship of angels. It is the manner of these factions to present doctrines that lack the testimony of eyewitnesses and Scripture. Quoting *John* 3:11 and *1 John* 1:1–3, Luther again appeals to eyewitness testimony stating that we speak of what we have seen, and that "which we have heard, which we have seen with our eyes, which we have looked upon and touched with our hands, concerning the word of life...that we proclaim to you." "Also predigen wir hie auch ynn diesem Artikel (spricht S. Paulus), das ich und alle Aposteln sampt funffhundert Brudern gesehen haben und mit mir einhellig zeugen."[351] The factions however prate about delusive visions, and the devil charms their eyes physically with a phantom that does not actually exist.[352] The Christian faith on the other hand is firmly rooted in the historicity of Christ's resurrection.

Given this position, Luther notes its inevitable consequence, namely, that Paul stakes everything on the fact that Christ arose from the dead – this is the chief article of Christian doctrine.[353] It is all-important that this article be maintained, for if it is in doubt, all the other articles will be useless and void because everything that Christ did was done for the sake of the resurrection and the future life. That is, this one article forms the foundation, the *reason,* and end of all other articles in the Christian faith, and if it is removed then the entire faith falls to the ground in pieces.[354] Importantly then in his fourth sermon (6 October, 1532) Luther comments on Paul's statement, "if Christ be not raised from the dead we of all men are most to be pitied," and states that Paul reasoned as follows: If Christ is not indeed risen, then it is impossible for the doctrine of the resurrection to have any value. It would also follow that Christian preaching is in vain. Reemphasizing the importance of the actual event of Christ's resurrection, Luther forcefully declares that it would be a mere dream to believe it if it had not actually occurred in human history. This would be nothing less than to be fooled and misled by an empty dream and phantom, and one for which people had to endure persecution

---

[351] WA XXXVI 504.26–35; 505.9–21.

[352] WA XXXVI 506.15–17.

[353] WA XXXVI 524.31–34. See also Luther's use of logical analysis 524.34–37ff. (Third sermon, preached in the afternoon of 22 September, 1532.)

[354] WA XXXVI 605.16–23. Luther included this in his ninth sermon, preached in the afternoon of 10 November, 1532.

and torture.[355] Our confidence is founded entirely upon the fact that Christ has risen from the dead, we already have life in him, and are no longer under the power of death.[356]

Luther continued the series on 1 December, 1532, claiming that human thoughts are such that we imagine we know the faith well enough and do not need the constant reminding of Holy Scripture. Even though we may think that our memories are sufficient, says Luther, we must avoid being mislead and be watchful and not snore. The Word must be continually cultivated among Christians so that they may defend their position and not allow the devil to gain a foothold, for he will not sleep or snore and will assail Christians on every possible side. They therefore must be armed with God's Word wherever they are, just as God commanded his people Israel to write and inscribe his commands everywhere before their eyes so that they could always see them and thereby resist temptation.[357] Otherwise if we simply imagine we are well acquainted with it, that in itself is slumbering, allowing the head to droop, and snoring in the very midst of the devil's spears. According to Luther, this is precisely what happened to the Corinthians. They became complacent and made subtle alterations to God's Word based on their own ideas and alleged that the resurrection had already taken place.[358] They did not go to where they were bid, but rushed into the articles of faith with their own reason and proceeded to make judgments on that basis. As a result they strayed further and further from the knowledge of God. This is like a blind man, Luther claims, who goes astray in broad daylight, unable to find his way back to the path. In this way others are also lead astray until nothing of God's Word is left and they deal only with their own invented dreams.[359]

Bringing the sermon series to a close Luther comments on verses 54–55. In these remarks he draws an important and often repeated connection (one which we will examine in detail below) between the resurrection and the visible means of grace. Christ, he says, is poison to hell, death, and the devil. He is not a foe of nature *per se*. He has compassion on our misery and wishes to help nature subdue its enemy. What Christ gives is a real divine antidote prepared by heaven and given to us through Christ's resurrection. Though it will be harmless to us, it will kill him who served us the poison to begin with. When we believe in Christ's resurrection the potion is already drunk which eliminates the poison injected into

---

[355] WA XXXVI 532.36–37; 533.25–31; 534.21–39; 535.11–26.

[356] WA XXXVI 549.19–21.

[357] WA XXXVI 625.24–36; 626.12–27.

[358] WA XXXVI 627.21–31.

[359] WA XXXVI 630.25–38.

our hearts, conscience, and body. We thus drink a salutary medicine in Baptism and the Sacrament which expels our poison. As God has not willed that this victory over sin, death, and the devil take place immediately, he begins to mix and prepare the potion to be a *purgatio* for us. That is, to refresh us but to be a poison and death for the devil. Luther adds that this is comparable to a potion prescribed by a physician; it is conducive to a patient's health, but poison to a fever. In the Church the Word, Baptism, and the Sacrament, are the only prescription for our sin and death. We must take it daily in order to drive the poison from our heart and take us from death and hell to eternal life. Only then does the heart grow in faith and learn to despise and overcome the hardships of life. Through Word and Sacrament victory is presented and offered, thereby weakening death and depriving it of its strength.[360]

The closing of his final sermon sums up the importance of everything he had said throughout the series. God had compassion on our misery and sent his own Son to enter the battle for us, and in doing so destroyed our enemies sin, death, and hell. He transferred this victory to us in order that we may say that it is truly our victory. The condition is that we must accept the gift sincerely and not make God a liar by attempting to overcome sin and death on our own. We should not be ungrateful, but should keep God's gift in our heart in firm faith, always being engaged in a song of thanksgiving concerning this victory in Christ: "und darauff frölich dahin faren, bis wir yn auch an unferm eigen leibe sehen, Dazu helff uns Gott durch den selben lieben son, dem fey ehre und lob ynn ewigkeit, Amen."[361]

We must make three observations of this sermon series before moving on. First and foremost, Luther claims that human reason is by nature ignorant concerning the articles of faith, a factor and the reasons for which we have already discussed in detail. Here Luther adds that when reason is confronted with true doctrine, it is unwilling to remain within the simplicity of the Gospel message presented in Scripture. It always, even in the saints, wishes to progress and develop with the consequence that it draws illegitimate conclusions. This situation necessarily involves reason's own rationalistic presuppositions provided, in part, from our own everyday experience. Thus he can say that it is truly foreign to our thinking to hear and accept the doctrine of resurrection in the face of present evidence that seems to contradict such a doctrine (the reasons for which we have already discussed). (These issues are significant as they relate to his notion of limits, a subject that will be dealt with in detail below.) Second, Luther confronts our limited experience with a recorded instance of resurrection, one having the strength of actual

---

[360] WA XXXVI 682.19–40; 683.15–38; 684.22–36; 685.28–29. (Sixteenth and seventeenth sermons, preached in the afternoons of 14 and 27 April, 1533.)

[361] WA XXXVI 695.35–38; 696.9–16.

eyewitness attestation. This element of the sermon series in my opinion plays *the* central role in its overall structure. He frequently points out that human reason is prone to stray from the simple words of Holy Scripture, and instead naturally creates its own articles of religion. The obvious problem with self-created ideas is their blatant lack of objectivity. In the eyewitness accounts of Scripture however we find an objective presentation of God's attitude toward mankind with which we are to bring our own, often bizarre, ideas into captivity. Thus in the face of death we are to be assured that Christ was the first fruit of those who will follow him in the resurrection. This is precisely Luther's intended meaning when he claims that faith must precede perception, for though we perceive only death and decay we must find solace in this pivotal event, and in the message proclaimed by those who were witnesses to that event. Third, Christ distributes the benefits of his death and resurrection only through Word and Sacrament. We therefore see a necessary connection in his thought between Christ's work and the sacred Sacraments of the church. Only here does God deal with our infirmities and this importantly (for our purposes) includes natural human reason. But how does God deal with reason in the Sacraments? This may seem like a queer notion on Luther's part, but it is an essential element of his understanding of reason's limitations, and it is to this significant aspect of his thought that we now turn.

CHAPTER

EIGHT

Reason Set Within Limits:
Luther's Notion of Marks and Signs

As we move to examine some important connections in Luther's thought between reason and visible signs, it might be advantageous first to review where he has so far directed reason in search for the divine. Briefly, he held that knowledge of this sort was lost in the fall and cannot be obtained except through the humanity of Christ, the God-man. Given this position, where does he direct the man (post-ascension) in search of Christ? Certainly we do not have direct access to Christ – and he alone reveals the heart of the Father – so how do we come to know him? Luther accomplishes the connection by drawing a line directly from Christ to the apostles. The apostles alone had the promise of the Holy Spirit, and they alone are called the foundation of the church; as such they must present the articles of faith. "Quare non sequitur, Apostoli hoc et hoc potuerunt, Ergo idem possunt eorum successores. Sed quidquid volunt docere aut statuere, debent autoritatem Apostolorum sequi et afferre."[362] The authority of the apostles can be found in no other place than Holy Scripture. Scripture alone, therefore, properly communicates information concerning Christ and thus the true knowledge of God. Receiving the apostles is accomplished only by being willing to read and hear the Word.[363] God has bound himself, so to speak, to the words of Scripture, and he is to be sought

---

[362] *Die Disputation de potestate concilii*, WA, XXXIX, i, 184 propositions 4–5 to 185 propositions 6–8.

[363] Martin Brecht, *Martin Luther: The Preservation of the Church 1532–1546* (Minneapolis, 1993) p. 112.

nowhere else. This is then the limit which God sets before human reason, that it seek him in no other place than his Word. Indeed, the very communion between Christians and Christ is created by their relationship to the Word.[364]

Though this sounds simple enough, Luther does not end the discussion at this point. As a matter of fact one could say he begins his discussion here, often using as a catalyst his repeated criticisms of the "imagination." As we will recall man's imagination i.e., reason and will, is always operative in Luther's view whether he is engaged in thoughts about God or thoughts about his civic duties. In other words, reason is never idle but always imagining something (again his use of imagination is roughly equivalent to his use of speculation). The importance of Luther's observations here consist in his firm belief that the imagination is opposed to God's Law, being inherently sinful and thus under the wrath of God. It cannot be freed by its own powers.[365] Reason is truly in darkness and therefore has need of the Word as a leader and a guide.[366]

Inextricably bound to the Word for Luther are the visible means of grace, Baptism and the Lord's Supper. So important are these visible signs to his understanding of human reason that one may know he is a Christian, persevering in true faith, only by their constant use. It is this aspect of his thought that we intend to examine here, as Luther sees Word and Sacrament as the very connection between the ascended Christ and his earthly church. Here, and only here, are we to approach him. That is, Christ has bound and limited his saving presence to the Word, oral and visible. With this in mind it is easier to understand Luther's insistence on the real presence in the later Sacramental debates. The Sacraments constitute the very hope of the Christian; that which actually delivers Christ, so to speak, to a sinful and needy human race. Christ still rules but all that is seen of this rule is in Baptism and the Sacrament, and all that is heard is the external Word. These are the only ways in which God rules and executes everything on earth.[367]

Luther's later distinction between the accomplishment of salvation by Christ on the cross and its transmission by the Sacrament is important in this regard. Luther acknowledges that salvation has been realized on the cross, once and for all. But even if Christ gave himself for us a thousand times and were a thousand times crucified for us, everything would be in vain if the Word did not come and distribute and offer it to me. He phrases it as follows: "If then I want my sins forgiven, I must not run to the cross, for there I do not find the forgiveness of sins

---

[364] Brecht, *Martin Luther: The Preservation of the Church 1532–1546* p. 113.

[365] WA XLII 348.31–36.

[366] WA XLIV 640.16–17.

[367] WA XXXVI 569.18–28.

attributed. Neither must I simply cling to the remembrance and knowledge of the suffering Christ...but to the sacrament or the gospel; it is there that I find the Word which attributes it to me, offers it to me, presents it to me and gives me that pardon acquired on the cross."[368] For Luther then the office of mediation is not limited to the incarnation but continues in the present intercession of Christ at the right hand of God.[369] This means that the glory of Christ is not to be enthroned above all creatures, but to love them with the same love which originally drove him to the cross on earth. Thus Lienhard says that "the rule of Christ, as he understands it, continues to operate under the sign of the cross. Christ rules in such a way as to call forth the irony of the proud and the irritation of the wise....He rules by offering himself to sinners in the bread and the wine of the Eucharist, just as once he ruled by the cross."[370]

Accordingly, as Christ allowed himself to be seen, heard, and touched in first century Palestine, so he allows his church to eat and drink his body and blood both physically and spiritually. By this eating, Luther maintains, we obtain just as much and arrive at the same point as the Apostles and eyewitnesses did with their handling, seeing, hearing etc. In the Supper he is just as near to us physically as he was to them, except in a different mode of presence.[371] The presence of Christ to the church is absolutely necessary for the origin and maintenance of faith. In other words, for Luther there must be a direct connection between the risen Christ and the church on earth.

In addition, Luther saw a connection between the necessity of Christ's humanity in the incarnation and the necessity of that same humanity for the church. Lienhard points out that, in contrast to Zwingli's belief that Christ's humanity would be useless if present today, Luther declares that the salvation of believers is and remains linked to the flesh of Christ. It is necessary that this be given to them as in it alone do they find their justification. We must receive Christ with his flesh because it is this flesh with which he accomplished our redemption. Answering the important question, Why does Luther insist on the body of Christ and on the real presence of this body? Lienhard answers:

> It is for him a fundamental concern which cannot be emphasized too much. We do not meet God outside of the man Jesus Christ, "in whom the whole fullness of God dwells bodily" (Col. 2:9). For that would be to move toward the naked God

---

[368] See Marc Lienhard, *Luther: Witness to Jesus Christ* (Minneapolis, 1982) pp. 199–200. The Luther passage is cited from WA XVIII 203.27–39.

[369] Lienhard, *Luther: Witness to Jesus Christ* p. 280. WA XL, ii, 6.19.

[370] Lienhard *Luther: Witness to Jesus Christ* pp. 238–239.

[371] WA XXIII 193.8–16.

of speculation, while God wishes to come near to us for our salvation in the form
of the flesh of the man Jesus, as he has appeared in history and as flesh present
in the physical elements of the gospel, announced and in the sacraments.[372]

He continues by observing Luther's insistence on God's "descent" rather than an
ascent by which believers are reunited to the body and blood of Christ. For Luther,
such an ascent would be a theology in which men are detached from reality in
order to rise up to the uncovered God, thereby falling back into vain and dangerous speculations. This descent is the abasement by which God, who has realized
salvation in Christ, comes today offering salvation by Jesus Christ in these humble
realities i.e., Word and Sacrament. It is interesting here that Lienhard makes the
connection with Luther's developed order of salvation. God first approached us
by the humanity of Christ, by the water of Baptism, the bread and wine of the
Eucharist, and by the proclamation of the gospel – only then does he ask us to
believe.[373] This seems to correlate with what we maintained above; namely, Luther
expressly insists that God reveals himself in order that we may learn to know
him, and this happens only through Word and Sacrament, the oral Word which
precedes to move us. That is, God works through the oral Word and Sacraments
through which he awakens in us knowledge of him. Man becomes acceptable by
justifying grace and the gift of the Holy Spirit, by which he knows God as Savior
– to truly know God is to know him as Savior.[374]

The Word for Luther not only reveals the true nature of God, but also binds
Christ to the elements of water, bread, and wine for our sakes. The foregoing may
add a slightly different cast to his assertion that it is one thing if God is present
and another if he is present for you.[375] For if Christ is present locally only at the
right hand of God, and not in the Supper, then the church and Christians have been
virtually abandoned to speculation – i.e., isolated from God. On Luther's account,
God has bound himself to the Supper and has bid us to come to that external place
where we are commanded to take our reason captive. We no longer have to seek
him in the dark. He makes this point in a Christmas sermon in which he tells the
congregation that they should not seek Christ at the right hand of God, but in the
Sacrament as in the manger.[376] While the fanatics had taught, in Luther's view,

---

[372] Lienhard, *Luther: Witness to Jesus Christ* pp. 220–223.

[373] Lienhard, *Luther: Witness to Jesus Christ* pp. 222–223.

[374] WA XLIII 606.31–42.

[375] WA XXIII 151.10ff. See also Lienhard, *Luther: Witness to Jesus Christ* p. 238.

[376] Martin Brecht, *Martin Luther: Shaping and Defining the Reformation 1521–1532* (Minneapolis,
1990) p. 315. WA 23.737.41. Brecht also notes here that Christ's body and blood cannot be considered secondary in comparison with the Word and faith, as they bring salvation and are therefore
necessary (see p. 299).

that nothing spiritual can be present where there is anything material and physical, he claims that just the opposite must be maintained: the Spirit cannot abide with us *except* in material and physical things![377] How else are we to understand what would otherwise, in a spiritual mode, be completely beyond human limitations of knowing? Word and Sacrament are necessary then for consoling minds and they aid in our battle against vain and innate speculations, "we are commanded only to hear and not act."[378] In fact, for Luther the origin of every temptation is when reason tries to reach a decision about God without the Word.[379]

Impediments to Reason

Having observed that reason is to encounter God in the visible means, we are now in the position to examine the reason for Luther's often forceful admonitions to that effect. Central to his understanding is his belief that affliction in general has a striking effect on fallen reason, one that directly influences its *reasoning* abilities. This brief discussion will give us another important angle on the nature of Luther's attacks on reason and will serve to clarify our ending remarks.

Brecht cites an incident in February of 1533 that will appropriately set the tone for this section. According to various reports, Luther had a severe dizzy spell in the castle church and he thought that his life would soon come to an end. He was so sure of impending death that he exhorted the present clergy to continue to make the preaching of the gospel their chief concern. A few days later he had a similar dizzy spell, but by the evening he had already recovered. Luther was able to depict his struggle with death as a completely normal thing, but what ultimately sustained him was Christ's promise, "Because I live, you will live also." The striking feature of Brecht's report is his important inclusion that this promise, so comforting to Luther, was not simply a self-evident truth for him, as his following remarks clearly betray: "Reason says, 'This is a big lie'."[380]

This particular theme of reason's opposition in the Christian life is not an insignificant one in Luther's thought. Indeed, to a large extent he is perplexed by the fact that reason *more than not* hinders the preservation of faith. Why? Because it gets confused by what God's Word says and what it actually sees. The wicked, for instance, always seem to prosper while believers are despised. Luther often

---

[377] WA XXIII 193.28–33.

[378] WA XL, ii, 410.34–39; 411.16–18.

[379] WA XLII 116.18–19.

[380] Brecht, *Martin Luther: The Preservation of the Church 1532–1546* p. 22.

concludes from this apparent incongruity that God allows adversity for believers so that they may learn and exercise their faith. Most importantly however, adversity teaches us to trust in the Word alone, to disregard visible things and things perceptible by the senses, and retain consolation against all judgments of reason: "Nam quae cernuntur oculis, sunt fallacia et evanida: Sed quae promissa sunt, et non videntur, sunt certa et firma."[381] He almost bemoans the fact that reason is bound to sense-experience and therefore bound to time, but declares that we are to persevere in faith because God's promise is secure. And even though we may be sure of this, says Luther, how does reason respond? "Praeclare quidem et pulchre ista dicuntur, sed ego contrarium experior. Non solum dormit, verum etiam stertit, imo plane nullus Deus est, qui curet aut respiciat nos."[382]

Elsewhere Luther asks once again why such awful experiences are thrown in our path, and simply replies: this is the manner of God's government, and such is the life of the saints in this world. Therefore there is need of wisdom and doctrine exceeding the whole grasp of human reason, by which I am able to say: "Baptisatus sum, absolutus sum a peccatis meis, comedi corpus, et bibi sanguinem Christi, habeo certissimum verbum Dei, ille mihi non mentietur, non fallet, utcunque omnia in contrarium ferri videantur."[383] Reason struggles in the flesh because it perceives the opposite of the promise, but we must overcome these struggles by God's sure signs of acceptance; when we seem to be deserted and the promise is called into doubt, then the flesh and understanding of the flesh and reason must be mortified and all human wisdom must be reduced to nothing. We must return to the Word, says Luther, but practically it is hard work to be reduced this way. Though we be led down to hell, we must rely with certainty on the promise made in the Word and Sacraments; these are the real experiences of life. If we only had reason and flesh in the midst of evil experiences we would surely end our lives.[384] We thus often conclude that we have been handed over to Satan and brought down to hell, but we should not make this conclusion, for if we had been forsaken there would be no survival even for an hour.[385] Luther concedes that in prosperous times even reason and the flesh rejoice and praise God's mercy and goodness, but in bad times it is mixed with weepings and complaints.[386] For in the midst of troubles, reason does not and cannot understand that when it is being put to the test that

---

[381] WA XLIV 226.19–28.

[382] WA XLIV 268.39–269.18.

[383] WA XLIV 270.1–7.

[384] WA XLIV 270.8–37.

[385] WA XLIV 70.2–14.

[386] WA XLIV 533.39–41.

these things are a purging. But one must fight against a corrupt reason and nature which can feel and say nothing else. Here we are to hold to Baptism and God's promise.[387] God wants us to confess our sins and believe his promise, and if reason did not resist this, as it does even in the saints, nothing would be in the way of our life becoming a Paradise. However, flesh wars against the Spirit, and it feels that God not only refuses to hear sinners but even hates them.[388]

Here we come to one of Luther's most common complaints against human reason. On his account, reason follows only things that are visible, that is, only what is happening at the present time. The result is, any misfortune that befalls us brings despair and doubt concerning the will of God toward us, and we feel at such times that we are being afflicted by an angry God. It is precisely at this point that Luther declares we are to slay our reason and close our eyes. What exactly, however, does he mean? Simply this: According to our understanding God forsakes us eternally in our sufferings and afflictions, but in the face of our angst we must fortify our hearts and cling and find rest in the clear words pronounced in Scripture and the Sacraments. Though it seems that God has rejected us in our suffering, Luther firmly believes that it is only through despair, mistrust, hatred, and murmuring against God that we learn to put our trust in the promise alone. Word and Sacrament lead us through that sea of perils and trials to the port, just as a fish is pulled along by means of a hook.[389] For we believe in the historic Christ whom we no longer see. Yet we have his Baptism, the Sacrament of the Altar, and consolation through the promise. So although we feel the opposite of the promise in the flesh we must here, *at these visible means,* struggle and do battle against unbelief and doubt.[390] Luther clearly recognizes the reality of struggling with unbelief in the saints.[391] He believes that for the benefit of Christian faith God troubles, mortifies, and leads them down to hell. In this way we are to learn to concentrate only on the promise presented in Word and Sacrament in contradiction to what we actually feel in our own hearts and consciences. Accordingly, the only book in which to learn and understand this strange work of God is Holy Scripture. Reason is therefore to bow before the promise and not be stricken with

[387] WA XLIV 585.12–33.

[388] WA XL, ii, 394.19–26.

[389] WA XLIII 395.3–22.

[390] WA XLIII 570.12–37.

[391] It is interesting that Luther believed Zwingli knew nothing about a weak and embattled faith, and therefore lacked a deeper experience of the Christian life. See Brecht, *Martin Luther: Shaping and Defining the Reformation 1521–1532* p. 297.

fear in the face of struggles.[392] When we seem to be deserted and reason calls the promise into doubt, then it is at this point that Luther claims it must be mortified and reduced to nothing.

These remarks might be better understood in light of what appears to be a verse of great comfort to Luther, *Isaiah* 42:3, which he quotes no fewer than eighteen times within his discussions concerning Jacob and Joseph alone. He states that faith is actually strongest at its weakest point. When we feel terrified, troubled, and dejected it is this weak faith – struggling against unbelief – which draws the last and deepest sighs. This is not the voice of triumph, but a groaning by which the afflicted heart sighs and seems to draw breath with great difficulty. This is what Isaiah refers to as the smoking flax and the reed that is not whole but crushed and shattered. God's power however is made perfect in such weakness. When the devil has brought us to the point that we can no longer do anything else, he has already lost. Only do not, says Luther, add your agreement by despairing. Here despair is not yet complete and there remains a spark which seems tiny to us but very large in God's ears, a shout that rises above all shouts and fills heaven and earth so that God cannot bear not hearing us and replying: "Why do you cry to me?"[393] So important is this that we should carefully impress on those who are afflicted that God is not angry with them, and that what they interpret as desertion is in fact acceptance and the surest proof of God's grace – since he "chastises every son whom he receives" – lest the son perish in the stupor and blindness of original sin, which men cannot see or understand on the strength of their own mental capacity.[394] Thus we are to comfort ourselves in such times that we feel terror and say to both the devil and our own hearts that Christ must have more weight than all our feelings and ideas. The basis for such a claim, Luther highlights once again, can only rest in the fact that Christ has risen from the dead.[395]

It is when reason reaches the lowest point that it tends to allow adversity to influence its inferential capabilities. Hence Luther claims that we should fight this tendency at the Altar and not give in by adding our agreement. Here at our (seemingly) weakest point we are to draw breath, though with great difficulty, with the aid of the external Word and Sacraments and rely solely on the benefits imparted through those efficacious means of God's wondrous grace.

[392] WA XLIV 586.20–29.
[393] WA XLIV 79.20–80.14.
[394] WA XLIV 474.10–14.
[395] WA XXXVI 541.18–24.

Necessity of Externals

We have already alluded to the question, How is reason to find an incomprehensible God post-ascension? The connection, as we have seen, that the mature Luther saw between the ascended Christ and means of grace appears to answer this question. According to him, God establishes a sign of grace in order that he may be recognized by sinners and that they might be saved (though it is common that they despise it). In fact, from the beginning of the world God has ordained some public sign toward which all people might look and find him e.g., the Tree, Circumcision, Baptism, etc. The essence of this argument for Luther is that by nature we have need of such marks and signs in order that they may lead us to a knowledge of God. Human reason is unable to find God unless these signs are instituted by him to lead us by the hand, so to speak.[396] It is virtually impossible to over-emphasize the importance of this concept within the later writings of Luther. He goes so far as to declare that these marks and signs are those by which God now manifests himself to the world, and must therefore be regarded more highly than any miracles. For it is here that God displays his boundless mercy by not allowing the human race to go astray in its own thoughts, as nothing could be more dangerous than the attempt to understand God's nature through unaided human wisdom. Reason by nature, says Luther, roams and seeks God through its own endeavors in an effort to find him. But God is found only where he has bound himself in these humble yet visible and tangible signs. "Hoc diligenter inculcandum est contra horribiles furias Satanae, qui non cessat seducere orbem, ornatus divina et Angelica specie, ut obscuret, aut penitus ex oculis removeat illa dulcissima signa gratiae, quibus se Deus patefecit generi humano." We should accordingly give hearty thanks to God for our ability to hear his Word, see his signs, and then make frequent use of them.[397]

Luther often condemns those who think they will obtain salvation through "spiritual" speculations without external things. For him, the Holy Spirit works nothing without externals and great attention must therefore be given to the Word and Sacraments. In fact, Luther asserts that we find no word of God in the entire Scripture in which something material and outward is not contained and presented.[398] It is in these visible means alone that God deals with us and presents himself to be observed.[399] So intimate a connection does Luther see between Christ and the means of grace that he gives the analogy that those who are in touch with

[396] WA XLII 624.39–625.2.
[397] WA XLII 651.35–652.25.
[398] WA XXIII 261.11–36; 263.1–25.
[399] WA XLIII 70.16–73.23.

Word and Sacrament are made sound, just as the woman was when she touched
Christ's own garment. Any attempt to find God another way is nothing less than
to ascend to heaven without ladders i.e., the Word.[400] Where do the fanatics get
the idea, asks Luther, that there is ever an accurate idea of God produced by
human reason without the Word? They must admit, he says, that they could not
have obtained ideas about the articles of faith from the Spirit before physically
and outwardly hearing and reading about them in Scripture. One can only get the
idea that there is a God, that God's Son is man, and all the other articles of faith
through the material, outward word of Holy Scripture.[401]

It appears that Luther intends Word and Sacrament to be the focal point for a
true knowledge of God, that sign with which we are to refresh the memory and
sharpen the attention span. This is evident for example when he quotes Christ's
words, "If anyone says: 'Lo, here is the Christ!' or 'There He is!' do not believe
it."[402] For Luther, Christ must be sought only where he has chosen to manifest
himself and wishes to be known, that is, in the Word, in Baptism, and in the
Supper; "Ibi certo invenitur. Verbum enim fallere nos non potest." The connection between his notion of reason and religious epistemology is highlighted very
clearly. It generally happens, says Luther, that reason disregards those signs and
turns aside to the harlot sitting at the gate. We are exhorted to remember to walk
on the way God himself has prescribed and not on one of our own choosing.
Luther emphasizes this for two reasons. (1) It is certain that a human being cannot find God through the use of his own unaided wisdom. (2) Satan is able to
transform himself into an angel of light, surrounding himself with majesty, while
producing signs and wonders to confirm his message. Given these factors, how
are we to avoid the very real danger of false doctrine, not only that originating
from natural man but also from that of demons? Luther did not believe that Satan
presents himself as a horrific figure, but as a being able to divert man's attention
towards his own ideas i.e., necessarily creating false doctrine. This is precisely
where Luther's notion of visible signs becomes the focal point of his discussions
on reason, not only for the unbeliever but equally for the Christian. According to
him, we will be free from the above dangers if, and only if, we follow the vis-

---

[400] WA XLII 11.25–29: "In has absurdas opiniones delabuntur animi, cum sine verbo de tantis rebus
volunt cogitare. Atqui nos ipsos nescimus....Ergo fanaticum est, sine verbo et involucro aliquo de Deo
et divina natura disputare, sicut solent omnes Haeretici; ea securitate de Deo cogitant, qua de porco
aut vacca disputant. Ideo etiam ferunt dignum premium temeritatis, ut sic periculose impingant.
Nam qui vult tutus esse et sine periculo in tantis rebus versari, is simpliciter se intra species, signa
et involucra ista divinitatis contineat, qualia sunt verbum eius et opera eius. Nam in verbo et operibus
se nobis ostendit" (XLII 11.11–25).

[401] WA XXIII 263.26–36.

[402] WA XLII 625.19–40.

ible forms which God has set before our eyes. The central visible form of course is Christ himself on the lap of his mother Mary and the suffering of the cross. But as we do not have local access to Christ we are bound to that which he has bound himself: Baptism, the Eucharist, and the spoken Word. Because we truly have Christ in these places, we cannot complain in any way that we have been forsaken. As such we must say:

> Ego sicut nescio ante adventum Christi aliquam Ecclesiam praeter illam, quae fuit in domo Abrahae, et circumcisione notata fuit: Ita post Christi adventum nihil scio, quam Christum, eumque crucifixum, qui se patefacit nobis in visibilibus formis, in usu clavium, in Eucharistia: Ibi scio, quod Deum invenio, ibi remissionem peccatorum consequor, et alibi nusquam.[403]

As one might predict then it is Satan's primary goal, on Luther's account, to lead us away from the forms prescribed by God. For we naturally tend to get lost in our own thoughts and illegitimate deductions about God's disposition toward us. The visible means are intended means by which we must focus our reason and attention on God's true character and will i.e., on the crucified Christ. This is clearly brought out in his strong declaration that we must adhere to and follow this sure and infallible rule: God in His divine wisdom arranges to manifest himself to human beings in a visible and definite form which can be seen with the eyes and touched with the hands. In short, plainly within the scope of the five senses – so near does the Divine Majesty place itself! "Has formas visibiles firmiter retinere summa sapientia est."[404]

Luther's thought here displays a noticeable consistency. Not only are limits on human reason important for fallen human beings, but they were also a strongly emphasized theme in Luther's understanding of Eden. We may recall in his *Genesis* lectures that Adam was bound to certain forms of worship and was not to move outside of those limits, and the tree is specifically mentioned as Adam's form of obedience to God. Even though Adam had innate knowledge of God, he was still commanded to bring his reason and will captive to the Word, visibly represented at the tree. This was Adam's temple, so to speak, where he was to bring his descendants and give thanks for God's goodness. Luther's emphasis remains the same concerning both man's pre- and post-fallen state. In fact we are only to know we are truly God's people by these outward signs. It must be pointed out that Luther's particular emphasis on the centrality of the incarnation remains clear. For those before the incarnation there was the promise, the Word, and circumcision; for us, there is Word and Sacrament. The importance of this

[403] WA XLII 626.4–8.
[404] WA XLII 626.15–20.

in his view is that only from these sources can we put forth sure arguments and demonstrations that we are indeed Christians.[405] In addition, it is by these signs that we know we are still the object of God's concern; thus they function as our light bearers toward which we look as dependable tokens of the sun of grace. The moment we leave them behind, our thoughts will inevitably lead us eternally astray from the true God.[406]

God condemns, says Luther, all erring thoughts outside the one and only revelation made in the Word and Sacraments. Because of this, God wishes to gather us around these forms so that we may have a sure and infallible sign by which we know we are saved, just as he promised he would do the same at the mercy seat among the people of Israel. We are therefore not to devise a special administration of the Sacraments. For God does not want us to go astray in our own speculations, but wishes to enclose us within these limits so that we are not tossed about by erroneous doctrines.[407] So sure in fact is Luther about this he boldly states that God has surrendered and revealed himself to us in these means. We are not to conquer God by the judgment of reason, but by holding firm to the promise presented to us in our Baptism. This is an element in Luther's thought most deserving of attention. According to him, even if God pretends he is unfriendly and angry with us then we must say: "Domine Deus, tu promisisti hoc in verbo tuo. Non mutabis igitur promissionem. Ego sum baptisatus, sum absolutus." If we persist God will be conquered by his own promise and will eventually say: "Fiat tibi sicut petivisti, quia habes promissionem et benedictionem, Ich muz mich dir ergeben. Constans enim et pertinax quaesitor et petitor est suavissimum sacrificium."[408]

In the same way Luther claims that we should cling to the Word of God only, "By it I shall die, and by it I shall live." There is an abundance of protection in the promise not only against the devil, the flesh, and temptation, but even against God himself. That is, if God appeared in his majesty and said, "You are not worthy of my grace; I will change my plan and not keep my promise to you," we should not yield to him, and it would in that case be necessary to fight most vehemently against God himself – as Job says "Though he slay me, yet will I hope in him." Luther continues here and even declares that if God should cast us into the depth of hell and place us in the midst of devils we should still believe we are saved because we have been baptized, absolved, received the pledge of salvation and the

---

[405] WA XLIV 6.26–31: "Inde colligas argumenta et demonstrationes, quibus certus fias te esse Christianum, esse baptisatum, et incedere in vocatione sancta et pia."

[406] WA XLII 184.38–185.20.

[407] WA XLIV 95.31–40; 96.1–6.

[408] WA XLIV 105.25–35.

body and blood of the Lord in the Supper.[409] It is in this very struggle that God demonstrates his most perfect will to his saints. We must not therefore seriously entertain our thoughts which suggest that we have been forsaken and rejected. It is true that nature cannot abstain from them any more than it can from impatience, wrath, and concupiscence, but they should only remain thoughts and not become axioms that speak the final word. One should rather follow the advice of the hermit to whom a youth complained that he continually experienced imaginations about lusts and other sins, to whom the old man replied: "Tu non potes prohibere, ne volitent super caput tuum volucres. Sed volitent tantum, et non nidificent in capillis capitis. Sint cogitationes, et maneant tales, sed non fiant conclusiones." Luther remarks that it is rather the mark of desperate men to make conclusions out of mere thoughts.[410]

Illegitimate Deductions

We will conclude this chapter by examining one final issue that Luther deemed fundamentally important, namely, skepticism. According to him, it is the innate desire to draw conclusions beyond the text that plays the central role in creating doubt and skepticism within the mind of the believer. This may seem obvious but his concern is that it is very difficult, in reality, for human beings to disregard their own wavering thoughts and concentrate rather on an objective source, one that often does not satisfy our desire for idle speculation. One major issue presented in Scripture that has riddled the human mind with doubt and despair, says Luther, is predestination. His comments on *Genesis* 26:9 are informative in this regard. They deal with the entire spectrum of our preceding remarks and will serve to show how Luther dealt with the issue of skepticism in relation to his pivotal notion of limits.

He begins by discussing doubt and the will of God, as there are people who are spreading false statements concerning God's foreknowledge or predestination. Luther was concerned about the doubt produced in the hearts of the faithful as a result of these issues. Briefly, their arguments run as follows: If I am predestined, I shall be saved whether I do good or evil; or, if I am not predestined, I shall be condemned regardless of my works. These arguments produce another sort, namely: What God has determined before must of necessity happen. Therefore every concern about religion and about the salvation of souls is uncertain and

---

[409] WA XLIV 97.38–98.9.
[410] WA XLIV 99.23–34.

useless. Provocatively, Luther counters by saying that if these things are indeed true, then the incarnation of the Son of God, his suffering and resurrection, and everything he accomplished for salvation are clearly done away with.[411]

It quickly becomes evident that Luther sees such inferences cutting right to the heart of Christian assurance, and if he was unclear about it in *De servo arbitrio* he certainly is not here. For him these questions are the very poison of original sin itself, with which the devil first led Adam and Eve into sin. As such they were not satisfied with the divinity that had been revealed and wanted to rise and know the unrevealed divinity. Our questions about predestination are exactly the same sort of devilish darts that threaten the very core of Christian assurance. If in fact we have been invited to probe into such issues, then for what end did it serve for God to send his own Son to suffer and be crucified for us? And of what use was it to institute the Sacraments if they are uncertain or useless for our salvation? For if someone had been predestined, he would have been saved without Christ and without the Sacraments or Holy Scripture.[412]

Central to Luther's complaint is fallen reason. We have already noted its continual desire to know God apart from Christ, and this is just another instance of that sinful impulse. But Luther makes it abundantly clear here that these questions, which originate in man's own imagination, are delusions of the devil with which he tries to make us doubt and disbelieve, in spite of the fact that Christ came into the world to make us completely certain of salvation.[413] We must oppose these thoughts, says Luther, with the true and sure knowledge of Christ, for although we change, God is unchangeable and his promise certain. Thoughts about predestination then are nothing more than sophisticated speculations of human reason couched in the appearance of profundity. The only appropriate response is to kill the ways of reason by focusing on the wounds of Christ and the blood that was shed for us, as from these our predestination will certainly shine clearly.[414] Here we come to the heart of the matter in Luther's view. In order to counteract our curiosity, God wished to show us his will by his self-revelation in the historic Christ. To emphasize that this revealed God truly represents the heart and will of the hidden God, Luther claims that he is in fact the same God, but has now condescended in such a way that he is squarely within the limits of human understanding. For Luther, he who sees Christ truly sees the Father.[415]

---

[411] WA XLIII 457.32–40.

[412] WA XLIII 458.3–19.

[413] WA XLIII 458.20–25.

[414] WA XLIII 460.36–461.16.

[415] WA XLIII 459.21–34.

We must therefore reject the natural inclinations of human reason and receive Christ in our hearts in his birth, miracles, and cross.[416] The way in which this is practically accomplished is through Word and Sacrament. It is through these external means that we are to jump outside even our own conscience and find our predestination by believing with our hearts, seeing with our eyes, and touching with our hands Christ's body and blood given us for the forgiveness of sins. Luther's insistence on tangible proofs is very significant, for human reason requires such proof in order to escape the devastation of its own thought. God has given the ultimate proof of his trustworthiness by delivering his own Son into the flesh and into death, and now distributes the benefits of his death in the Sacraments in order that we may know he is truthful. God's gift on Luther's account would mean nothing if it were confirmed with spiritual proofs; he has therefore confirmed it with tangible proofs. For we see the water, we see the bread and wine, and we see the minister – only in these physical forms does God truly reveal himself, for our own benefit, lest we get lost in the hellish depths of our own ideas.[417]

Concluding Remarks

In order to grasp the significance of Luther's thought we must keep in mind his insistence that human reason is *never idle*, as his synonymous use of "imagination" strongly suggests. Reason finds it virtually impossible to concentrate solely on the promise, thereby filtering out contrary conclusions. It therefore has need of an outward sign as a leader and guide. It must be stated from the outset that these remarks have to be kept in the context of Luther's overall thought. That is, he clearly recognizes the logical importance of the eyewitness attestation to Christ's resurrection and explicitly claims that it is the cornerstone of Christian belief, without which nothing that follows would have objective grounding.

Luther believed that God cannot be known outside of Christ's humanity, and any attempt to know him otherwise is necessarily to move toward the God of speculation i.e., a god of our own making. God must first descend in order that we avoid this very real danger. He therefore approached us in Christ's humanity, revealed his true character, and eliminated any metaphysical notions on man's part concerning his person. However, Luther believed the church even now depends upon that same humanity in order to avoid the danger of total isolation and specu-

---

[416] WA XLIII 459.35–460.2: "Idque unicum et praesentissimum remedium est istius horribilis morbi, quo homines in inquisitione Dei procedere volunt speculative, et ruunt tandem in desperationem aut contemptum."

[417] WA XLIII 462.14–27.

lation. Thus Word and Sacrament are seen as the very connection between the ascended Christ and his church. He first approached us in his humanity and now does the same in Baptism, the Eucharist, and the proclamation of the gospel. He works solely through these means as they alone properly communicate information about himself; only then does he call for belief. The reason for this position is that, for Luther, a proper knowledge was a necessary requisite for faith. God has promised to meet us at the elements and commands us to bring our thoughts and reason captive at this external place. We are to seek him there as we would have sought him in the manger.

In the midst of adversity, however, reason often jumps to conclusions based on its own created premises, and either concludes that it has been forsaken or that there is no God at all. It is here that Luther declares we are to close our eyes and slay our reason. But this simply means that we must concentrate on the promise presented in the visible means, a promise we already know to be well-established, itself based on Christ's resurrection. Thus when we feel deserted we are to reduce these illegitimate conclusions to nothing. That is, we are to disregard inferences based on our own subjective experience and seek rather inferences based on the objectivity of Christ's resurrection, thereby appropriating his saving presence in the Sacraments. Properly understood then, Luther does not advocate that we should simply close our eyes and believe in a promise without external support. He believes that the resurrection has overwhelming attestation and that it merits allegiance even in the face of our own contrary experience. The Sacraments on this account become a visible focal point for sinful human beings to bring their reason in subjection to the sure promises of forgiveness and eternal life given in and through their use.

PART THREE

Faith and Reason

CHAPTER
NINE

Luther's Faith/Reason Antithesis:
Another Look

Before we can move on to discuss the precise relation between reason and faith, we need to define first as best we can Luther's notion of faith. However, it is necessary to keep in mind that this study is highly restricted, and we will not therefore attempt an overall examination of faith in Luther's works. This will result in the unfortunate, yet necessary, fact that many important features of Luther's thought in this area will have to be ignored. What is of specific concern here is the nature of the apparent antithesis between reason and faith throughout Luther's later works. With these restrictions in mind, let us turn to the subject of faith.

The Essence of Faith

First, what is the relation of knowledge to faith? According to Luther, as we have already seen, proper knowledge is a necessary prerequisite of faith; without it, faith would be utterly meaningless.[418] But we have also seen that, for knowledge to exist, something mind-independent must be presented to the senses. Thus for

---

[418] "Ergo haec confessio sive cognitio ad remissionem peccatorum est necessaria, ut credamus et confiteamur nos peccatores esse et totum mundum esse sub ira Dei" WA XL, ii, 370.20–22. "Fidem nihil aluid esse quam veritatem cordis, hoc est, rectam cogitationem cordis de Deo" WA XL, i, 376.23–24. "qui primum notitia sui iustificat nos, deinde creat cor mundum, parit novos motus, donat certitudinem illam, qua statuimus nos placere Patri propter ipsum, donat item certum iudicium, quo probamus ea, quae prius ignorabamus aut prorsus contemnebamus" WA XL, i, 579.14–17.

Luther faith is conceived solely through teaching, and by that he means it originates when the mind is instructed about what the truth is. It will be helpful to
recall one of his most explicit remarks in this regard:

> Hoc genus doctrinae quod revelat filium Dei, non discitur, non docetur, non
> indicatur ulla sapientia hominum nec per ipsam legem, sed per Deum revela-
> tur, Primum externo verbo, deinde intus per spiritum. Est itaque Evangelium
> verbum divinum quod de coelo descendit et per spiritum sanctum revelatur
> qui et ad hoc missus est, Sic tamen, ut verbum externum praecedat. Nam nec
> Paulus ipse habuit revelationem internam, nisi prius audisset verbum externum
> e coelo, nempe hoc: 'Saule, Saule, quid me persequeris?' etc. Primum ergo au-
> divit verbum externum, deinde sequutae sunt revelationes, cognitio verbi, fides
> et spiritualia dona.[419]

His contrast between faith and hope will serve to illustrate his meaning. While
faith comes into being through teaching, hope is conceived by exhortation and
comforts the man who has already been justified by faith. If the torch of faith
did not first illuminate the will, hope could not persuade the will.[420] Accordingly,
faith and hope differ in their subjects because faith is in the intellect and hope
is in the will. And although they cannot be completely separated in fact they do
differ in function. For faith commends and directs the intellect (though not apart
from the will) and teaches what must be believed, and is therefore teaching and
knowledge proper. Hope is exhortation because it arouses the mind to be brave
and resolute; faith is a theologian and a judge. As its object, faith has truth and
it instructs us to cling to truth with a sure confidence.[421] With faith we bravely
encourage, illuminate, instruct, and rule the will.[422]

So what does Luther mean when he says that the believer must have a correct
understanding and an intellect *informed* by faith[423] or, that it is only faith, not
reason, which can think correctly about God? His meaning is simply this: Man
can think correctly about God only when he believes God's Word. Faith is nothing else but the truth of the heart, that is, the right knowledge of the heart about

---

[419] WA XL, i, 142.14–22.

[420] WA XL, ii, 28.25–29.

[421] WA XL, ii, 26.11–25. "Ut igitur Dialectica et Rhetorica mutuas sibi invicem operas tradunt, ita
fides et spes. Est igitur ea distinctio fidei et spei in Theologia, quae est intellectus et voluntatis in
Philosophia, Prudentiae et Fortitudinis in Politia, Dialectices et Rhetorices in sermone." WA XL,
ii, 28.21–24.

[422] WA XL, ii, 29.15–17.

[423] WA XL, ii, 28.9–10.

God.[424] Elsewhere Luther defines faith as right reason and a good will.[425] What he means by these definitions is that faith believes what God says and regards him as truthful, wise, righteous, and merciful, thereby attributing glory to him. Without faith God loses his majesty or divinity. According to Luther God requires nothing greater of man than that he attribute to him glory and divinity i.e., that he regard God as God – not an idol – who has regard for him, listens to him, shows mercy and helps him. "Et illam gloriam posse tribuere Deo est sapientia sapientiarum, iustitia iustitiarum, religio religionum et sacrificium sacrificiorum. Ex his intelligi potest, quanta iustitia sit fides, Et per Antithesin: quantum peccatum incredulitas." In this sense Luther can say that faith is man's supreme sacrifice and something truly omnipotent, for it consummates and is the creator of the Deity *in us*.[426] What is central to Luther's understanding here is that faith kills unbelief and hatred of God.[427]

More specifically, faith is the firm and sure thought or trust that through Christ God is propitious, and his thoughts concerning us are ones of peace, not of wrath or affliction.[428] Accordingly, faith in its proper function has no other object than Jesus Christ who was put to death for the sins of the world: "Agnoscit igitur fides quod in ista persona, Iesu Christo, habeat remissionem peccatorum et vitam aeternam. Qui hoc obiecto excidit, non habet veram fidem, sed fucum et opinionem et vertit oculos a promissione ad legem, quae perterrefacit et in desperationem eum adigit."[429] Faith attaches itself to Christ's promise i.e., the essence of faith is that it confidently lays hold of and gives assent to the promise.[430] (Therefore faith and promise are naturally and inseparably bound together as there would be no

---

[424] WA XL, i, 376.23–24.

[425] WA XL, i, 415.22–24.

[426] WA XL, i, 360.17–35.

[427] "Hoc ergo primum agendum est, ut per fidem occidamus incredulitatem, contemptum, odium Dei, murmurationem contra iram, iudicium, omnia verba et facta Dei, tum occidimus rationem." WA XL, i, 365.24–26.

[428] WA XLII 564.5–7.

[429] WA XL, i, 164.22–30. "Sic et Christus in Ioanne definit iustitiam fidei. 'Ipse Pater', inquit, 'amat vos'. Quare amat? Non quia fuistis Pharisaei in iustitia legis irreprehensibiles, circumcisi, bene operantes, ieiunantes etc., Sed quia 'Ego vos elegi de mundo', nihilque fecistis, nisi 'quod me amastis et credidistis, quod a Patre exivi'. Placuit vobis hoc obiectum, scilicet Ego, missum a patre in mundum. Et quia hoc obiectum apprehendistis, ideo amat vos Pater et placetis ei." WA XL, i, 371.26–32. This also underscores Luther's assertion that with regard to the unrevealed God there is no faith, no knowledge, and no understanding. What is above us is none of our concern. WA XLIII 458.38–40.

[430] WA XLII 565.12–15. "Ergo sola fide iustificamur, quia sola Fides apprehendit hanc victoriam Christi." WA XL, i, 444.13–14.

advantage of one without the other.[431]) For those then, says Luther, who complain that they cannot believe yet are convinced that the articles of the Creed are true and happened as reported should not despair about their unbelief; for if you do not doubt that the Son of God died for you, you surely believe, because to believe is nothing else than to regard these facts as the sure and unquestionable truth.[432] Luther puts this another way by stating that faith is that which stretches out its hand when God offers something and simply accepts what he offers.[433] Thus for him the part that fulfills the whole of theological knowledge is the fact that God gives grace to the humble, so that those who cry out, "Miserere mei, Deus," are truly pleasing to God. This is, in fact, what Luther claims his theology adds to the Law, namely, the particle "Mei" – this is precisely what the gospel so earnestly inculcates.[434] The implication of the above is that those who suppose faith to be a useless reflection or a knowledge such as demons have do not know that it means to believe and give assent to God when he promises and swears. For Luther, true faith draws the following conclusion: "Deus est mihi Deus, quia mihi loquitur, mihi remittit peccata, non irascitur mihi: Sicut promittit ego sum Dominus Deus tuus."[435]

His departure from Augustine at this point is notable. In its connection to justification, McGrath has observed that faith in Augustine's understanding is primarily an adherence to the Word of God; thereby implying a strongly intellectualist element. But Augustine argues that this faith must be supplemented with *caritas* or *dilectio* if it is to justify man. Given that fact, it is love rather than faith which brings about the conversion of man. (An important corollary is that *cupiditas* is seen as the root of all evil while *caritas* is the root of all good.)[436] Though Luther too has a firm intellectualist element within his overall understanding, he does demand a distinction between what faith alone does and those virtues with which it is closely connected. As we have seen faith alone lays hold of the promise, that is, believes God when he gives the promise, stretches out its hand when God offers something and accepts it. "Hoc proprium solius fidei opus est." For him love, hope, and patience are concerned with other matters and have other bounds

---

[431] WA XLII 451.36–38.

[432] WA XLIII 460.14–22.

[433] WA XLII 565.37–39.

[434] WA XL, ii, 336.20–34; 337.16–19.

[435] WA XLIII 243.28–35.

[436] Alister E. McGrath, *Iustitia Dei: A History of the Christian Doctrine of Justification* (Cambridge, 1986) Vol. I, p. 30. McGrath thus states that "it is for this reason that it is unacceptable to summarize Augustine's doctrine of justification as *sola fide iustificamur* – if any such summary is acceptable, it is *sola caritate iustificamur.*"

within which they remain. The importance of his distinction is the fact that these virtues do not lay hold of the promise (as faith alone does) but rather carry out the commands. In other words, it is love which deals with God when he commands by carrying out those commands and obeying them. "Sicut autem promissio et lex, sic fides et charitas, sic finis fidei et charitatis est distinguendus, et pestilens illa glosa explodenda de fide formata charitate, quae charitati tribuit omnia, fidei adimit omnia."[437]

By taking hold of the promise, faith restores to some extent that lost image and similitude of God man once possessed. We may recall that in the Garden, according to Luther, man not only had the ability to reason but also had a likeness of God, that is, a will and an intellect by which he understood God and even desired what God desired. On his account, if man had not fallen he would have lived forever, happy and full of joy, and would have had a will that was glad and ready to obey God. Through sin this was lost, but is now renewed to some extent through faith. For we are beginning to know God and our will is to some extent incited to praise, to thank, and to confess him.[438] It is not surprising then that Luther believes that Satan's priority is to cause us to doubt God's Word. As the source of all righteousness is faith i.e., taking God's words to be truth, so the source of all sin is unbelief and turning away from God. Once Satan has diverted our attention from God's Word sins against the Second Table necessarily follow.[439]

Within the general category of doubting God's Word, as far as Luther understands it, must be included man's inquisitive discussions about otherwise clear statements in Scripture. For instance, we have Christ's clear declaration concerning the Lord's Supper in which he says: "This is my body which is given for you" and "This is the cup of the New Testament in my blood." When the fanatics depart from a trust in the simplicity of these propositions and discuss how these

---

[437] WA XLII 565.39–566.2, 15–18.

[438] WA XLII 248.9–19: "Fuit enim in Adam ratio illuminata, vera noticia Dei et voluntas rectissima ad diligendum Deum et proximum....Hoc autem nunc per Euangelium agitur, ut imago illa reparetur. Manserunt quidem intellectus et voluntas, sed valde viciata utraque. Euangelium igitur hoc agit, ut ad illam et quidem meliorem imaginem reformemur, quia in vitam aeternam vel potius in spem vitae aeternae renascimur per fidem, ut vivamus in Deo et cum Deo, et unum cum ipso sumus, sicut Christus dicit....Ad hunc modum incipit imago ista novae creaturae reparari per Euangelium in hac vita, sed non perficitur in hac vita. Cum autem perficietur in regno Patris, tunc erit voluntas vere libera et bona, mens vere erit illuminata et memoria constans." WA XLII 47.33–34; 48.11–16, 27–30.

[439] WA XLII 122.10–24: "Atque hoc etiam Satanae astus ostendit. Neque enim Heuam statim sollicitat suavitate pomi. Summam virtutem hominis primum invadit, fidem in verbum. Radix igitur et fons pecatti est incredulitas et aversio a Deo, Sicut e contra fons iusticiae et radix est fides. Et Satan primum abducit a fide ad incredulitatem. Hoc ubi confecit, ut non crederet Heua praecepto a Deo tradito, facile fuit etiam id perficere, ut involaret in arborem et pomum decerptum comederet. Nam peccatum per incredulitatem consummatum in corde sequitur etiam externa inobedientia."

things can be, they inevitably come to a gradual denial of Christ's word and even attack it, just as happened to Eve in Paradise. Thus Luther notes that when Arius speculates that God is the simplest unity, he comes up with preposterous deductions until he at last maintains in so many words that Christ is not God. This is in spite of the fact, says Luther, that John clearly declares "The Word was God," or that Christ commands Baptism in the name of the Father, Son, and Holy Spirit, and that we have been commanded to believe in Christ, to worship him, and to pray to him. What is more absurd, asks Luther, than the fact that we pass judgment on God and his Word, when it is we who ought to be judged by God? We should rather follow this rule as a holy anchor: that after it has been established that what we have and profess is the Word of God, we give it our assent in simple faith and do not engage in curious disputes. Therefore when we hear God saying something, we are simply to believe it and not debate about it; in so doing we take our intellect captive in the obedience of Christ.[440] Faith's highest single virtue on this account is its willingness not to pry into the benefit or necessity of what one believes. That is, it refuses to encircle God or demand why, for what purpose, and from what necessity he commands or enjoins something, but is perfectly content to give God the glory and believe his simple Word.[441]

Before we move on then let us briefly summarize the essential elements of faith according to Luther. First of all, faith is a knowledge of the facts concerning Christ's life, death, and resurrection – without which of course faith could not exist. Second, and central to Luther's understanding, faith is that which apprehends Christ's merits for itself. In this way we acknowledge that God is truthful and trustworthy, for as Luther points out, one cannot deal doubtfully with God. Because God is not a liar or changeable, it is the highest form of worship to be convinced that he is truthful. And in order to substantiate this to a weakened and sinful mankind, God has given the strongest proof of his trustworthiness by offering his own Son into the flesh and death, and has instituted the Sacraments so that we may be sure that he does not wish to be deceitful.[442] Simply put then, faith is the knowledge that Christ has died for the sins of the world coupled with the all important trust that he has died for, and forgiven, *my* sins (personal appropriation). Luther aptly sums up the simplicity of faith's confession as follows:

[440] WA XLII 118.11–32.

[441] WA XXIII 249.22–28: "Darumb warnet uns wol S. Paulus fur solcher schlangen 1 Cor. etc. und spricht: 'Ich furchte, das gleich wie die schlange mit yhrer teuscherey Hevam betrog, also auch ewer verstand möcht verderbt werden von der einfeltickeit die ynn Christo ist'. Ists nicht war? Diese schwermer furen uns von dem einfeltigen synn dieser hellen einfeltigen wort 'Das ist mein leib' durch yhr teuscherey?" WA XXIII 251.10–15.

[442] WA XLIII 462.15–18.

Lex, nullum ius in me habes, ideo frustra accusas et condemnas me. Credo enim in Iesum Christum, filium Dei, quem Pater misit in mundum, ut nos miseros peccatores oppressos legis tyrannide redimeret. Is suam vitam profudit et prodegit largissime pro me. Itaque sentiens terrores et minas tuas, o Lex, immergo conscientiam meam in vulnera, sanguinem, mortem, resurrectionem et victoriam Christi, praeter hunc nihil plane videre et audire volo.[443]

With these basics outlined we can now examine Luther's apparent antithesis between faith and reason.

Faith and Reason as Opposites

Ibi pii fide mactant bestiam maiorem mundo Atque ita Deo gratissimum sacrificium et cultum exhibent....Et ad hoc piorum sacrificium et cultum omnes omnium gentium religiones, omnia omnium monachorum et iustitiariorum opera collata prorsus nihil sunt. Per hoc enim sacrificium primum necant rationem, hostem Dei omnium maximum et invictissimum, quia contemnit Deum et negat eius sapientiam, iustitiam, virtutem, veritatem, misericordiam, maiestatem et divinitatem.[444]

Quare, ut dixi, quilibet Christianus summus est Pontifex, quia primum offert et mactat suam rationem et sensum carnis, Deinde tribuit Deo gloriam, quod sit iustus, verax, patiens, miserator et misericors. Hocque est iuge illud sacrificium vespertinum et matutinum in novo Testamento, Vespertinum: mortificare rationem, Matutinum: glorificare Deum. Sic Christianus quotidie et perpetuo versatur in illo duplici sacrificio et usu eius, Et nemo satis praedicare potest pretium et dignitatem sacrificii Christiani.[445]

These provocative words come from the same man who demanded proof and well-reasoned arguments from his adversaries to substantiate their claims. How are we to harmonize such conflicting statements? It might seem that either Luther is completely unaware of his many demands for reasonable arguments, or he is an inconsistent fideist of the most extreme type. However, it is also possible that the explanation of these troubling statements lies somewhere else. Let us examine one such possibility.

We have already seen that Luther regards faith as constituting the sole righteousness of the believer, and conversely, that unbelief is the greatest of sins – in

---

[443] WA XL, i, 563.31–33; 564.11–14.

[444] WA XL, i, 362.26–31; 363.10–11.

[445] WA XL, i, 370.12–18.

fact the root of all sin. As a result, faith justifies because it renders to God what is due him and very simply says: "Ego credo tibi Deo loquenti." Whoever says this is righteous. The apparent antithesis between reason and faith consists of the fact that reason often regards the things that God says as impossible, untrue, foolish, and absurd. For what, Luther asks, is more foolish and impossible than when God says to Abraham that he is to get a son from the body of Sarah, which is barren and already dead? In fact when God proposes the doctrines of faith, he always proposes things that are impossible and absurd if you wish to follow the judgment of reason. For instance, it seems ridiculous to reason that the body and blood of Christ are truly presented and given in the Lord's Supper, that Baptism is the washing of regeneration and renewal in the Holy Spirit, that Christ the Son of God was conceived and carried in the womb of the Virgin, that he was born, that he suffered the most ignominious of deaths on the cross, that he was raised again, that he is now sitting at the right hand of the Father, and that he has authority in heaven and on earth. Here Luther claims that reason judges the same way about all the articles of faith, because it does not understand that the supreme form of worship is to hear the voice of God and to believe; reason rather supposes that what it chooses on its own and what it does with its good intention and devotion is pleasing to God. Therefore when God speaks, reason regards his Word as heresy and as the word of the devil, for it seems absurd. This is in fact, according to Luther, the very theology of the sophists and sectarians, who measure the Word by the judgments of reason.

It is in this connection that Luther's language becomes particularly harsh. He says that faith by nature actually slaughters reason and thereby kills the beast of the whole world. Abraham for example killed it by faith in the Word of God, though reason did not immediately assent to this Word. In reality it fought against faith in him and regarded it as ridiculous that Sarah, who was not only ninety years old but barren by nature, should give birth to a son. However, faith won the victory in him and killed and sacrificed God's bitterest and most harmful enemy. Thus all devout people, claims Luther, enter into this same darkness of faith and, killing reason, they say: "Tu ratio stulta es, non sapis quae Dei sunt, itaque ne obstrepas mihi, sed tace, non iudica, sed audi verbum Dei et crede." In this way the devout, by their faith, kill a beast greater than the whole world and offer a highly pleasing sacrifice and worship to God. And what is the precise nature of this sacrifice? That faith slays reason because it despises God and denies his truthfulness, mercy, and majesty. By their sacrifice the devout ascribe glory to God and thus regard him as just, good, faithful, and truthful, believing that he can do everything his Word claims. "Quod est Deo acceptissimum obsequium. Ideo nulla maior, melior aut gratior religio cultusve inveniri potest in mundo quam fides."[446] In short, faith alone attributes glory to God and through it we kill unbelief, contempt of God, and murmuring against his wrath and judgment; it is then that we kill reason.[447]

Luther's comments are not so surprising or irrational if we take into consideration his general epistemology, according to which factual knowledge obtains only through the external world; that is, the very concepts available for reason's consideration arise solely through our own severely limited sense-experience. We do not on his account have any *a priori* knowledge of a factual nature, and this of course most importantly includes a saving knowledge of God. Because concepts of a factual nature originate in such a way reason regards the statements of God, for instance that we will never truly die, utterly foolish and even heretical (the reasons for which we have already discussed). But given the basic fact that our everyday knowledge lacks *a priori* status we should not, on Luther's account, regard God's propositions as absurd or devoid of meaning: It is entirely *possible* in other words that God can do exactly what he says. Therefore reason, in its refusal to consider these as open possibilities – instead thinking the opposite of what it should by taking the *a priori* line that such propositions are ridiculous – is actually betraying its own *ir*rationality. It is, in this case, actually being highly *unreasonable*, because in reality it cannot say with absolute certainty that God's statements are ridiculous. Faith, in ascribing to God this possibility, is *itself* right reason; faith actually restores to some extent reason's created function. It is not the case therefore that reason *per se* is destroyed according to Luther; but rather that reason, in taking its rationalistic assumptions as absolute truth, is properly brought to ashes by faith in that faith alone destroys the unreality of such self-appointed majesty. (We have already noted that reason, post-fall, by its very nature is hopelessly turned inward.) In this case it can only be considered an irrational self-love that constitutes the Christian's evening sacrifice. With this established we must now turn our focus to an important corollary in the faith/reason relation.

---

[446] WA XL, i, 361.14–29; 362.11–.31; 363.10–15: "Contra operarii carentes fide multa faciunt....In summa: deturbant Deum e sede sua et sese in locum ipsius collocant. Neglecto enim et contempto verbo Dei eligunt cultus et opera quae ipsis placent. His Deum delectari somniant et se pro illis mercedem recepturos ab eo sperant. Hi rationem, atrocissimum Dei hostem, non mactant sed vivificant auferuntque Deo maiestatem et divinitatem et eam operibus suis tribuunt" (363.16–27).

[447] WA XL, i, 365.24–30.

Faith and Reason Engaged in Combat

Perhaps the most significant aspect of Luther's faith/reason relationship is his re-peated motif concerning the two caught up in a seemingly endless battle. In fact most of his extended treatments of this relationship are set within the context of combat, in which faith takes on a strongly eschatological overtone.

Among other sources, Luther's sermon series on *1 Corinthians 15* yields some very important information for this discussion. Commenting on verse 24 – "Then comes the end, when he delivers the Kingdom to God the Father after destroy-ing every rule and every authority and power" – he says that St. Paul is speaking of Christ's kingdom on earth. That is, a kingdom of faith in which Christ rules through the Word and not in a public and visible manner. It is like beholding the sun through a cloud; one sees the light but not the sun itself. In a like manner, Christ now rules undivided with the Father, and it is one and the same kingdom. After the clouds have passed however both light and sun are viewed simultane-ously in one and the same object. Christ's rule on earth consists in the fact that it is dark and hidden at present, or concealed and covered, comprehended entirely in faith and in the Word. One does not see any more of this rule than Baptism and the Sacrament, and all that is heard is the external Word – these, in other words, are the only power and might with which he rules and executes everything on earth.[448]

We might like to see, says Luther, Christ reign as an earthly king surrounded by external splendor and power, but he wishes now to reign quietly and invisibly in our hearts, solely through the Word. Through this Word he wants to protect and preserve us amid our weakness over and against the world's might and power. Yet this kingdom on earth is identical with the one which will later be in heaven, only now it is hidden and not open to view. A florin, for instance, in a purse is a genuine florin and remains such when I take it out and hold it in my hand; the difference is that it is no longer concealed. Christ will similarly take the treasure which is now veiled to us who know nothing of it except what we hear and believe and reveal it openly before the eyes of the whole world. But we do nonetheless truly posses this treasure. The point in this is that it all happens in faith alone through Word and Sacrament. Here we believe and do not doubt that we are God's children, that he is our king who reigns over us and protects us against all enemies and frees us from every need, even though we do not see this but rather feel the reverse. That is, sin weighs us down, the devil terrifies and torments us, death kills us, the world persecutes us, and everything overwhelms and oppresses us. Today the order needs to be that we believe and not see i.e., not to perceive

---

[448] WA XXXVI 569.18–28.

Christ's rule with the five senses like an earthly king, but to disregard these and give ear solely to what God's Word tells us until the hour comes when Christ will present himself publicly in his majesty and sovereignty. Then we will see what we now believe and life with God will be manifest, before our view, as an uncovered treasure such as we now yearn for and look forward to.[449]

Importantly, Luther claims here that when St. Paul says Christ will deliver the Kingdom to the Father he means to say that he will discontinue faith and the hidden essence, and present his own to God the Father and openly transfer us into the Kingdom – which he has already established and now administers daily – so that we will behold him clearly without veil and obscurity. When this happens it will no longer be called a kingdom of faith but a kingdom of clarity and manifest being. And though this is indeed the same kingdom, it is at present called the kingdom of Christ because God in his majesty is now hidden and has given all to Christ so that he may bring us to himself through his Word and Baptism. God has hidden himself in Jesus Christ so that we must now seek and acknowledge God only in him. But when Christ accomplishes all that he is to accomplish e.g., when death and sin are abolished, when he has brought us to behold the Father in divine majesty, and when we no longer need to administer his gospel, Baptism, and remission of sin, nor learn to recognize him, then will it truly be called God's kingdom.[450]

We need to take note of two key elements in his exegesis in order to widen our discussion on the faith/reason battle. (1) Faith takes on an almost eschatological overtone here. That is, the kingdom of faith is one that does not now have visible access (meaning through the senses) to God's majestic kingdom.[451] God rules solely through Word and Sacrament, and in that sense it must be considered hidden or concealed. In other words, the kingdom of faith is offset against the kingdom in which God will be uncovered and fully manifested. Thus in that sense faith is in things unseen and that which is yet to be.[452] (2) Because God's kingdom is concealed we feel that sin weighs us down, the devil terrifies us, the world persecutes us, and death eventually gets its way, but it is in this restricted

---

[449] WA XXXVI 569.29–39; 570.16–32.

[450] WA XXXVI 570.33–39; 571.15–29.

[451] These same elements are related in his *Galatians* commentary (1535) in which he states that, because Christ does not become visible to any of our senses, it is a great effort to cling firmly to the promise in the midst of trial and conflict. In fact, at such times Christ appears to have deserted us. See WA XL, i, 580.15–27; 581.9–10.

[452] Again, Luther's foundation for belief in a present and future kingdom rests on the fact that we possess reliable and sure eyewitness accounts of Christ's resurrection. Only on that basis can we lay claim to the forgiveness of sins and the future life.

sense that Luther urges us to believe in things unseen and even contradictory to what we see and feel with the senses. We can be sure that Christ will put an end to these miseries and present himself publicly and in majesty.

Luther's faith/reason relationship then can be properly said to revolve around the following struggle: the believer's fight to retain what little faith he possesses in the midst of a world that appears to discredit the Gospel's claim (a fight Luther often characterizes with *Isaiah* 42:3, "A bruised reed he will not break, and a smoldering wick he will not snuff out"). For we already have at least two strikes against us. One, the fact that reason cannot progress beyond judging and concluding in accordance with what it immediately sees, hears, and feels, with the result that we are often paralyzed by fear; and two, the fact that reason naturally creates and loves its own subtle ideas and argumentation in addition to what it reads in the Word. But in the face of this situation, faith must transcend such feeling and understanding and make its decision contrary to these and hold fast to whatever the Word submits (again, because Luther insists that theological knowledge must be derived *a posteriori* through scripture), for Christ must have more weight than all our feelings and highly valued ideas.[453] We have already made note of Luther's example concerning the resurrection, namely, that we are asked to believe it, but reason does no more than to observe the facts as they appear to the eye and concludes on that basis there is no truth to such an incredible claim. Or, when man feels his sin and fails to embrace the words of forgiveness through Christ, but rather examines his sin and relies on the Law and works he surely removes himself from the forgiveness which should have been apprehended through faith.[454] In other words, according to Luther, when you no longer accord the Word greater validity than your every feeling and seeing, then you can no longer be helped. These are articles of faith that are not based on human reason or wisdom (the reasons for which we have discussed in detail), and we should therefore judge solely by the Word regardless of how we feel, and say: It is true I feel God's wrath, the devil, death and hell, but the Word proclaims that I have a gracious God through Christ who is my Lord over the devil and all creatures. And it is also true that I and all other men will rot in the ground, but the Word informs me that I shall rise and live eternally. This is the knowledge and wisdom of faith which renders the wisdom of the world foolishness.[455] How do we know that Scripture speaks

---

[453] WA XXXVI 541.18–24.

[454] WA XXXVI 493.12–32.

[455] WA XXXVI 494.26–31; 495.3–14: "Si autem rationem et oculos tuos consulueris, diversum iudicabis. Vides enim multa in piis quae te offendunt, vides eos quandoque labi, peccare, infirmos esse in fide, iracundia, invidia et aliis malis affectibus laborare –: Ergo Eclessia non est sancta. Nego consequentiam. Si meam vel proximi personam inspicio, nunquam erit sancta. Si autem Christum,

of something beyond our own limited feeling and experience? Because, Luther continues, the Lord Jesus Christ has already been raised from the dead in order to prove that the message is real.[456] However, Luther flatly concedes that adhering to faith in the face of seeing the opposite of the promise sets the stage for an exhausting battle.[457]

Yet faith is not such a slight object as one might assume, but rather a valiant hero who holds to the Word. It is in fact so active and mighty that it tears heaven and earth apart and opens all graves in the twinkling of an eye, and if you remain with it you shall live eternally and become lord over all things, even though this faith is feeble and your feeling to the contrary strong. That is, you shall live eternally so long as you do not live according to your own ideas and reason but according to Scripture. For there is no other consolation than the promise found in the Word which says: "hörestu wol, das Christus fur dich aufferstanden und deine sunde und tod vertilget hat etc." We may feel differently, but that does not matter to God any more than it matters to a mother that her child is weak and scabby. Though it is weak and cannot help itself, so long as it rests on its mother's lap and in her arms it need not ever worry.[458] Accordingly, Luther claims that the victory of Christ is utterly certain and the defects thus do not lie in the fact itself, but in our own incredulity. It is difficult in other words for reason to believe such inestimable blessings, but must be grasped only by reason illumined by faith because it is faith alone which takes hold of Christ's merits for itself.[459]

Luther explains elsewhere that the sophists are unaware that faith is a change and renewal of the entire nature so that the ears, the eyes, and the heart hears, sees, and feels something very different from what others perceive. The reason for this is that faith is a vigorous and powerful thing; it is not idle contemplation, nor does it float on the heart like a goose on water. It is rather like water that has been heated and is now no longer cold but hot. In a similar manner, faith fashions a different mind and different attitude and thereby makes an altogether changed

---

Propiciatorem et Purgatorem Ecclesiae, inspicio, tota sancta est; hic enim peccata totius mundi sustulit." See WA XL, i, 445.12–18. Luther's Christo-centric position regarding the nature and reason for faith always remains clear.

[456] WA XXXVI 496.29–33: "Des sollen wir uns nu halten und trösten, ob wirs wol nicht so gewaltig gleuben, als wir solten, und nicht so starck wil ym herzen sich fülen lassen, wie wir gerne wolten, doch das wir uns nur daran halten und ymer treiben und nur nicht aus dem herzen lassen, Gleich wie wir das auch schwechlich gleuben, das wir durch Christum herrn sind uber welt und Teuffel, sondern viel mehr das widderspiel fülen, Aber des trösten wir uns, soviel wir können, das wir das Wort haben, welchs ist uber alle macht und weisheit." WA XXXVI 497.8–14.

[457] WA XXXVI 497.31–32.

[458] WA XXXVI 497.33–39; 498.3–30.

[459] WA XL, i, 444.22–24; 447.15–22.

human being. Faith on this account is an active, difficult, and powerful thing. Luther's meaning is clear as he explains that, while reason is prone to concern itself with things that are present, faith apprehends the things that are not present and, contrary to reason's suppositions, regards them as being present. This, says Luther, is why faith does not belong to all men as does the sense of hearing, for few believe. In fact it is the mark of the divine promises that they are in conflict with reason and thus difficult to accept. Because those of the devil are in agreement with reason, they are readily accepted without hesitation. Mohammed, for instance, promises those who keep his law a temporal kingdom and after this life physical pleasures; this the heart quickly accepts and firmly believes. The reason for such easy acceptance is the fact that reason is delighted by the lie i.e., delighted by the flattery and glorifying of its own virtues. But in so doing we do not kill the harmful tendencies of human reason; on the contrary, by turning inward in such a manner we give it life. In the notable instance of Abraham's command – "Go out from your country, from your kindred, and from your father's house to an unknown place; I shall be your God" – reason immediately draws back, for it considers it utterly stupid to forfeit those things that are present in order to strive after things that are not. It fears the possible dangers and flees in a search for security. In short, reason is captivated by counterfeit performances and empty outward appearances.[460]

This leads us to another notable feature of the combative nature of the faith/reason relation as Luther understands it, namely, that once the cogitations of reason combine with the Law, faith immediately loses its virginity. For nothing is more hostile to faith than the Law and reason, and they cannot be overcome without great effort and work; but we must overcome them if we are to be saved.[461] Thus when our conscience is terrified by the Law and is wrestling with the judgment of God, we are not to consult either reason or the Law, but rely only on the sweet message of forgiveness for our comfort:

---

[460] WA XLII 452.13–453.12. "Siquidem ratio non intelligit, quid fides et vera pietas sit, ideo negligit et contemnit eam et naturaliter afficitur superstitione et hypocrisi, id est, iustitia operum. Ea, quia maxime fulget et floret, potentissima Imperatrix est orbis terrarum." WA XL, i, 666.28–31.

[461] WA XL, i, 204.17–21. "Sed quando ad experientiam venit, tum invenis Evangelium rarum et e contra legem assiduum esse hospitem in conscientia. Ea enim est assueta legi et sensui peccati et illum sensum ratio etiam adiuvat." WA XL, i, 209.20–23.

Ibi omnino sic te geras, quasi nunquam de lege Dei quidquam audieris, sed ascendas in tenebras, ubi nec Lex nec ratio lucet, sed solum aenigma fidei quae certo statuat se salvari extra et ultra legem, in Christo. Ita ultra et supra lucem legis et rationis ducit nos Evangelium in tenebras fidei, ubi Lex et ratio nihil habent negotii.[462]

Godly people, Luther claims, do in fact experience how willing they are to hold to the Word in full faith when it is heard, and how willing they are to erase their opinions concerning the Law and their own righteousness. But in the midst of this, there exists a genuine struggle in the flesh that resists the Spirit with great force; reason and the flesh simply want to work together. The notion that one must observe the Law cannot be completely banished from us and will remain even in the hearts of the godly. Given this fact, there is a perpetual struggle in believers between the hearing of faith and the works of the Law because the conscience is always murmuring that it is too easy for salvation to be granted solely through the hearing with faith in the promise.[463] Our capacity to understand is limited and our faith weak, and this creates such a struggle that we cannot accept the gift when it is offered. But just let your conscience murmur, says Luther, and hold your ground until you conquer the "Oportet." As faith gradually increases that opinion about the righteousness of the Law will decrease – this however is not accomplished without a great battle.[464]

Conclusion

In light of these comments the underlying tension between faith and reason should now be apparent. Faith is in things unseen in the sense that believers do not immediately see God's kingdom as they do an earthly kingdom. The resurrection of the dead, the forgiveness of sins, in short the consolation of the gospel, seems to contradict our own limited experience – the only experience *immediately* accessible for the cogitations of reason. Reason, therefore, in the present face of death and an afflicted conscience concludes that the claims of the gospel are at

---

[462] WA XL, i, 204.21–27: "Itaque procul hic absit ratio, inimica fidei, quae in tentationibus peccati et mortis nititur non iustitia fidei seu Christiana, quia eam penitus ignorat, sed propria aut ad summum iustitia legis" (204.15–17).

[463] WA XL, i, 345.31–35; 346.13–15. "Eaque est generalis opinio rationis humanae in omnibus Sophistis et toto mundo de religione et iustitia, quod paretur operibus legis. Illam perniciosissimam opinionem nullo modo patitur sibi eximi ratio, quia non intelligit iustitiam fidei...Natura enim omnes sentiunt legem iustificare." WA XL, i, 477.12–27; 478.12.

[464] WA XL, i, 346.17–22.

best an ill contrived fairy-tale. What this amounts to is the fact that reason (and philosophy) follows only those things that are visible to the senses *at present*. And even though we do in fact have ample Apostolic eyewitness testimony concerning Christ's resurrection reason is driven, due to its inherently crippled nature, not only to pay attention primarily to what it perceives at the present time but also to get lost in its own subjective creativity. But Luther declares that if one is to live eternally, he must not live according to his own ideas and reason but according to Scripture. This is simply to reiterate what has been pointed out already; namely, that theological knowledge is obtained only *a posteriori* through Scripture and thus must be diligently adhered to when we feel the opposite of its promises.

His comparison between man's pre- and post-fall memory may add some clarification to this point. Very simply, he alludes to the fact that man's memory is no longer persistent.[465] In paradise, reason was naturally enlightened with a true knowledge of, and desire for, God. These qualities were an inherent part of Adam's make-up and therefore always present in his person. Due to the fact that they are no longer within fallen man, his memory of God's Word is not rigidly persistent in the face of immediate contrary circumstances. And though the gospel now brings about the restoration (somewhat) of that original image, it is a constant struggle to keep the sure knowledge of Christ's victorious resurrection at the forefront of our minds as it faces a world that appears to confute the gospel's claims. It is interesting that this element of his thought finds a strong corollary, according to Ozment, in the young Luther. He has noted that, when the intellective powers meditatively reside in the works of God, intellective activity is "remembering." He argues as follows:

> As Luther emphasizes, to forget the manifest past works of God *(praeterita exhibita)* is simultaneously to forfeit confidence and trust in the promised future works of God *(certitudo futurorum)*. Oriented neither to the past nor to the future works of God, oblivious to what God has done and promises to do, one's 'stability' in the present is threatened. For concurrent with the failure of memory is the failure of *intellectus* and *voluntas,* and vice versa...The works

---

[465] For example the following: "Quare imago Dei, ad quam Adam fuit conditus, fuit res longe praestantissima et nobilissima, cum scilicet nulla lepra peccati neque in ratione neque voluntate haesit. Sed et interiores et exteriores sensus omnes fuere mundissimi. Intellectus fuit purissimus, memoria optima, et voluntas sincerissima..." WA XLII 46.16–20. "Ad hunc modum incipit imago ista novae creaturae reparari per Euangelium in hac vita, sed non perficitur in hac vita. Cum autem perficietur in regno Patris, tunc erit voluntas vere libera et bona, mens vere erit illuminata et memoria constans." WA XLII 48.27–30.

of God exhibited in the past and promised in the future form the indispensable objective context in which a *substaculum vitae*, i.e., a 'place' in which the whole man can stand with assurance, is made possible.[466]

Significantly, the mature Luther firmly retains the substance of this throughout his later works, directing the memory – and therefore reason (or intellect) – towards Word and Sacrament for its grounding or stability. Without such a focus, reason necessarily moves freely and without compulsion within the *sub*jectivity of its own thinking. The resurrection is thus the pivotal objective content for reason to focus on according to Luther because it is that event alone that substantiates Christian belief. And he is just as adamant in these later years that the failure of the memory is also the failure of *intellectus* (or *ratio*) and *voluntas*.

In the midst of this struggle to keep the memory persistent, faith fashions a different mind and attitude, thereby completely changing the human being. Once again, reason is naturally delighted by the glory of its own virtues and actively seeks to keep them alive, while faith concentrates solely on God's Word; simultaneously slaying those destructive inward tendencies of reason and agreeing with God's pronouncement on mankind. This is what Luther means when he says that the blessings of the gospel must be grasped only by reason illumined by faith, because it is faith alone which reckons God just in his verdict, and it alone which takes hold of Christ. In this sense the believer must have a correct understanding and an intellect informed by faith, by which the mind is governed amid afflictions so that in the midst of evils it hopes for the things that faith has commanded and taught. Based on this Luther can say that faith is like dialectic, which conceives the idea of things that are to be believed.[467] This simply means, as we have pointed out, that faith kills reason's unreasonableness. For Luther, the victory of Christ is certain and the defects do not therefore lie in the facts themselves e.g., Christ's resurrection and his promise, but in man's own incredulity.

Luther phrases this another way by saying that because reason follows only those things that are visible, it must in this instance be killed in order to make room for the Word and faith. The unfortunate necessity of conflict is illustrated by Luther here because reason, in his view, cannot be killed in this way except through despair, mistrust, hatred, and murmuring against God. The eventual result of such struggle is that the heart, after everything external has been removed

[466] Steven E. Ozment, *Homo Spiritualis: A Comparative Study of the Anthropology of Johannes Tauler, Jean Gerson, and Martin Luther (1509–16) in the Context of Their Theological Thought* (Leiden, 1969) pp. 110–111.

[467] WA XL, ii, 28.9–14. Luther continues by saying that hope is like rhetoric, which develops, urges, persuades, and exhorts to steadiness, so that faith does not collapse in temptation but keeps the Word and holds firmly to it.

(in other words those things by which reason tends to form judgments), clings to and finds rest in the Word and Sacraments alone. These external means are truly blessed because they inhere in the Word and fasten our faith, and are the focal points by which God leads us through our sea of perils and trials to the port, just as the fish is pulled along by means of a hook.[468] Again, Luther's understanding of the Sacraments comes to the center as an absolutely essential element in the faith/reason relation. For it is there at Word and Sacrament that the battle against unbelief and doubt, produced by reason's false judgments, takes place: "Ego enim credo in Christum, quem non video, sed habeo eius Baptismum, Sacramentum altaris, consolationem per verbum et absolutionem. Atqui nihil video eorum, quae promittit: Imo sentio contrarium in carne? Ibi ergo luctandum est et pugnandum adversus diffidentiam et dubitationem."[469] According to Luther we are opposed by half of our very selves, that is, by reason and its powers. But just as God initially gives us faith through the Word so he exercises, increases, strengthens, and perfects it in us by that same Word. On this understanding Luther can affirm then that the supreme worship of God that man can offer, the Sabbath of Sabbaths, is to examine and hear the Word.[470]

---

[468] WA XXIII 263.4–5; XLIII 395.14–22. Heiko Oberman makes a suggestion along similar lines in the following: "The benefit of the eucharistic controversy cannot be overlooked. Faith in the Word of God is essential for overcoming the spiritual-psychological focus on the inwardness of pious communion. What makes this so significant is that the Enemy, an expert on the single soul, loves individualism. He can penetrate the psyche and control it. He can twist and cripple even the believing Christian so that, lost in introspection, he despairs of God and the world. But there is one thing the Devil cannot do: he cannot become really present flesh. The call of the words of institution liberates the Christian from the clutches of self-analysis." See *Luther: Man Between God and the Devil* (London; 1989) p. 243.

[469] WA XLIII 570.12–16.

[470] WA XL, i, 129.28–29; 130.14–17.

CHAPTER
TEN
─────

Faith, Logic, and Fideism:
Luther's Response

Concluding our survey of the faith/reason relation we will now assess Luther's relationship with the fideist tradition. Does Luther's faith/reason understanding fall within the fideist tradition, and, if not, where does his peculiar approach lead? Here we are asking the age old question, as formulated by Tertullian, "What has Athens to do with Jerusalem?" Would Luther in his later years answer this question with an unequivocal "nothing?" Or further, might he concede with Pascal, "The heart has its reasons which reason does not know," thereby implying that some people have to take steps to dull their reasoning faculties in order to be able to believe?[471] On the face of things it certainly seems as though he might.

Before we can accurately deal with this important issue it is necessary that we have some sort of a working definition of "fideism." Kai Nielsen, in his lucid article on the subject, provides in my opinion a core definition to which every fideist (despite their apparent differences in expression) will claim some sort of allegiance. To be a fideist, Nielsen claims, one generally believes that fundamental religious beliefs rest solely and completely on faith. Finite and sinful man cannot come to know God by the use of his unaided reason, and this implies for the fideist

───

[471] Michael Peterson, William Hasker, Bruce Reichenbach, David Basinger, *Reason and Religious Belief: An Introduction to the Philosophy of Religion* (New York, Oxford; 1991) p. 33–34. The authors of this text phrase the question as follows: Granted that we may have to make use of reason in understanding the faith, is it also true, in any sense, that having faith at all depends (or should depend) on having good reason to believe that one's faith is true? This is, according to these authors, the real core of the faith/reason problem.

the parallel assertion that belief and unbelief are intellectually on a par. Religious experience is therefore ambiguous as to the reality of its object, and the existence of God can never be established by empirical investigation or philosophical demonstration. God, according to this view, remains an utter mystery and a thorough scandal to the intellect i.e., intellectually speaking a belief in God is absurd. The believer can only trust that he is not "whistling in the dark" and not believing in something thoroughly illusory when he accepts the God revealed in Scripture as an ultimate reality. He must simply take the leap of faith without any intellectual assurance that he is leaping in the right direction.[472]

To help set the stage for our discussion, let us briefly note a few of Nielsen's criticisms of the fideist position. He points out that if the believer does not understand the utterances about God *at all* he cannot accept or reject them, for he literally would not understand *what* he is accepting or rejecting. If these utterances are in fact to be meaningful at all they must be intelligible to at least some men. But if we do not understand what "God" means or what it would be like for "There is a God" to be true or false, then to say that we accept God on faith is logically equivalent to saying we accept the assertion "There is an Irglig" on faith. That is, before we can make the leap, or before we can accept a claim on faith or refuse to accept it on faith, we must at least have some minimal understanding of *what* it is we are accepting or rejecting. It is apparent from this that faith cannot at this level be a way to understanding. "Faith cannot insure the meaningfulness of religious utterances; quite the contrary, faith presupposes that the discourse in question is itself meaningful (intelligible)."[473] And if the fideist still maintains that it is a *fact* that there is a God, that he created the world, that he loves us etc. – and it seems that if he indeed has a truly Christian theology he *must* hold to these propositions – then how can we meaningfully assert that they are statements of fact if we have no idea of what it would be like for such statements to be either true or false? It is generally accepted that in order for a sentence to serve as the

---

[472] Kai Nielsen, "Can Faith Validate God-Talk?" in *New Theology* (ed.) Martin E. Marty and Dean G. Peerman (New York, 1964), No. 1, p. 131–132.

[473] Nielsen, "Can Faith Validate God-Talk?" p. 135. "It is this last question [i.e., granting religious utterances are intelligible why should we accept them when we cannot establish their truth or even establish that they are probable?] that Pascal, Kierkegaard, and Barth wrestle with, while (in effect) assuming that there is no puzzle about the *meaning* of religious utterances. But it is just this logically prior question that disturbs contemporary philosophers when they think about religion, and to this question it would seem that fideism is no answer at all nor is it a way around the problem. We are, whether we like it or not, left with the crucial question: Are religious utterances intelligible, can we meaningfully assert or deny there is a God? This logically prior question remains a question of first importance in an examination and defense of religion" (p. 136).

vehicle for a factual assertion, we must be able to say what would count for the truth or falsity of this putative assertion. It must, in other words, have *that* much meaning (this of course includes scientific assertions).[474]

These and similar critiques are generally accepted by modern scholarship as betraying the logical illegitimacy of the fideist position. To be sure, the religious adherent cannot simply pass over these issues without severely begging the more logically central questions. But in dealing as such with the sixteenth century Luther, are we not in effect expecting him to address questions that were not part of the philosophical conversation of the day? I do not think so. The fact that modern emphases, for instance meaning, was not the issue in Luther's day does not free him from the damning criticisms of recent philosophers if he did in fact hold to a fideist position. And given the nature of much Luther scholarship one could easily get the impression that he was in line with such a tradition.[475] For does not Luther himself seem to make it clear that faith to some extent "slaughters" reason, in effect ultimately reducing his position to fideism? It may be obvious at this point that to answer the question decisively we need only elaborate on what has already been said throughout the present thesis. We will therefore digress somewhat to recap very briefly the significance of the position argued in preceding chapters, and then return to attempt to answer the question. (Note: For the sake of brevity, I will attempt to follow only the *logical* progression of Luther's thought, thereby filtering out other less relevant – to this particular question – issues.)

First, Luther's theory of knowledge is such that the external world is required for the origin of any concepts of a factual nature. In other words, something must be presented before the senses in order for a concept of that particular thing (whatever it may be) to exist. Or, to put it another way, a concept of a particular will not have any *factual* content unless there indeed exists – external to the mind – the object to which the concept properly refers. Concepts of a factual nature, and therefore factual understanding in general, depend on the external world (we noted roughly this same theory in Ockham's epistemology). And absolutely vital to our present inquiry is the fact that, for Luther, religious knowledge is in *no way* exempt from these constraints. In fact as we have noted in several places, some of his harshest words are directed against those who claim to have *direct* illumination and visions from God himself. In order for religious concepts to

---

[474] Nielsen, "Can Faith Validate God-Talk?" pp. 138, 143.

[475] See for one example (in addition to the works already mentioned) N. Arne Bendtz, "Faith and Knowledge in Luther's Theology" in *Reformation Studies: Essays in Honor of Roland H. Bainton* (Richmond, Virginia, 1962) ed. Franklin H. Littell, pp. 21–26. Bendtz states his aim as follows: "In spite of the fact that Luther often has been called an 'anti-intellectualist', it is the aim of this paper to show that Luther operates in his thinking both as a philosophical realist and as a religious fideist" (p. 21).

have any objective value for Luther they must be known according to the limitations of human comprehension (thus Luther's insistence that we obtain theological knowledge *a posteriori* through Scripture); any claim that entails the suspension of these human constraints is nothing more than a delusion of the devil or a dream produced by reason's fertile imagination.

So what is the status of reason's ability to know God according to Luther? Due to his epistemological demarcation between observation and speculation as means to knowledge, Luther did not in general accept the conclusions of natural theology as valid logical inferences. They do not strictly entail that God, let alone the Christian God, actually exists. Thus his departure from Aquinas is notable, in that St. Thomas saw a real interconnectedness of reality. As Ozment points out, the underlying metaphysical presupposition of Thomist epistemology is a conviction that real relations hold between God, the mind of man, and the world of finite things. That is, God, man, and the world are connected to one another by the structure of reality itself. "They related to one another like tendons to bones and muscles, not like a bride to a bridegroom or a friend to a friend; the relationship was organic, not covenantal." It was this assumption that provided the basis for Aquinas' *a posteriori* proofs for God's existence; "finite effects led necessarily to their origin, because they were really connected with it."[476] Because Luther did not accept this metaphysical interconnectedness of reality, he insisted that if there is to be genuine knowledge of God it must arise from a more concrete, objective source. That source, as we have repeated almost *ad nauseam,* is found in Christ and Christ alone. It is only at the lap of the Virgin and at the foot of the cross that we have a true picture of God's character from which to draw valid conclusions. The importance of this strong emphasis in his writings for the modern debate is the fact that Luther regarded Christ as the sole starting point for all assertions about the character and nature of God. *This is* God's self-revelation. Only from there can we progress to a genuine knowledge of the Father, that is, from the known to the unknown, not vice versa. Had God not chosen to condescend into the midst of human frailty we would simply have no epistemologically solid ground for belief in him.

---

[476] Steven Ozment, *The Age of Reform 1250–1550: An Intellectual and Religious History of Late Medieval and Reformation Europe* (New Haven and London, 1980) p. 54. See also Etienne Gilson, *History of Christian Philosophy in the Middle Ages* (London, 1955) pp. 368–372. Thus Aquinas can argue: "Ad tertium dicendum quod per effectus non proportionatos causæ non potest perfecta cognitio de causa haberi: sed tamen ex quocumque effectu manifeste nobis potest demonstrari causam esse, ut dictum est. Et sic ex effectibus Dei potest demonstrari Deum esse, licet per eos non perfecte possimus ipsum cognoscere secundum suam essentiam." *Summa Theologiæ,* Ia, 2, 3, in *St. Thomas Aquinas Summa Theologiæ,* vol. 2, *Existence and Nature of God* (New York and London, 1964) ed. Timothy McDermott p. 11.

But, of course, we must ask the obvious question, How do we know that Christ
is truly God? Is this not in itself a matter known only to faith? It must be said
that if it is known only to faith (whatever that may mean) then we are back to the
dilemma we detailed above and are, therefore, no closer to resolving the faith/
reason conflict. Given that, is there anything else, external to the proposition itself
which simply affirms God's presence in Jesus Christ, that might support the claim
to Christ's deity? Luther thought in fact there is, and his appeal to the historic
event of Christ's resurrection is of decisive importance in this regard. That one
event in effect provides the validation of his belief in God, for without the reality
of the empty tomb all theological discourse would prove irrelevant. He makes his
case very clear, as we have already seen, by stating that the proof for the validity
of Christian theology rests entirely upon, and flows directly from, Christ's historic
resurrection. It is this event that provides the proof for his earlier claims to deity
and thus the authority to forgive sins, etc. (again, Luther sees Christ's resurrection
as self-authenticating). Accordingly, for Luther St. Paul stakes everything on the
fact that Christ arose from the dead – this is the chief article of Christian doctrine[477] e.g., this one article forms the foundation, the *reason* and end of all other
articles in the Christian faith, and if it is removed then the entire faith falls to the
ground in pieces.[478] However, we may appropriately ask Luther at this point how
we, separated from the event by hundreds of years, can know that Christ truly rose
from the dead? Luther's reply to this is lucid and straightforward, and is simply
answered by an appeal to apostolic eyewitness testimony. Paul thus appropriately
cites his own experience and points to the eyewitness accounts of many people
still living concerning the resurrected Christ. Significantly, Luther declares in
this connection that it is the mark of a reasonable man to prove what he says not
only with words, but also with concrete examples both of himself and others.
Therefore, in Luther's view Paul's enumeration of eyewitnesses is a completely
reasonable procedure: Peter and the Twelve to whom Christ showed himself alive
so that they saw and heard him in his external physical body. He was then later
seen by more than five hundred people, many of whom are still alive and will
bear witness to the event. On the other hand, according to Luther, the factious
spirit will never be able to prove his story irrefutably with Scripture and then with
people who witnessed the events themselves. We may thus cheerfully defy his
account and challenge him to step forth and produce such proof.

Assuming then from our previous discussion that reason can know God in
Christ – indeed this seems to be the focal point for Luther's later distinction between the *Deus absconditus* and the *Deus revelatus* – how does this mesh with

[477] WA XXXVI 524.31–34.
[478] WA XXXVI 605.16–23.

his odd phraseology regarding reason's fatal opposition to faith? As the preceding chapter should have made clear, the nature of the antithesis between the two seems to reside in the fact that reason is hopelessly turned inward, and by this Luther not only means that it is captive to its own subjective speculation as to the nature of God, but also that its attention span often encompasses only that which is immediately present (primarily in the religious context). As a result it has a difficult time believing God's promise that these present hardships will be eradicated, and instead finds itself collapsing under the weight of sin, death, and the devil. Faith, by regarding God's Word as true and trustworthy, establishes a new attitude in the mind of man about Scriptural propositions of deliverance from sin and death. Faith is then that which, in the heat of battle with reason's presuppositions, clings steadfast to the historic event of Christ's death and resurrection, and appropriates the benefits of that victory in Word and Sacrament. Here, the benefits of Christ's death are distributed and the memory is trained to be persistent in hope. It is literally in this struggle between faith and fallen reason that a different mind and attitude is being fashioned – a struggle which slaughters reason's self-love and moves it towards an utter dependence on God's precious and life-giving words. Thus, so far, there is no epistemological gulf between faith and reason i.e., there is no dualism in Luther by which man knows some things by reason and others only by faith.

However, having established this, there is one other important element in this connection that needs to be touched upon. It concerns the fact that, according to Luther, faith is unequivocally a gift of God, mediated through the working of the Holy Spirit i.e., man cannot possess faith apart from the Spirit of God. So how does this important aspect of his thought relate to our suggestion above that reason is able, indeed *has* to be able, to know God in Christ? What is the relation between reason, faith, and the Holy Spirit?[479] Or, given the fact that reason can comprehend the propositions about God in Christ, why is the Holy Spirit required not only for the initial conception but also for the continuation of faith? Here we return to an aspect that we alluded to at the very beginning of the thesis, namely, Luther's close connection between man's fallen reason and his equally corrupt will. We might recall the oddity, at least from a modern standpoint, of his definition of "right reason" in that it consists of both a right knowledge of God *and* a right will toward God. Although in Luther's mind man generally has dominion over the creatures of the earth, he does not specifically have a free will in those

---

[479] "Nam ratio sine Spiritu sancto est simpliciter sine cognitione Dei." WA XLII 291.30.

matters that pertain to God.[480] Our will is extraordinarily depraved so that we do
not trust the mercy of God and do not fear God, but are unconcerned, disregard the
Word and the will of God, and follow the desire and the impulses of the flesh.[481]
This is in fact, according to Luther, the most serious loss, that man's will no longer
wants and does any of those things God wants and commands.[482] The loss is such
that our will makes a devil out of God and shudders at the mention of his name,
especially when it is troubled by his judgment. Just as reason is overwhelmed by
ignorance of many things, so the will has not only been confused but has been
turned away from, and is now an enemy of, God. It actually enjoys, says Luther,
rushing to evil.[483] (We have briefly mentioned that in speaking of this manifold
corruption Luther often subsumes his condemnations under the one word *ratio*.
He asks, for example, how a reason which hates God can be called sound, except
in a mundane sense? As for its attitude toward God it is full of ignorance and
detestation of his will.[484] This is shown in Adam and Eve as they soon obtained
a desire for what was forbidden by God and aspired to become obedient to the
devil.[485] In a similar fashion Luther condemns reason and will under the one
term "imagination," meaning that the very formation of man's thoughts is evil.
Man devises them with the utmost care and effort, selects, fashions, and regards
them as something highly profound.[486] Nevertheless, reason and will are restored
to some extent through faith, for we are beginning to know God and our will is
incited to praise, to thank, and to confess God.[487] Thus, *in this sense,* right reason
and a good will *is* faith in Christ.[488])

We have previously seen that Luther believes God has deposited his very wisdom in the words of Holy Scripture, and that, as of necessity, the Holy Spirit is
bound to and works only within its limits. Therefore, knowledge of our sin and
condemnation comes only through God's external Word, and that knowledge is
the beginning of our salvation. What Luther means by this is that it is only then
that we completely despair of ourselves and give to God alone the glory for our

[480]"Sed vere est sicut lutum in manu figuli, positus in mera potentia passiva, et non activa. Ibi enim
non eligimus, non facimus aliquid, sed eligimur, paramur, regeneramur, accipimus, sicut Iesaias dicit:
'Tu Figulus, nos lutum tuum." WA XLII 64.33–36.

[481] WA XLII 86.21–23.

[482] WA XLII 106.16–18.

[483] WA XLII 106.32–107.5.

[484] WA XLII 107.32–38.

[485] WA XLII 128.38–41.

[486] WA XLII 291.22–28; WA XLII 348.27–36.

[487] WA XLII 248.17–23.

[488] WA XL, i, 415.22–24.

righteousness. "Hoc cum in corde fixum est, magna pars fundamenti salutis nostrae est iacta." Thereafter we have the clear and firm assurance that God does not cast aside sinners e.g., those who recognize their sin and desire to come to their senses, who thirst for righteousness or the forgiveness of their sins through Christ.[489] So according to Luther's model, man cannot come to a true knowledge of God apart from the working of the Spirit because such "knowledge" consists in the fact that the sinner not only understands the propositions of Scripture, but *also* that he acknowledges God's pronouncements therein as true and just. This necessarily requires, due to Luther's anthropology, not only reason but also the will,[490] which is (due to sin) inherently and fundamentally opposed to God's Word. (We have already observed the reasons for this, namely, that reason and will are hopelessly turned inward and love above all else the self-created propositions of the imagination.) To counter this the Spirit must work through the Word to change man's attitude or mind concerning its sinful status before its creator. Luther regards this tranformation a change of man's entire nature in that he now bows humbly before God's judgment and finds hope and salvation in the wounds and suffering of Christ.

The importance of these points consists in the fact that Luther's understanding of "knowledge" in salvation entails more than just comprehending Scriptural propositions concerning Christ and the cross, and that more is nothing else than the phrase "for me." What this amounts to is that Luther's conception of faith involves personal appropriation in addition to historical knowledge – they simply cannot be separated. Yet this also means that Luther takes for granted the fact that the non-Christian can not only understand the propositions of Christianity, but also that he can be offered reasonable grounds for its central soteriological claims e.g., the historic resurrection.

Let us sum up our findings then as follows: It is untenable to place Luther within a camp that attempts to argue from effect to a Cause (Thomism). On the other hand, I think it is also quite clear that he cannot in any sense be defined as a fideist. Faith for Luther, at its very core, consists in proper knowledge of God's saving act in Christ towards mankind. But in order to know one has the right object of belief he has to be able to provide factual data and argumentation for his central claims, and these claims cannot involve internal logical contradictions; a set of conditions which according to Luther the major world religions cannot fulfill. Accordingly any religious claim failing these external conditions is to be regarded as nothing but a delusion or fantasy of the believer. There ultimately is one deciding factor between competing religious claims, and that is none other

---

[489] WA XLII 291.5–14.
[490] WA XL, ii, 27.14–16.

than the empty tomb, and Luther appeals to this frequently as reasonable grounds for Christianity's validity. It is my opinion that although Luther did not formerly develop an apologetic the weight of evidence suggests that he would be driven, due to reasons provided throughout this thesis, to utilize arguments based on the historical reliability of the eyewitness accounts concerning Christ's resurrection, proceeding only *from there* to a knowledge of God. Had the resurrection not actually occurred, as Luther often points out, Christianity would of necessity be conclusively falsified. The sharpness of his christological focus seems to be unparalleled in the middle ages, and in this sense it must be considered as a major thrust forward, not only in terms of its soteriological force but also in terms of its epistemological clarity. Here it seems for the first time that christology comes to the foreground in almost every issue in theology *and* philosophical theology, thereby providing an historical, and therefore falsifiable, defense of the Christian faith.

CHAPTER

ELEVEN

Conclusion

So far we have seen several key elements at work in Luther's understanding of reason which, viewed within the overall context of his thought, clear up much our bewilderment over his strange and often irrational sounding remarks. The illusion of irrationality in fact immediately begins to disintegrate as we examine his epistemology. This analysis reveals that he places himself well within an empiricist tradition concerning our knowledge of the external world, maintaining as he does that human beings are not born with factual knowledge, including knowledge of God. Factual knowledge obtains only by contact with the external world via the senses, in an *a posteriori* manner. It is evident that Luther implicitly accepts our knowledge of everyday events and objects as secure and doubt free, a position that importantly includes our knowledge of history – e.g., matters of these sorts are completely within the confines of human comprehension. Consequently, valid reasoning concerning matters of a factual nature is limited to that which originates from sense-perception. This is in contrast to those epistemological rationalists who hold that cognition is the criterion of truth, such that its judgments demand universal assent. Truth of a factual nature, in Luther's understanding, can only be known to be the truth by its connection to the empirical world.

It is interesting that Luther sees his epistemology as justified by the *Genesis* passages on Paradise and the Fall, and it becomes apparent from his particular exegesis that his empiricism is consonant with, even *necessitated by*, the notion of original sin. That is, before the Fall it could be said that man had innate knowledge of the cosmos and its Creator, and that reason therefore had the raw knowledge from which to draw valid inferences. The reality of the Fall however is that men have completely lost any immediate, internal, knowledge of either the external world or of God. Sin has thus brought on the awful situation that man is now forced to *learn* about the world, God, and himself through that which is external to his own mind. The obvious result of reason's fallen state is that knowledge itself is severely limited (in comparison to man's state in Paradise), which automatically entails the fact that reason's capabilities of inference are equally restricted. Luther's epistemological position should thus not be seen primarily as a positive statement regarding the origins of knowledge, but rather as a position necessitated by man's expulsion from Paradise i.e., as a result of evil.[491] Thus his high view of reason's original state consistently becomes the measuring rod by which he criticizes its fallen state.

As it turns out his criticisms are almost entirely directed toward reason's pure rationalizations concerning the articles of religion, a position not the least unreasonable given his epistemology. If the external world is requisite to form concepts of a factual nature, how are we to conceive God, or even know there is a God, without some similar external source of information? Certainly, as Luther repeatedly points out, the only thing one can demonstrate from the reasoning of the philosophers concerning religion and metaphysics is their widespread disagreement. It therefore seemed to him impossible to classify such speculative "thinking" as genuine knowledge at all. And as much as he had reacted against the view that reason is virtually limitless in power, he would doubtless – for the exact same reasons – have protested with equal vehemence against the view soon to emerge in the so-called Enlightenment (especially its reduction of Christianity to ethics by necessity of the universal laws of reason). Its particular elevation of reason to the position of omnicompetent[492] would have been a direct affront to Luther's philosophical sense, being as it is almost completely devoid of any realistic efforts to understand the nature and potential limits of reason. I think it can be safely said that, unlike Luther, many of those who both preceded and followed him took little or no pains at all in asking the basic question of what reason actually is.[493] He was certainly no antagonist to reason *per se* by asking these critical and necessary questions.

In addition to the above epistemological limitations, Luther envisaged another serious detriment to the proper functioning of reason involving the corrupt will.

---

[491] As a side note it is interesting that there would soon be, after Luther's death, nothing more distasteful than the whole notion of original sin to the epistemological rationalists of the Enlightenment. Reason in this period is seen as virtually limitless in its scope of significance. See Alister E. McGrath "Enlightenment" in his (ed.) *The Blackwell Encyclopedia of Modern Christian Thought* (Basil Blackwell, Oxford, 1993) p. 154. See also Hugh Ross Mackintosh, *Types of Modern Theology* (London, 1937) p. 16.

[492] McGrath, "Enlightenment" p. 152.

[493] Mackintosh, *Types of Modern Theology* pp. 16–17.

The problem consists in the fact that reason is commonly unwilling to seek an objective source before making its conclusions about the character of God, and instead is driven to speculation via its own rationalizations and imagination, with the result that it creates its own premises from which to draw its inferences. And because reason values these ideas so highly, it becomes difficult for it to subject them to the scrutiny of a source that could endanger their viability. According to Luther, in other words, a love for our own presuppositions is often the greatest hindrance to reaching reasonable conclusions. (Thus Luther's condemnation of the whole man, reason and will, with the one word *ratio*.) It is not the case therefore in Luther's view that we are simply unable to reason properly: it is more accurate to say that we are often unwilling to take the time and effort to learn about God and subject our thoughts to the scrutiny of his revealed Word. Faith is, on this account, precisely that which subjects the unreasonableness of the human mind to the revealed Word of God: it is the faculty that bows before its creator and simply cries out, "Thou art my beloved Lord and Master, I am thy disciple."

If I am correct in my evaluation, Luther has an entirely legitimate view of reason from an epistemological point of view. His reasoning is determined by his epistemology, with the result that a *reasonable* argument is only one that proceeds from well-established fact, and any reversal of this procedure is tantamount to arguing from groundless premises. This is, for instance, exactly why he rejects astrology as a genuine body of knowledge; there are no empirical grounds for its over-generalized assertions. The same criticism can be leveled against the various world religions, as they all present views about the nature of God which cannot in principle be brought under empirical examination. In the case of the Christian religion, on the other hand, Luther is utterly convinced that it has the empirical support of eyewitnesses concerning the very Word of life. The resurrection constitutes the foremost proof of his claim to deity and thereby the ground for all Christian discourse. If those reports are substantially defective then everything the church has taught throughout the centuries is nothing more than a dream. In terms then of the purely logical grounding of Luther's faith, his theological system cannot be said to flow from propositions based in metaphysics. All theology flows rather from the historic event of Christ's resurrection. As pointed out in the last chapter, it is upon this foundation that we can unequivocally deny the charge that Luther's understanding of the faith/reason relation is fideist in nature: the centrality of the incarnation in other words eliminates the viability of that position.[494]

---

[494]To anticipate the next chapter somewhat, this point betrays a crucial weakness in Gerrish's model – despite his remarks to the contrary– in that it seems by its very nature to imply that Luther sees no real bridge from ordinary human comprehension to knowledge of God.

These important aspects of Luther's thought are, in my opinion, the same ones that preclude the assertion that he held to a "double-truth" theory so often connected with later nominalism. Though his remarks in, for instance, *Die Disputation de sententia: Verbum caro factum est (Joh. 1, 14)* may give the surface impression of such a theory, a close examination of both this disputation and his overall thought reveals that Luther did *not* believe knowledge gained by observation is in contradiction to that found in Scripture. This can be illustrated from his epistemology and his critique of natural theology. Concerning these general issues he maintained that knowledge of God cannot be properly deduced from premises based on the workings of nature without overstepping the rules which govern proper logical discourse i.e., it is an illegitimate move to infer from the abstractions of nature a knowledge of God; properly speaking, there are no logical grounds for that type of inference. Although his skepticism of natural theology could in principle lead one to adopt a double-truth theory (as doubtless it sometimes did in the medieval tradition), for Luther it actually highlights the necessity of the incarnate Christ. If knowledge of God is to be obtained at all it has to come from the incarnation, and Luther's later development of the two natures and the historical orientation of the resurrection suggests that he believed knowledge of this sort was possible on objective, historical grounds, meeting the requirements for genuine knowledge as he understood it. Needless to say, this also precludes the assertion that there exists an insurmountable gulf between knowledge of facts and knowledge obtained only through faith. I think this is generally the approach he was attempting to forge in his 1539 disputation on *John 1:14,* although it must be admitted that he was still arguing to a large extent within the confines of certain medieval dilemmas e.g., the apparent logical illegitimacy in the proposition that God is man. It is however the overall tenor of Luther's thought that surpassed these and other related philosophical dilemmas of his time. At any rate, had Luther affirmed a double-truth theory it would be difficult to understand why he so frequently switches the focus to the problematic nature of language and its relation to logic.

It is interesting that his assessment of language is very closely related to his assessment of reason. On his account, the purpose of language is to communicate or "fit" the facts as best it can, and we should therefore strive to keep our use of it within those measurable objectives.[495] Language and logic are inseparably

---

[495] This trend may also be seen in keeping with the nominalist tradition. Oberman observes that in Ruprecht Paque's analysis of the origins of nominalism he – although still too much in the tradition of the German *via antiqua* – finds the modernity of nominalism in the view of language as 'nachträgliches Zeichensystem für schon fertig vorliegende und verstandene Realitäten'. See Heiko Oberman "The Shape of Late Medieval Thought" in *The Pursuit of Holiness in Late Medieval and Renaissance Religion* (Leiden, 1974) edited by Charles Trinkaus and Heiko Oberman p. 14, n. 1.

bound together inasmuch as logical relations obtain only within and between propositions of thought, speech, or writing. But the fact that human language is limited in the way it expresses reality, demonstrates to some extent that the way in which we use it can itself be one of the foremost contributors to many of our philosophical dilemmas. Luther, to a certain extent, attempted to point out some of those problems by noting that his opponents were utilizing syllogisms with terms inadequately dissimilar to their respective subjects e.g., terms within the major and minor premises. These various factors suggest that his remarks, so often a point of controversy, to the effect that we must create a new language for theological use must not be taken to mean that we can redefine words at whim, but that these words should fit the facts at hand as best they can. In the case of God – the subject matter of theology – they should accurately reflect Scriptural mandate, the only source for such knowledge.

To conclude we should ask the inevitable question, Has Luther not at least been over-enthusiastic and possibly over-generalizing in his condemnations of reason? Here we could possibly present two more objections. On the one hand, we could say that his criticisms of reason are themselves nonsensical. But given the above analysis – not to mention a few striking similarities between Luther's core position and various modern approaches – I do not think that we can say his reservations concerning reason's scope of significance are *un*reasonable. One may not like his characterizations of reason's unchallenged presuppositions e.g., his inflammatory language, but his overall position is, in my estimation, clear. What one *can* on the other hand justifiably say in criticism of Luther is that he failed to provide us with a more systematic analysis of the philosophical issues latent in his conception of reason. Unfortunately, all we get (like many other aspects of his thought) is snippets here and there, but no detailed assessment as can be found in many of his predecessors. This lack of systematization creates a good deal of frustration for those attempting to understand his position. However, though these criticisms may be justified, it is important to keep in mind that Luther's writings were significantly determined by the ever present threat of losing the rediscovered gospel, and it was therefore necessary to concentrate his efforts defending that message rather than on a reworking of philosophical theology. What may in fact be more beneficial than criticizing Luther on the above points is to reconsider his overall contributions to the history of Christian philosophy and how that influenced later methods of theologizing. In so doing we may find that Luther's contributions, especially in philosophical theology, are more significant than once thought. (It is curious, for instance, that Luther is either passed over in historical examinations of the philosophy of religion or, more frequently, completely misunderstood.) And we may also find that he speaks directly to our present day dilemmas concerning the relation of reason and science to Christian faith.

Doubtless some of my own conclusions will need to be amended as these philosophical aspects of his thinking receive more attention. To be specific, additional work needs to be completed in the area of Luther's theory of language and its relation to logic. Questions such as, How exactly do theological terms succeed in meaning and how is that different, if at all, from the way our everyday terms (e.g., chairs and tables) succeed in meaning? and, How closely is a term's meaning related to its reference? should be examined in some detail. Though these issues may seem modern they are nonetheless central, and their clarification would go a great distance in answering both the question of Luther's relation to his forerunners and his relevance to the modern age.[496]

Having given my own general conclusions we are finally at an appropriate place to examine the secondary literature on the subject. As stated at the beginning, we have delayed a detailed critique of these sources until the position of the present thesis was laid out in full. Now that we have done so, my critique of other attempts will be easily understood.

---

[496] One particular issue that would be interesting to examine is Luther's various comments, especially those in his 1539 disputation on *John 1:14*, regarding what may be viewed as a proposal for a many-leveled logic and its similarity to some of the approaches put forth in this century. Obviously, the positions would differ in many respects, but the similarities may be just as informative.

PART FOUR

Secondary Literature: Another Look

CHAPTER TWELVE

Gerrish's Thesis Revisited

Earlier on we pointed out that one cannot properly due justice to "reason," with all of its implications, without dealing first with epistemology and logic. Given that, it is not just a little bewildering that we find no extended treatment of these essential aspects within Gerrish's evaluation of Luther, or for that fact within any of the other works that have dealt with this subject. Clearly, it is not sufficient to pass them over by simply asserting, as Gerrish does, that Luther subordinates the epistemological question to the soteriological. As we have already shown, this is tantamount to collapsing two distinct, equally important, questions. The question that must be asked is, What is Luther's *implicit* epistemology (subordinate or not)? Only then should we ask if Luther in fact subordinated the epistemological question to the soteriological. They are, in short, completely different questions. So before we go on to critique what Gerrish actually does say, we need to highlight the fact that his thesis is flawed from the outset, failing as he does to take the above issues seriously.

Now to what he does suggest. Perhaps the most important and telling aspect of his thesis is his proposed governing framework for interpreting Luther's remarks. The framework is highly important because it virtually determines his overall approach and findings. It consists of, I will argue, an improper elevation of Luther's two kingdom theory and the forgiveness of sins. He phrases it as follows:

> ...it would be a serious failure should the scholar overlook the fact that organizing principles really are there in Luther's thinking, which often explain apparent inconsistencies and show how the great variety of his theological ideas are bound together. In particular, recent Luther-research has stressed the manner in which the entire structure of the Reformer's theology is determined by the

doctrine of the 'two-kingdoms' and of the forgiveness of sins. It is these two fundamental conceptions which give Luther's thinking such inner harmony as it has, and it is these same two conceptions that bring order into his apparently incompatible utterances on reason.[497]

This framework brings him to the odd position that Luther's attitude towards reason rests upon a "fundamental dualism" between the Kingdom of Christ and the Kingdom of the World.[498] "Reason," he says, "is properly exercised within the limits of the *regnum mundi,* and must not presume to trespass upon the *regnum Christi.*"[499] As such it would seem that the kingdoms are simply not to be mingled. In fact, he adds that reason is so tied down to its own sphere of activity that it has no perception of spiritual matters, as the religious dimension lies beyond its reach.[500] One of the outcomes of this view is his perplexing, *un*-Lutheran, distinction between reason and what he calls "realm of the spirit."[501] Since reason belongs to the flesh it cannot be the instrument of translating man into the realm of the spirit. The spiritual world, in other words, is "wholly incommensurate"

---

[497] Brian A. Gerrish, *Grace and Reason* (Oxford, 1962) p. 8.

[498] Gerrish makes this clear in several places: "One thing is certain: many of the time-honored lines of criticism are beside the point. It is not sufficient to say, 'Luther was an irrationalist: he attacked reason', and leave it at that. One must stop to inquire *why* he attacked reason, *in what respects* he attacked reason, and *what he meant* by 'reason'. And a careful scrutiny of the sources makes it plain that the crucial issue concerns Luther's fundamental dualism" (p. 25). In his chapter "Luther's Attitude Towards Philosophy" he states the same: "Basically, the conclusions to our separate discussions of reason, philosophy, and Aristotle are the same. The ambivalence of Luther's attitude towards all three is to be explained by reference to his dualism of an Earthly Kingdom, on the one hand, and a Heavenly Kingdom, on the other" (p. 41). See also p. 119.

[499] Gerrish, *Grace and Reason* p. 69.

[500] Gerrish, *Grace and Reason* pp. 71–72.

[501] Montgomery's remarks to this effect are instructive: "Luther very definitely distinguished two kingdoms, the earthly and the spiritual, and in fact considered this distinction to be one of the most valuable aspects of his theology. But does this distinction dichotomize the world into a secular realm where reason and proof operate, and a spiritual realm where evidence has no place? This is precisely the impression given by virtually all modern interpreters of Luther. Especially revealing is Robert Fischer's declaration that for Luther 'such insights ['reason, experience, common sense'] operate in what would later be called the phenomenal realm; they do not penetrate the noumenal'. The use of the terms 'noumenal' and 'phenomenal' (borrowed from the Kantian critical philosophy, which is itself dependent upon a Platonic separation of the realm of 'ideas' or 'ideals' from the phenomenal world of sense experience) is most significant: Luther is painlessly being absorbed into the idealistic-dualistic frame of reference characteristic of virtually all contemporary Protestant thought." See John Warwick Montgomery, "Lutheranism and the Defense of the Christian Faith," *Lutheran Synod Quarterly* vol. 11, no. 1, Special Issue (Fall, 1970) p. 25. Montgomery refers to Fischer's article "A Reasonable Luther," in *Reformation Studies: Essays in Honor of Roland H. Bainton* ed. F. H. Littell (Richmond, Va., 1962) p. 39.

with the powers of natural reason.[502] Unless I have failed to understand Gerrish at this point, it seems that this entails the assertion that the two-kingdoms are *epistemologically* incommensurate, a position consonant with a Platonic dualism. If my analysis however is correct, the view that Gerrish presents is precisely what Luther uncompromisingly rejects. Luther sharply condemns any investigation into the spiritual realm not only because it is epistemologically problematic, but also because it is spiritual suicide. The very fact that the religious dimension (or the "Spiritual Kingdom") lies beyond the reach of reason is exactly why Luther un-ambiguously and incessantly forces us back to God's *visible* self-revelation, the incarnation.[503] One wonders how – if at all – Luther's christology, so central to his thinking, fits in with Gerrish's dualistic picture. That is, does not his thesis inevitably have the effect of transferring Luther's christology to a mere second-ary status? Although Gerrish would probably deny this consequence, as he does recognize that knowledge of God is found in Christ alone, I fail to see how his framework does not force Luther into a schizophrenic position. According to his position Luther would have to, in principle, simultaneously deny any contact between the earthly and heavenly realms yet affirm that we have a secure source of knowledge in the historic Christ. Such a position seems to me to be difficult to maintain.

This particular problem is perhaps the most crucial defect in Gerrish's work. I think it has been adequately shown that Luther's christological emphasis must take logical precedence over other, less central, notions. Montgomery has ac-curately pointed out that the incarnate Christ is the connection between the two kingdoms and is, therefore, he who *links* the two realms epistemologically in Luther's thought. But this also means that the incarnation eliminates any theologi-cal schizophrenia, as it offers a genuine bridge from ordinary human experience to the divine truth of God's revelation.[504] Luther insists that it was provided, not

---

[502] Gerrish, *Grace and Reason* pp. 71–72.

[503] David Steinmetz makes a similar observation regarding Luther's contention with Zwingli: "Luther, however, is suspicious of what he considers to be an excessive spiritualizing tendency on Zwingli's part. Christianity, after all, is not a Gnostic religion. It is a historical religion which stresses the activ-ity of God in time and space. The central message of the New Testament in Luther's view is that God has assumed humanity in Jesus of Nazareth; he has identified himself with the fragile elements of the earth. Christianity glories in a God found in dust. Therefore, for Luther a realistic understanding of the incarnation and a realistic doctrine of the eucharist imply and demand each other. A theology which seeks refuge in the calm and unverifiable realm of the spirit, which appeals too quickly to sign, symbol, sage, myth, and legend, is a theology which is unwilling to face the utter humiliation of God in the eucharist." See *Luther in Context* (Bloomington, 1986) p. 82.

[504] "The incarnational center of Luther's theology eliminates entirely the possibility of making him an advocate of the "two-fold truth" – a kind of 16th century Averroes. In the sharpest possible opposition to Platonic dualism – and to the related modern dichotomies of Kantianism and of Lessing's ditch

only for our redemption, but also in order that we may have an empirical, *non-speculative,* source for our knowledge of God. In his view, as we have pointed out, we are not to rise and know God "spiritually" at all, but are to approach him at the bottom rung of the ladder where he has "condescended to speak with us in human fashion." In other words, God has graciously met our epistemological and soteriological needs in the incarnation, a pivotal event which for Luther is nothing less than his real entrance into human history. It is precisely *because* reason is so tied down to its particular sphere of competence (to use Gerrish's phraseology) that the incarnation is so central to Luther's view of reason. Christ is that epistemological point of contact with the incomprehensible God.

Given Gerrish's dualism it is not surprising that he thinks Luther subordinates the epistemological question to the soteriological.[505] Luther on his account brings reason in direct relation to the forgiveness of sins. In its arrogance reason devises a host of religious exercises in the expectation of making itself acceptable to God. Accordingly, Gerrish claims that even when Luther speaks of speculation he is merely utilizing another expression to state the same thing. "Here is the focus of his interest in reason, and it is this which provides us with the key for understanding his violent censure."[506] Again, "this is the heart of Luther's criticism, reason's attitude is essentially arrogance. This single charge sums up the whole of Luther's indictment."[507] Such an egotistic religion, he states, expresses itself in legalism.[508] The necessary outcome of all of this is his decisive assertion that Luther's critique of reason is "theological through and through." "'Faith' and 'reason' stand, so we have maintained, for two different types of religiousness, two different ways of *salvation;* and 'rationality' (if we dare use so vague a term) is not more characteristic of the one type than the other."[509] Gerrish claims that reason is seen by Luther as a threat to *sola gratia,* and *faith* must not, therefore, be the antithesis of reason; rather, his notion of *grace* must be the essence of the

---

between historical fact and absolute truth – Luther declares that Jesus Christ, in His own person, offers immediate access to the Divine. One begins with the earthly and finds the heavenly." See Montgomery, "Lutheranism and the Defense of the Christian Faith" pp. 25–26.

[505] Gerrish, *Grace and Reason* p. 55.

[506] Gerrish, *Grace and Reason* p. 82–83.

[507] Gerrish, *Grace and Reason* p. 103. "Again we must say that the sum of Luther's objections lies in the charge of pride or arrogance. Like Paul, Luther contrasts faith with that 'boasting' which is invariably an accompaniment of all attempts to earn salvation by good works. Reason's religion of works is symptomatic of that fundamental self-love which leads a man into the blasphemy of seeking his own even in God and of imagining that any merely human goodness can be perfect enough to put God in his debt" (p. 107).

[508] Gerrish, *Grace and Reason* p. 110.

[509] Gerrish, *Grace and Reason* p. 135 (emphasis mine).

antithesis. Gerrish's position at this point, however plausible it may sound, in reality both begs the question of epistemology and improperly elevates Luther's connection between man's arrogance and his reason. Luther's criticism of reason, as we have clearly shown, is not in fact distinctly theological at all. It is rather, in its essence, an epistemological critique of reason's limitations:[510] arrogance in and of itself should thus not be over-emphasized.

Gerrish also makes ambiguous the precise relation between faith and reason. He suggests, for instance, that Luther probably follows Ockham in drawing a sharp division between the two spheres (i.e., faith and reason). However, we have already observed two flaws in this notion. First and foremost, his characterizations of Ockham are misleading. For one, the thesis that Ockham's epistemology is "pessimistic, sceptical, destructive"[511] is now generally regarded as false. So Gerrish's statement that Luther was positively influenced by an epistemologically destructive view is simply incorrect. Second, and equally important, even if Ockham did hold a sharp division between what can be known by natural reason and what can be known only by faith, it has become clear that Luther's apparent antithesis is not epistemological in nature – indeed the nature of his later christology precludes that assertion. I think it is more accurate to say that the nature of the tension between faith and reason as Gerrish perceives it is perhaps more a product of his own methodology than Luther's. This is evident when he states, for one example, that reason is not the appropriate "organ" of knowledge in the Spiritual Kingdom. If by organ he means "source" I can concur. However, it is apparent that he actually does mean to say that faith is a distinct organ of knowledge. "It is faith, not reason, that receives the Word. The distinction between the two spheres of knowledge, with its accompanying distinction between two organs of knowing, is rigidly maintained."[512] If there really is an incommensurability between the two kingdoms as he seems to suggest then he is, in a sense, forced to say that faith is

---

[510] As we have detailed, Luther rejects epistemological rationalism and what he sees as an illegitimate use of deductive reasoning as forcefully as he rejects works-righteousness. He critiques on epistemological grounds, for instance, his opponents' reasoning on the real presence and their corresponding misunderstanding of the Personal union.

[511] Gerrish, *Grace and Reason* p. 55.

[512] Gerrish, *Grace and Reason* p. 20. I am not quite sure in this connection how the above statement meshes with the following: "For Luther's concern was with *justifying* faith – faith, not as a mode of cognition, but as the *organon leptikon* of salvation" (p. 58). How exactly does 'mode of cognition' differ from 'organ of knowing'? This is, it must be said, one of the features of Gerrish's study that perplexes me i.e., his lack of precision with philosophical and theological terminology. At any rate, I do not think that the confusion comes from Luther.

somehow a distinct organ of knowledge. But I think we have shown that Luther does not view the faith/reason problem from this strange dualistic perspective. Again, Luther's christology eliminates faith operating epistemologically.

Another example of Gerrish's ambiguity concerns the way in which he oscillates on the notion of reason's subordination. While at times he identifies reason and faith as virtually the same in the believer,[513] his claim elsewhere e.g., that reason may be of service in spiritual matters provided it is kept "subordinate" to faith and is first illuminated by the Holy Spirit, makes their precise relationship unclear.[514] It must be said that Luther does not generally focus on reason being subordinate to faith *itself* at all;[515] rather, it is clear that he demands that reason should be taken captive to the *object* of faith, Christ. But again, I think that Gerrish's failure to analyze properly the issue of reason precludes any precision as to the nature of Luther's position on the faith/reason relation. It is difficult, in other words, to see how one can properly understand the latter without a clear understanding of the former.

Finally, Gerrish is highly ambiguous about the nature of faith as Luther understands it. He seems to overlook the fact that (as he also did concerning the notion of reason) the concept of faith is not in the least neutral. The particular nuances of "faith" seem to change from one author to the next. Yet Gerrish nowhere provides a systematic definition of it in conjunction with his treatment of reason (in fact, if I am right, he nowhere provides a systematic definition of reason).

---

[513] For instance the following: "Clearly, what has happened is that the notion of 'regenerate reason' tends to coalesce with the notion of 'faith' itself. This, doubtless, hardly makes for lucidity. For sometimes regenerate reason seems able to do anything faith could do; sometimes it is severely limited. In the Commentary on Galatians we will find passages where regenerate reason does the distinctive work of 'saving faith'; yet elsewhere Luther tells us that, even when illuminated, reason cannot understand the articles of faith (the Trinity and the Manhood of Christ), though it can sometimes understand the Ten Commandments and the religion of the Jews. For the most part, when Luther is not simply using 'regenerate reason' as another name for 'faith', he is thinking of it as the organ of orderly thought being exercised upon the matter provided by the Word" (p. 24). "The governing principle of conduct in the believer is no longer natural reason, but reason enlightened by faith. Faith virtually takes the place of reason: right reason in spiritual matters *is* faith." He continues on the next page: "Faith is, indeed, for Luther a mode of cognition – though not only this, nor even primarily...In the course of the comparison [between faith and hope] Luther affirms that faith is 'in the understanding' *(in intellectu);* that it is a kind of 'knowledge' *(notitia);* that its object is 'truth' *(veritatem);* that it is an 'instructor and judge' *(doctor et iudex);* and so on. Elsewhere he calls faith 'right thinking about God' *(recta cogitare de Deo).* And reason, he says, is wrong thinking" (see pp. 81–82).

[514] Gerrish, *Grace and Reason* p. 81.

[515] One problem in this connection is that Luther uses the term faith in different ways. Sometimes he simply means the personal appropriation of Christ's merits, while others he is referring to a body of doctrine.

To conclude, I can summarize my critique of Gerrish as follows: (1) He improperly employs the two kingdom theory as a guide to Luther's overall thought. (2) His governing framework creates a dualism that ultimately subordinates Luther's christology to a secondary position (regardless of his intent). Simply put, his artificial elevation of the two-kingdoms as his governing methodology weakens the impact of Luther's (logically prior) emphasis on Christ:[516] in effect this also eliminates Luther's notion of objectivity and with it his emphasis on certainty. According to the model presented in this thesis, the nature of Luther's christology necessarily precludes any epistemological separation between the two-kingdoms. Luther's christology thus bears all the marks of a well thought-out position – though perhaps lacking in formality – which adequately answers both the soteriological *and* epistemological question. (3) Perhaps the most obvious criticism I can offer is Gerrish's tendency to beg the more important implicit epistemological questions. One's position as to the extent of reason's abilities seems explicable only in terms of these wider philosophical questions. (4) A combination of an almost anti-epistemological stance and an improper elevation of the two-kingdoms forces the conclusion, in my opinion, that the faith is walled-off from any empirical justification. This means that within Gerrish's model, notwithstanding his attempt to absolve him, Luther is at *least* a fideist. Again, we have adequately demonstrated that he does not stand within the fideist tradition.

In light therefore of my analysis of Luther's position on epistemology, logic, and the centrality of his christology, I think it has been adequately shown that Gerrish's thesis has – as well as the other approaches that roughly agree with Gerrish – improperly elevated certain features of Luther's thought and effectively misrepresented his mature position. It has been my position throughout this thesis that Luther's christology is the fulcrum around which every other aspect of his thought revolves, and that very importantly includes the issue of reason. For Luther, the crucified God is the only remedy for fallen reason, a remedy that finds its concreteness in the Word and the visible means of grace.

---

[516] In addition to Ian Siggins' valuable remarks quoted in our Introduction, Marc Lienhard also states that – in contrast to his adversaries who were concerned primarily with the transcendence and immutability of God (thus making the incarnation secondary) – Luther held that the image we have of God is dictated by the incarnation and it is that which lies at the very basis of our knowledge of God. *Luther: Witness to Jesus Christ* (Minneapolis, 1982) p. 225.

Bibliography

Adams, Marilyn McCord. *William Ockham*. Indiana, 1987.

Althaus, Paul. *The Theology of Martin Luther*. Philadelphia, 1981.

Aquinas, St. Thomas. *Summa Theologiæ*. In St. Thomas Aquinas Summa Theologiæ. Vol. 2, Existence and Nature of God, ed. Timothy McDermott. New York and London, 1964.

Bendtz, N. Arne. "Faith and Knowledge in Luther's Theology." In *Reformation Studies:* Essays in Honor of Roland H. Bainton, ed. F. H. Littell, 21–29. Richmond, Va., 1962.

Bergvall, Ake. "Reason in Luther, Calvin, and Sidney." *The Sixteenth Century Journal* XXIII/1 (1992): 115–127.

Bielfeldt, Dennis. "Luther, Logic, and Language: An Inquiry into the Semantics of Theological Language in the Writings of Martin Luther." Ph.D. diss., University of Iowa, 1987.

Black, Max. *Models and Metaphors*. Ithaca, New York, 1962.

Blanshard, Brand. *Reason and Analysis*. London, 1962.

Boehner, Philotheus. *Collected Articles on Ockham*, ed. Eligius M. Buytaert. New York, 1958. — (ed.) *Ockham: Philosophical Writings*. Indianapolis, 1990.

Brecht, Martin. *Martin Luther: Shaping and Defining the Reformation 1521–1532*. Minneapolis, 1990. — *Martin Luther: The Preservation of the Church 1532–1546*. Minneapolis, 1993.

Brody, Baruch A., ed. *Readings in the Philosophy of Religion*. New Jersey, 1974.

Brown, Stephen F. "A Modern Prologue to Ockham's Natural Philosophy." *Sprache und Erkenntnis im Mittelalter* (Miscellanea Mediaevalia 13.1, ed. A. Zimmermann), (Berlin, 1981): 107–129.

Cairns, David. *The Image of God*. London and Glasgow, 1973.

Copleston, Frederick. *A History of Philosophy*. 8 vols. London, 1976.

Courtenay, William J. "Late Medieval Nominalism Revisited: 1972–1982." *Journal of the History of Ideas* XLIV (Philadelphia, 1983): 159–164. — "Nominalism and Late Medieval Religion." In *The Pursuit of Holiness in Late Medieval and Renaissance Religion: Papers from the University of Michigan*

Conference, eds. Charles Trinkaus and Heiko A. Oberman, 26–59. Leiden: Brill, 1974. — "Nominalism and Late Medieval Thought: A Bibliographical Essay." *Theological Studies 33* (Baltimore, Md., 1972): 716–734. — "The King and the Leaden Coin: The Economic Background of 'Sine qua non' Causality." *Traditio XXVIII* (New York, 1972): 185–209. — "Token Coinage and the Administration of Poor Relief during the Late Middle Ages." *The Journal of Interdisciplinary History III* (Cambridge, Mass., 1972): 275–295.

Cranz, F. Edward. "Cusanus, Luther and the Mystical Tradition." In *The Pursuit of Holiness in Late Medieval and Renaissance Religion*, eds. Charles Trinkaus and Heiko A. Oberman, 93–102. Leiden, 1974.

Cross, Richard. "*Alloiosis* in the Christology of Zwingli." *The Journal of Theological Studies* Vol. 47, Part 1 (April, 1996): 105–122.

Davis, Charles T. "Ockham and the Zeitgeist." In *The Pursuit of Holiness in Late Medieval and Renaissance Religion*, eds. Charles Trinkaus and Heiko A. Oberman, 59–65. Leiden, 1974.

Dillenberger, John. *Protestant Thought and Natural Science*. Westport, CT, 1960.

Ebeling, Gerhard. *Lutherstudien Band II: Disputatio de Homine*. Tübingen, 1977. — "Luther and the Beginning of the Modern Age." In *Luther and the Dawn of the Modern Era*, ed. Heiko A. Oberman, 11–39. Leiden, 1974.

Evans, G.R. *The Language and Logic of the Bible: The Earlier Middle Ages*. Cambridge, 1984. — *Problems of Authority in the Reformation Debates*. Cambridge, 1992.

Fischer, Robert. "A Reasonable Luther." In *Reformation Studies: Essays in Honor of Roland H. Bainton*, ed. F. H. Littell, 30–45. Richmond, Va., 1962.

Flew, Antony and Alasdair MacIntyre, eds. *New Essays in Philosophical Theology*. London, 1955.

Gerrish, Brian. *Grace and Reason*. Oxford, 1962. — "Martin Luther." In *The Encyclopedia of Philosophy*, vol. 5, 109–113. New York, 1967.

Gilson, Etienne. *History of Christian Philosophy in the Middle Ages*. London, 1955.

Glare, P. G. W. *Oxford Latin Dictionary*. Oxford, 1982.

Goddu, Andre. *The Physics of William of Ockham*. Leiden — Köln, 1984.

Hägglund, Bengt. *The background of Luther's Doctrine of Justification in Late Medieval Theology*. Philadelphia, 1971. — *Theologie und Philosophie bei Luther und in der Occamistischen Tradition*. Lund, 1955.

Harbison, E. Harris. *The Christian Scholar in the Age of the Reformation.* New York, 1956.

Hepburn, Ronald W. *Christianity and Paradox.* London, 1958.

Janz, Denis R. *Luther on Thomas Aquinas: The Angelic Doctor in the Thought of the Reformer.* Stuttgart, 1989.

Johnson, Wayne Gustave. "Martin Luther's Law-Gospel Distinction and Paul Tillich's Method of Correlation: A Study of Parallels." Ph.D. diss., University of Iowa, 1966.

Knowles, David. *The Evolution of Medieval Thought* 2d ed., eds. D. E. Luscombe and C. N. L. Brooke. London and New York, 1988.

Krumweide, Hans-Walter. "Martin Luther: Die Kompetenz der Vernunft." *Jahrbuch der Gesellschaft für Niedersächsische Kirchengeschichte* Vol. 83 (Blomberg, 1985): 55–74.

Leff, Gordon. *William of Ockham: The Metamorphosis of Scholastic Discourse.* Manchester, 1975.

Lewis, Charlton T. *A Latin Dictionary.* Oxford, 1879.

Lienhard, Marc. *Luther: Witness to Jesus Christ.* Minneapolis, 1982.

Lohse, Bernard. *Martin Luther: An Introduction to His Life and Work.* Edinburgh, 1987. — *Ratio und Fides.* Göttingen, 1958. — "Conscience and Authority in Luther." In *Luther and the Dawn of the Modern Era,* ed. Heiko A. Oberman, 158–183. Leiden, 1974.

Losee, John. *A Historical Introduction to the Philosophy of Science.* Oxford and New York, 1993.

MacKinnon, James. "Martin Luther." In *Encyclopædia Britannica,* vol. 14, 491–498. London, 1955.

Mackintosh, Hugh Ross. *The Doctrine of the Person of Jesus Christ.* Edinburgh, 1956. *Types of Modern Theology.* London, 1937.

Marius, Richard. *Martin Luther: The Christian Between God and Death.* Cambridge, MA, 1999.

McGrath, Alister E. *Intellectual Origins of the European Reformation.* Oxford, 1987. — *Iustitia Dei: A History of the Christian Doctrine of Justification.* 2 vols. Cambridge, 1986. — *Luther's Theology of the Cross.* Oxford, 1985. — *Reformation Thought: An Introduction.* Oxford, 1988. — "Enlightenment." In *The Blackwell Encyclopedia of Modern Christian Thought,* ed. Alister E. McGrath, 150–156. Oxford, 1993. — "Forerunners of the Reformation? A Critical Examination of the Evidence for Precursors of the Reformation Doctrines of Justification." *Harvard Theological Review* 75 (1982): 219–242.

— "The Anti-Pelagian Structure of 'Nominalist' Doctrines of Justification." *Ephemerides Theologicae Lovanienses* 57 (1981): 107–119. — "The Influence of Aristotelian Physics upon St. Thomas Aquinas' Discussion of the 'Processus Iustificationis'." *Recherches de theologie ancienne et medievale* 51 (1984): 223–229.

Montgomery, John Warwick. *In Defense of Martin Luther.* Milwaukee, 1970.

— "Lutheranism and the Defense of the Christian Faith." *Lutheran Synod Quarterly* vol. 11, No. 1, Special Issue (Fall, 1970): 1–39.

Mullally, Joseph P. *The Summulae Logicales of Peter of Spain.* Notre Dame, Indiana, 1945.

Nielson, Kai. "Can Faith Validate God-Talk?" In *New Theology,* eds. Martin E. Marty and Dean G. Peerman, 131–149. New York, 1964.

Nilsson, K. O. *Simul: Das Miteinander von Göttlichem und Menschlichem in Luthers Theologie.* Forschungen zur Kirchen und Dogmengeschichte 17. Göttingen, 1966.

Oberman, Heiko A. *The Harvest of Medieval Theology: Gabriel Biel and Late Medieval Nominalism.* Cambridge, Mass., 1963. — *Luther: Man Between God and the Devil.* London, 1989. — "Headwaters of the Reformation: Initia Lutheri — Initia Reformationis." In *Luther and the Dawn of the Modern Era,* ed. Heiko Oberman, 40–88. Leiden, 1974. — "The Shape of Late Medieval Thought: The Birthpangs of the Modern Era." In *The Pursuit of Holiness in Late Medieval and Renaissance Religion,* eds. Charles Trinkaus and Heiko A. Oberman, 3–25. Leiden, 1974.

Ockham, William. *Prologus in Expositionem super viii libros Physicorum,* ed. Philotheus Boehner, *Ockham: Philosophical Writings.* Indianapolis, 1990. — *Quaestiones in lib. I Physicorum,* ed. Philotheus Boehner, *Ockham: Philosophical Writings.* Indianapolis, 1990. — *Quodlibetal Questions,* trans. by Alfred J. Freddoso. 2 vols. New Haven and London, 1991.

Olsson, Herbert. *Schöpfung, Vernunft und Gesetz in Luthers Theologie.* Uppsala, 1971.

Ozment, Steven. *Age of Reform 1250–1550: An Intellectual and Religious History of Late Medieval and Reformation Europe.* New Haven and London, 1980. — *Homo spiritualis; A Comparative Study of the Anthropology of Johannes Tauler, Jean Gerson and Martin Luther (1509–1516) in the Context of Their Theological Thought.* Leiden, 1969. — "Mysticism, Nominalism and Dissent." In *The Pursuit of Holiness in Late Medieval and Renaissance Religion,* eds. Charles Trinkaus and Heiko A. Oberman, 67–92. Leiden, 1974.

Pannenberg, Wolfhart. *Basic Questions in Theology*, vol. 2. London, 1967.

Pelikan, Jaroslav. *The Growth of Medieval Theology (600–1300)*. Chicago and London, 1978. — *Reformation of Church and Dogma (1300–1700)*. Chicago and London, 1984.

Pelikan, Jaroslav and Helmut T. Lehmann. *Luther's Works: American Edition*. 55 vols. Saint Louis and Philadelphia, 1958–.

Peterson, Michael and William Hasker, Bruce Reichenbach, David Basinger. *Reason and Religious Belief: An Introduction to the Philosophy of Religion*. New York and Oxford, 1991.

Rosenbladt, Rod. "The Christology of Chemnitz and Contemporary English Philosophical Scepticism." Ph.D. diss., University of Strasbourg, 1980.

Rupp, Gordon. *Luther's Progress to the Diet of Worms*. London, 1951. — *Patterns of Reformation*. London, 1969. — *The Righteousness of God: Luther Studies*. London, 1953.

Sasse, Hermann. *This is My Body: Luther's Contention for the Real Presence in the Sacrament of the Altar*. Adelaide, S.A., 1977.

Schwiebert, Ernest G. *Luther and His Times: The Reformation From a New Perspective*. Saint Louis, 1950.

Siggins, Ian D. Kingston. *Luther*. New York, 1972. *Martin Luther's Doctrine of Christ*. New Haven and London, 1970.

Spade, Paul Vincent. *The Cambridge Companion to Ockham*. Cambridge, 1999.

Spitz, Lewis W. *The Renaissance and Reformation Movements*. St. Louis, 1971. — "Further Lines of Inquiry for the Study of 'Reformation and Pedagogy'." In *The Pursuit of Holiness in Late Medieval and Renaissance Religion*, eds. Charles Trinkaus and Heiko A. Oberman, 294–306. Leiden, 1974. — "Headwaters of the Reformation: Studia Humanitatis, Luther Senior, et Initia Reformationis." In *Luther and the Dawn of the Modern Era*, ed. Heiko A. Oberman, 89–116. Leiden, 1974.

Steinmetz, David C. *Luther in Context*. Bloomington, 1995. — *Luther and Staupitz: An Essay in the Intellectual Origins of the Protestant Reformation*. North Carolina, 1980. — *Misericordia Dei: The Theology of Johannes von Staupitz in its Late Medieval Setting*. Leiden, 1968. — "Luther and the Ascent of Jacob's Ladder." *Church History* 55 (1986): 179–192.

Strauss, Gerald. "Reformation and Pedagogy: Educational Thought and Practice in the Lutheran Reformation." In *The Pursuit of Holiness in Late Medieval and Renaissance Religion,* eds. Charles Trinkaus and Heiko A. Oberman, 272–293. Leiden, 1974.

Swinburne, Richard. *Faith and Reason.* Oxford, 1981.

Taylor, A. E. *Aristotle.* London and Edinburgh, 1919.

Waismann, Friedrich. "Verifiability." In *Logic and Language* 1st series, ed. A. G. N. Flew, 117–144. Oxford, 1963.

Warnock, G. J. "Reason." In *The Encyclopedia of Philosophy,* vol. 7, ed. Paul Edwards, 83–85. New York and London, 1967.

Watson, Philip S. *Let God Be God! An Interpretation of the Theology of Martin Luther.* Philadelphia, 1950.

Wood, A. Skevington. *Captive to the Word.* Paternoster Press, 1969. – zur Mühlen, Karl-Heinz. *Reformatorische Vernunftkritik und neuzeitliches Denken: Dargestellt am Werk M. Luthers und Fr. Gogartens.* Tübingen, 1980.

CPSIA information can be obtained
at www.ICGtesting.com
Printed in the USA
LVHW081307070319
609843LV00018B/341/P